Praise for *Rac(e)ing to Class*

"With a growing focus on poverty, race, and equality in America, Milner's timely and sophisticated book deserves widespread discussion and debate. His subtle and sensitive analyses are just what we need. Don't miss this book!"

—Cornel West, Professor of Philosophy and Christian Practice, Union Theological Seminary

"Too many teachers think that ignoring the racial identity and social class backgrounds of their students is the best way to show that they are concerned about all of their students equally. Milner powerfully argues precisely the opposite. He makes a convincing case that teachers need a deeper understanding of the intersections of race and poverty so that they can better counter the out-of-school factors that hinder student learning. This book is crucial reading for educators at all levels."

—Mary Pattillo, Harold Washington Professor of Sociology and African American Studies, Northwestern University

"In my view, the kind of education and teacher education that Milner proposes is the only way that we will be able to provide a high-quality public education to everyone's children in the United States. This clearly written and very practical book should be required reading for every educator and aspiring educator as well as for those who prepare educators."

—Ken Zeichner, Boeing Professor of Teacher Education, University of Washington

"We should thank Rich Milner for *Rac(e)ing to Class*, a smart and accessible book that invites us to have a conversation about race and poverty, in schools and around [them], so that we may build schools rich in wisdom. *Rac(e)ing to Class* is honest, provocative, and compelling; a call to action, an invitation to talk, for parents, community, students, teachers and preservice educators."

—Michelle Fine, Distinguished Professor of Psychology and Urban Education, The Graduate Center, CUNY

"In this comprehensive and timely text, Milner takes head-on the issue of how poverty impacts education, and details why understanding and ameliorating the effects of poverty on education is a moral imperative. Importantly, Milner offers thoughtful solutions and strategies for teachers and school districts to better support the learning of students in poverty, drawing on his vast experience in classrooms as a teacher, teacher educator, and scholar. This book is one of the most thoughtful and important books on poverty and education on the market."

—Na'ilah Suad Nasir, Birgeneau Chair in Educational Disparities, Graduate School of Education, and H. Michael and Jeanne Williams Chair of African American Studies, University of California, Berkeley

"Classroom teachers, principals, and school leaders must read this book; it provides an illuminating model and framework for educators that vividly challenges us to reenvision what we think and do about poverty, race, and achievement in classrooms across the United States. We need this book."

—Terry Harris, Coordinator, Department of Educational Equity and Diversity, Rockwood School District, St. Louis, Missouri

Rac(e)ing to Class

Rac(e)ing to Class

*Confronting Poverty and Race
in Schools and Classrooms*

H. Richard Milner IV

Harvard Education Press
Cambridge, Massachusetts

Library of Congress Control Number 2014953102

Paperback ISBN 978-1-61250-786-6
Library Edition ISBN 978-1-61250-787-3

Published by Harvard Education Press,
an imprint of the Harvard Education Publishing Group

Harvard Education Press
8 Story Street
Cambridge, MA 02138

Cover Design: Ciano Design
Cover Photo: © Randy Faris/Corbis
The typefaces used in this book are Minion Pro and Myriad Pro

Reflecting Back . . .

*This book is dedicated to the loving memory of
my first teachers, my grandparents—Eunice Milner, Jessie Milner,
Annie M. Williams, and Henry "Nick" Williams.*

With love, Richie

Looking Forward . . .

*This book is dedicated to my twin daughters,
Anna Grace Milner and Elise Faith Milner,
born July 30, 2010. You are my heartbeat and the perfect gifts!*

Love, Daddy

Contents

Foreword

Atelling measure of any nation is how it treats its most vulnerable and marginalized citizens. This is particularly the case in a nation that places itself on high moral ground where appropriate responses to misery and suffering are concerned. In the United States, efforts to respond to national and international catastrophes, widespread loss of life, human indignities, and people in distress have been one of our calling cards. The United States often describes itself as the moral compass of the world, especially with respect to human rights and dignities. We have castigated nations the world over (e.g., China, Iraq, North Korea, and Libya) for human rights violations, and we have challenged them to be better in serving their most needy citizens, most often women and children.

It is against this backdrop that the United States has to confront some of its own citizens, namely its poor, and more specifically children. In this important work Professor H. Richard Milner offers conceptual and practical approaches that educators and teacher educators can incorporate in serving students in poverty. What Milner poignantly informs us is that if individuals have any chance of being lifted out of poverty, the quality of their schooling—from ideological, pedagogical, and policy perspectives— must be considerably transformed.

The point that Milner drives home in this work is that poverty matters in this country. It matters because it shapes life opportunities, destroys life dreams, can have a stranglehold on generations of families, and extracts hope from even the most optimistic of individuals. Even more concerning is the widening gulf between those with massive wealth and those without the means to meet life's most basic necessities. Wealth disparities in the United States are at an all-time high. According to an analysis by the

AFL-CIO, the CEO to worker ratio was 331:1 in 2013, and the CEO to minimum wage ratio was 774:1.[1] At a time when many people continue to work multiple jobs, yet still fall short in making ends meet, there is a greater need for compassion and understanding of children and families living in poverty. The sobering reality is that approximately sixteen million children currently live in poverty across this nation. These are some of the highest numbers we have seen in close to two generations.

Moreover, Milner effectively communicates in this book how poverty has a more concentrated and chronic influence on families and communities of color. Milner informs us that poverty cuts across all ethnic and racial lines, but we cannot dismiss the disproportionate manner in which poverty affects African American, Latino, Asian, and Native American populations. Milner is bold in taking on this challenge because many educators are much more comfortable discussing poverty than race. Milner courageously brings us back to this uncomfortable space and tells us that the nexus between race and poverty cannot be overlooked.

In 1989 critical race theorist Kimberlé Crenshaw discussed the salience of intersectionality.[2] In her work she contended that social identities interact on multiple levels, contributing to systematic injustice, social and economic inequality, and layered oppression. Moreover, she stated that intersectionality operates from a framework that assumes the typical conceptualizations of oppression within a society, such as racism, sexism, homophobia, and belief-based bigotries, do not act independently of one another. Milner echoes Crenshaw's work here, because he reminds us that we cannot look at issues of poverty apart from race. Moreover, he offers a framework that is thought provoking, solutions based, and empirically and conceptually sound for practitioners, researchers, and policy makers. Milner challenges educators to be mindful of the intersecting ways that race and poverty have a profound influence on the school experience of many young people in the United States. In this work, Milner is more than a reformer; he is a champion of one of the nation's most vexing challenges—the racialization of poverty. He is compassionate yet bold, forceful, and informative, and inspires us all to do better in preparing educators to work with this deep-seated problem, the intersection of race and poverty. Milner's charge will leave all educators asking, "How can I do more?"

Why does Milner push educators to look at the race and poverty nexus? Mounds of data on poverty convey a troubling reality. In 2010, according to the National Poverty Center, 27.4 percent of blacks and 26.6 percent of Latinos were living in poverty compared to 9.9 percent of non-Hispanic whites and 12.1 percent of Asians.[3] Furthermore, the center reports that poverty rates are highest for families headed by single women, particularly if they are black or Latina. In 2010, 31.6 percent of households headed by single women were poor, while 15.8 percent of households headed by single men and 6.2 percent of married-couple households lived in poverty. Children represent a disproportionate share of the poor in the United States; they are 24 percent of the total population, but 36 percent of the poor population. In 2010, 16.4 million children, or 22.0 percent, were poor. The poverty rate for children also varies substantially by race. The Children's Defense Fund (CDF) reports that the largest group of poor children is Latino (5.8 million), followed by white, non-Hispanic (5.2 million) and black (4.1 million).[4] Not only are children of color disproportionately poor, the youngest children of color are most at risk of challenges associated with poverty. According to CDF data, in 2012 approximately one in three children of color were poor—11.2 million—and more than one in three children of color under age five were poor—3.5 million. Even more staggering is that black children were the poorest proportionately (39.6 percent), followed by American Indian/Native Alaskan children (36.8 percent) and Hispanic children (33.7 percent). Nearly half of black children under age five and more than one in three Hispanic children the same age were poor. And the CDF reports that in six states (Kentucky, Michigan, Mississippi, Ohio, Oregon, and Wisconsin), half or more of all black children were poor in 2012. Nearly half the states had black child poverty rates of 40 percent or more.

These troubling statistics remind us that there is a need for educational practitioners who possess the knowledge, skills, and dispositions to effectively teach students who live in poverty. Moreover, we need to think about these children in a nuanced, anti-deficit, and compassionate manner. What is not helpful are reductive "how-to's" about children in poverty. The danger in such prescriptions is that they offer simplistic and pathological accounts of children living in poverty, and fail to recognize the skills, abilities, and resilience that are demonstrated by millions of poor children every day. Indeed, Milner reminds us that children living in poverty are not poverty stricken when it comes to intellectual ability, work ethic, resilience, survival skills, and determination. It is a message that educational practitioners must constantly keep in mind.

The disheartening data on children in poverty requires us to examine the poverty-race nexus and to evaluate what it means for classroom teachers. No longer can educators look at these students as "other people's children." There must be a willingness to tie the fates of teachers and their students. Dr. King famously stated in his letter in a Birmingham jail that "we are caught in an inescapable network of mutuality, tied in a single garment of destiny. Whatever affects one directly, affects all indirectly." It is in that spirit that educators must come to understand the structural conditions that contribute to poverty, and how many policies and practices reify them. Milner discusses the policies and structures that contribute to poverty, but he does not leave educators to figure out solutions. He offers accessible frameworks, research-based practices, and anecdotal accounts of how educators can think, care, and act. The famous abolitionist Frederick Douglass stated it well when he proclaimed, "Where justice is denied, where poverty is enforced, where ignorance prevails, and where any one class is made to feel that society is an organized conspiracy to oppress, rob and degrade them, neither persons nor property will be safe." It is abundantly clear that the United States must respond to its most marginalized citizens in a different way. Moreover, the role that educators can play in rethinking and reframing children in poverty cannot be overstated. The importance of the moment is upon us and each educator must be prepared to answer the call in a compassionate and caring manner. This book is certain to be hailed by change agents at all levels of our education system who are looking for authentic ways to identify and assist some of our most vulnerable populations.

—*Tyrone C. Howard*
Professor of Education,
University of California, Los Angeles

Acknowledgments

IN THE MIDST OF BUSY DAYS—inundated with meetings, deadlines, and too many unrealistic expectations—I sometimes have to pause and remind myself why I do my work and on whose behalf. As I reflect, I realize how blessed and fortunate I am to have the skill, ability, and *opportunity* to engage in work that I believe is my calling: research and discovery, knowledge sharing/dissemination, and service for/with students who are grossly underserved in education. Although my journey in this work seems to intensify almost every day, I never forget that I am a product of opportunity and possibility, and I will forever remember the people—especially students, friends, family, and colleagues—who have taught me and continue to teach me about engaging in work that truly transforms lives, policies, programs and practices.

I am grateful to my authentically caring, dedicated, and supportive wife, Shelley Banks Milner, who believed in the potential of this project from the very start. I am better in *every* single way because of you!

I am also grateful for and to my parents, Henry III and Barbara Milner, and my in-laws, Dick and Margaret Banks, who have stood (firmly!) in the gaps so many times to support us when I traveled, had a pressing deadline, or needed help. When *everything* else fails and when *everyone* else walks out, the four of you remain constantly consistent. Thank you!

I am also thankful to my aunts and uncles; my godmothers, Christine Hill and Dr. Sarah Favors; my sister, Tanya; and brother, Reginald, for all your love and support over the years. Although the work is daunting, challenging, and sometimes even frustrating, you remind me that the rewards of living a meaningful life overwhelmingly outweigh the difficulty. Thank you for your reassurance.

In general, I am grateful to my professors and mentors at my undergraduate institution, South Carolina State University. In addition, Gail McCutcheon, Anita Woolfolk Hoy, Tyrone Howard, John Singer, Mark Gooden, Cynthia Dillard, Terry Husband, Mike Jackson, and Robert Ransom have been "difference makers"—true mentors and friends—to me since my time at The Ohio State University. Thank you!

I would also like to acknowledge the uncompromising support of our team members in Pitt's Center for Urban Education. I am fortunate to work with an extraordinary dean, Alan Lesgold, and outstanding colleagues, including brilliant doctoral students, at the University of Pittsburgh. Your dedication to our vision and mission are admirable, and I am thankful for your support, work ethic, dedication, leadership, and heart in our fight for equity and social justice in urban education and beyond.

I am also fortunate to have other colleagues in my life who understand me, endorse my work, and push me to do my best. There are too many colleagues to name, but I am grateful.

I have had the honor of learning from and with many teachers, students, school leaders, and community members in my journey. You have taught me much, and I hope this book represents well your voices, triumphs, and struggles.

Finally, words cannot adequately express my gratitude to Douglas Clayton, my editor at Harvard Education Press, who pushed me to make this book better and who nudged me to finish it. The potential you saw in *Start Where You Are* ignited a fire that propelled me to write books that benefit educators and consequently students in real school districts across the globe. Thank you for forcing me to speak to my *intended* audience. And to the staff at Harvard Education Press, thank you. You are a dream team! This book is better because of you.

Introduction

No one who works full time should have to raise [his or her] family in poverty.
> —*President Barack Obama, February 12, 2013, during remarks given before signing an executive order raising the minimum wage for federal contract workers to $10.10 per hour.*

We pledge ourselves to liberate all our people from the continuing bondage of poverty, deprivation, suffering, gender and other discrimination.
> —*Nelson Mandela*

Just because a child's parents are poor or uneducated is no reason to deprive the child of basic human rights to health care, education and proper nutrition.
> —*Marian Wright Edelman*

Even though the economy is growing, too many middle-class families still feel like they're working harder and harder and can't get ahead . . . Inequality is still growing in our society. Too many young people aren't sure whether they'll be able to match the living standards of their parents. We have too many kids in poverty in this country, still.
> —*President Barack Obama, while nominating Jason Furman to replace Alan Krueger as the chairman of the White House Council of Economic Advisers*

OVER THE LAST FEW YEARS, as I have raised my twin daughters, I have spent a considerable amount of time studying aspects of early childhood—attempting to more deeply understand the educational ecology of early learning, particularly child development related to academic and social skills. As I have visited early childhood educational facilities (pre-kindergarten and kindergarten) on the first day of school, I have learned

1

that while some young children are fussy and a bit anxious about transitioning into these formal educational systems, most of them are eager to start school. These young children come with their backpacks filled with new supplies. They are excited to wear their new outfits (sometimes ones they have been able to select themselves), and they are eager for the new learning and social adventures ahead of them. Although some children are outwardly upset about leaving their parents for the first time, I have often observed parents who are more upset than their children. Indeed, most children seem to begin their educational experience curious and enthusiastic about school. However, after a few years (and sometimes after only a few weeks or months), many children begin to dislike school. They move from cognitive, intellectual, and social spaces of curiosity, engagement, and excitement to being disaffected, underwhelmed, and disengaged by what appeared to be a promising environment.

What turns students who were ready for and cheerful about the potential of school into ones who hate it? What happens in the educational process that changes students' minds and hearts about school and consequently educational opportunities? In what ways are schools complicit (albeit unintentionally) in the disengagement and disinterest of students? While one could argue that students from any language background, socioeconomic status, race, or culture could become disinterested in schools that underserve them, some students are more school dependent than others, and the consequences for these children can be devastating both short and long term. Due to structural and system inequities, for children who are living in poverty, whose first language is not English, or who are of color, education is an essential component of their upward mobility. Yet schools too often do very little to ensure these students succeed. My question about why some students *fall out of love* with school really is linked to how schools work, more so than what any one teacher does. Teachers tend to teach based on the culture established in their school or district or how they were taught themselves in the educational system. So the question is, how can we restructure schools and support teachers in ways that also support all students, building and shaping their interests, skills, knowledge, and overall connectedness to education? In other words, what is essential in education to cultivate the interests and enthusiasm of all children—especially those who are grossly underserved in schools? I make a conscious decision throughout this book to differentiate between *schooling* and *education*. Shujaa and his colleagues make an important distinction between the kinds of experiences afforded students when they experience education rather than schooling. Those who are schooled are coerced into assimilating into contexts that do not allow them to build the types of attitudes, dispositions, skills, and knowledge necessary for them to analyze, critique, and contribute to their communities when education is in place.[1]

In this book, I attempt to shed light on the complexities of race, poverty, and education and to specify practices educators—especially teachers—can employ to more effectively meet the needs of all learners. But my focus is not only teachers and their practices. I also illuminate broader structural challenges and recommendations that have direct influence on practices inside schools and classrooms. Although often treated and addressed separately in education and society, race, (social) class, and poverty are inextricably linked. I draw from my own and others' research and practices to make sense of these intersections with the ultimate goal of helping teachers teach all students more effectively and helping systems support teachers in doing so. *Every child matters, regardless of his or her race, gender, sexual orientation, language, religion, geography, zip code, social status, or poverty status*, and it is essential for those of us in education to demonstrate this through what we say, our discourse, and also what we do, our practice. But because racism still exists in society and thus schools, many students of color living in poverty tend to be doubly challenged and pressured to navigate schooling. In this book I aim to recenter interests, attention and actions of preservice and inservice teachers, leaders (principals, superintendents), coaches, counselors, researchers, policy makers and other professionals in preK–12 as well as higher education on poverty and race to ensure that every child—regardless of race or socioeconomic level—has an equitable opportunity to build the knowledge, skills, attitudes, dispositions, and insights for success. The success that I stress in this book is not limited to student financial or material possessions but also encompasses a heightened sense of themselves—the many assets they and their families and communities possess—as well their responsibilities to contribute to and improve their communities.

Consider the comments an elementary teacher expressed in a professional development session I conducted several years ago:

> I'm going to share with you what I suspect most of my colleagues really want to say but are too nice to. We work with young children, and we

love all our children just the same. Our principal invited you here to talk to us about *specific strategies* to teach our poor children. I was devouring what you had to say—you were right on target—until you got to this race stuff. Race has nothing to do with how to teach my kids living in poverty. What does it matter? Really!

Frustrated and a bit agitated, the teacher began to doodle for the remainder of the session, which focused on the intersections of race, poverty, and social class.

Given the comments of this teacher, it is important to remember that many white children also live below the poverty line. This book is concerned about meeting their needs as well as students of color. Frankly, I care about the educational success of all students—including white students. So, to be clear, this book also focuses on white students living below the poverty line. What some people fail to understand is that "white" is a race. So, when I talk about poverty and race in this book, I am discussing how poverty manifests and connects with issues of race for various groups of people—including white students. However, as I will illustrate throughout the book, white students living in poverty may experience education and schooling differently than black and brown students in similar circumstances. Thus, I will not pretend that issues of race emerge inside and outside of school in the same way for students living in poverty.

The comments of the elementary teacher above are not unique. I consistently encounter this type of thinking from people training to become teachers in different types of teacher education programs (mostly in higher education); those who have been teaching for years in elementary, middle, and high schools; and even some colleagues who study and teach aspects of education, often referred to as teacher educators. Educators tend to feel much more comfortable focusing on poverty (and to a lesser degree, social class) than on race. But why? Why is it *still* so difficult for people to engage race inside and outside of education? This is both a rhetorical question and one I attempt to address in this book.

UNDERSTANDING STUDENT EXPERIENCES IN AND OUT OF SCHOOL

In a landmark study commissioned by the federal government, James Coleman reported that schools had relatively little influence on student achievement and consequently students' life chances.[2] He found that out-of-school factors such as poverty were by far the central determinants of student success. However, Caldas and Bankston argued that Coleman's research generally "treated inequities in outcome as results of the family resources that individual students bring to school."[3] Caldas and Bankston's research attempted to measure the extent to which in-school variables such as peer pressure shaped the behavior of students receiving free and reduced-price lunch. Their conclusions countered Coleman's findings in some important ways. Perhaps most important, they argued for the "importance of taking characteristics of school populations, as well as individual school characteristics, into consideration as significant influences on individual academic achievement." Thus, while teachers and other educators may be quick to point to outside factors such as the lack of parental involvement as the reason students underperform, in-school realities and experiences also play a role. I will expand on this latter point throughout the book.

Whether one is considering in-school or out-of school experiences, test performance is at the heart of how most think about student and teacher success. Sadly, it seems that we are obsessed with student test results, although students are much more than numbers aggregated from test score measures. It is important to note that a sole focus on student achievement on standardized tests likely does little to help us address developmental and process-oriented needs of students. In other words, focusing on outputs without thinking seriously about the systems, programs, practices, policies, and processes that lead to the outcomes—that is, the inputs—seems to be ineffective. Moreover, pressures that teachers, school leaders (and other educators), and students are under to show gains on tests can make it difficult for them to concentrate on what should be at the heart of teaching and learning: educational experiences that build on the assets of students, pique their curiosity and interest in learning, and cultivate mind-sets and practices to improve community. As Darling-Hammond explains:

> The Reagan era introduced a new theory of reform focused on outcomes rather than inputs—that is, high-stakes testing without investing—that drove most policy initiatives. The situation in many urban (and rural) schools deteriorated over the decades. Drops in real per-pupil expenditures accompanied tax cuts and growing enrollments. Meanwhile student needs grew with immigration, concentrated poverty and homelessness, and increased numbers of students requiring second-language instruction and special educational services. Although some federal support to high-need schools and districts was

restored during the 1990s, it was not enough to fully recoup the earlier losses, and after 2000, inequality grew once again.[4]

My point here is not to be politically polarizing. A careful review of educational policy on the federal level would reveal that administrative moves by *both* liberals and conservatives have struggled to meet the needs of our most vulnerable students. Rather, the aim is to understand that focusing on outputs over inputs (whether inside or outside of school) seems to be resulting in more harm than good, especially for children living in poverty.

The collective body of research on poverty and education that informs school practice—mostly aimed at explaining why many students who live in poverty are less successful than those who do not—emphasizes three different areas, each explored herein:

1. Out-of-school factors such as unemployment, family income, parental styles, parental educational level, geography, and resources in the home, such as the number of books available to children
2. In-school factors such as instructional practices, resources and the lack thereof in school, administrative practices, school culture, and the nature of relationships between teachers and students as well as between teachers and parents, families, and community members
3. The effects of out-of-school factors on outcomes and experiences in school

I challenge educators to think about these three areas as they work to meet the complex needs of all their students. That is, what out-of-school factors are essential for educators to more deeply understand to support their students? How do we improve practices within schools to respond to the realities that students and their communities and families experience outside of school? And in what ways can we build collective partnerships and synergies to improve the effects of these outside factors on students' school experiences? These are complex questions. However, our ability to address them, as I discuss, is likely at the core of how we will realize *true* reform—change that makes a difference.

Consider the frustration of an aspiring high school principal I met a few years ago regarding his inability to "control" what happened in students' lives outside of school:

It's tough because I can't follow the kid home and tell the parent how to raise him. Kids go home to parents who don't care. They go home to parents doing drugs and not checking their homework and all. The parent will cuss you out if you call to talk to [him or her] about the kid. And then they [students] have the streets too especially in the inner city. Kids are shooting craps all day [gambling], staying out late, robbing people, and even selling drugs. How can I compete with all that? Why am I expected to do what the parent should be doing? Parents don't have time to spend with their kid because the parents are at work all day and night and don't even get home in time enough to put their kid to bed.

These remarks are consistent with those of many educators I have studied and encountered over the years—especially those already teaching. I have heard not only principals but also teachers express deep frustration because they believe out-of-school factors make it almost impossible for them to teach effectively in the classroom. They see the families and communities of students as liabilities—deficient, insufficient, and incapable of supporting students for the expectations they will face inside of school. They ask, How can I teach my students when their home lives are in turmoil? In many ways, teachers and principals wonder how to teach students whose home lives and experiences are different from theirs. They find it difficult to recognize that every student, every family, every community has assets and strengths on which they should build. I explore these frustrations throughout this book in the hopes that educators become better equipped to respond to them. Moreover, although I focus on the fact that educators often critique students, their families, and their communities, I also consider the unfair critiques and expectations of teachers working diligently to support students. Too often, teachers are blamed for issues, factors, and situations far beyond their control. I challenge us to identify and build on the many assets of teachers and to support them, just as we do students, in getting better.

GETTING REAL ABOUT RACE

Dating back to the pivotal and germinal work of Dubois and Woodson, researchers and theorists have attempted to unravel the intertwining nature of race and education.[5] Race is not a straightforward, linear construct. For as long as discussions have focused on race and education, people have attempted to figure out just what race means and how to address it to improve the educational experiences of those who have historically been marginalized and undereducated in schools across the United States. Educators tend to struggle to address race and how it informs their work with students, parents, communities, and colleagues.

In the courses I teach at various universities on race, I often remind my students that they should no longer refer to "color" when in fact they are talking about race because race is much more than skin color. Race is constructed physically, socially, legally, and historically. The meanings, messages, results, and consequences of race are developed and constructed by human beings, not by some predetermined set of scientific laws or genetics. Genetically and biologically, individuals are more the same than they are different. According to Nakkula and Toshalis, "there is no biologically sustainable reason for establishing 'races' as distinct subgroups within the human species . . . Race is a concept created in the modern era as a way of drawing distinctions between people such that some might benefit at the expense of others."[6]

Following is a closer look at these four constructs:

- *Physically constructed.* Based on skin pigmentation, people in society construct ideas, characteristics, images, and belief systems about themselves and others. These physical constructions are sometimes inaccurate, but they remain nevertheless. It is important to note that physical constructions of race vary from one society to the next. For instance, constructions of race in Africa and Asia are different from constructions of race based on phenotype in North America.
- *Socially constructed.* Based on a range of societal information and messages, people categorize themselves and others. These social constructions are linked to preferences, worldviews, and how groups of people perform. They are based on a range of perspectives drawn from people's interpretation of history and law, and they shape how we think about individuals and groups of people.
- *Legally constructed.* U.S. laws have helped us construct what race is. Landmark cases and legal policies such as the Naturalization Law (1790), *Plessy v. Ferguson* (1896), *Takao Ozawa v. United States* (1922), *Brown v. Board of Education* (1954), and *Milliken v. Bradley* (1974)

have all influenced our constructions and definitions of race in U.S. society.

- *Historically constructed.* Historical realties of how people have been treated and have fared in a society steeped in racism and oppression also shape the ways in which people understand, talk about, and conceptualize race. For instance, Jim Crow laws, slavery, and racial discrimination influence how people conceptualize and understand race.

People's beliefs about race informed by the areas outlined above shape what they do and do not do in practice. Although race is a central construct used to examine educational outcomes, policies, and practices, the depth and breadth of its applications are limited in public and academic discourse. For instance, people often talk about an "achievement gap" and disparities between white and black/brown students. However, race is not treated in any substantive way beyond reporting the data outcomes. Rationales for why race is so difficult to address go beyond the scope of this book, but my experience working with more than a thousand educators over the years is that race is a tough topic for people to discuss in "mixed" company. Some may fear that focusing on race will force them into conflicts with friends or colleagues that they are underprepared to address. Others are concerned that they are not being politically correct in talking about race. Still others wonder if they will be judged and deemed prejudiced based on their conversations and discursive inputs about race.

However, while race may be difficult to address among educators, *it may be one of the most important issues to consider,* particularly in schools where students of color are grossly underserved. When schools collectively decide to engage race to understand its intricacies in relation to their students, growth among both the faculty and students becomes more viable and visible. Based on my experiences, when the topic of race emerges, educators tend to automatically think the focus is on nonwhite people. What should be clear in reading this book is that white is a racial category as well, and we will grapple with whiteness just as we critically examine experiences of people of color.

Recent debates and decisions about the relevance and sustainability of affirmative action have left many to wonder if race should be considered in admission and hiring practices. A resounding shift seems inevitable. Opponents of affirmative action believe that as a country we all, across different racial and ethnic groups, have reached a "level playing field" and, accordingly, affirmative action should end.[7] Others believe social class, not race, should be used in "preferential" decision making with student assignment policies. Although much of this discussion takes place in society, outside of the traditional preK–12 school setting, these issues emerge powerfully in the ways in which educators (teachers, principals, counselors, coaches) construct and confront their work in schools. Thus, educators' experiences, worldviews, mind-sets, and belief systems (what they believe about affirmative action and social class, for instance) shape how they work with their students. White educators may even believe that students of color are now somehow at an advantage in society and that their own biological children may be disadvantaged.

Some educators in schools do engage in conversations about race, but I have observed that most of the discourses are superficial at best: "I am worried about my black boys" or "I'm not sure why I can't get the parents of my brown students to come to parent-teacher conferences." Rarely are the conversations regarding race *real*. By "real," I mean that these beliefs expressed through educators' language rarely address racism, discrimination, and the effects of structural inequity on individual students. In other words, it is difficult to have substantive conversations about race regarding individual students and their parents and families without thinking deeply about the broader collective, societal systems that directly impact the individual. For instance, how often are educators willing to talk about the fact that racist housing policies have kept people out of particular neighborhoods? Or how many educators understand the links between race, student assignment policy, property taxes, and education? How often do educators discuss how racist hiring practices have kept certain groups of people out of jobs in particular communities? It is easy to blame parents for their lack of attentiveness to their children. It is simple to proclaim that parents in a particular "culture" do not care about their children. It is much more difficult, however, to admit that discrimination still mars the experiences of some. Put simply, people of color who do not respond well to sustained and ingrained racism and discrimination can find it difficult to be "model" parents to their children. People tend to do the best they can in the circumstances they face and inhabit.

To be clear, my point is not to present people of color living in poverty as victims who are weak and incapable of working through the racist and classist systems described above. To the contrary, many of these people actually succeed in spite of unjust policies, practices, and circumstances. Moreover, racism is not the only culprit in the narrative about why some groups of people struggle, but it certainly is one reason. And it can be tough for people who have not experienced racism or discrimination to understand and empathize with others. At times, readers may disagree me, but my goal is not for readers to agree with every point made. My aim is to shepherd readers—educators—into reflective, proactive, and responsive spaces to move beyond complacency and beyond neutrality. Complacency is unacceptable if educators are committed to improving education for all. Moreover, neutrality is a conscious stance that works against social justice. In short, educators are either fighting for equitable education for all students, or they are fighting against it. *There is no neutral space in this work.* In these chapters I attempt to guide educators into real conversations about concrete issues regarding race. Such discussions can be murky and challenging, but I encourage readers to persevere. I know firsthand that engaging educators with race can be a game changer for children. It is within educational institutions where educators seriously engage issues of race that I have seen the most pervasive and positive changes and improvement for students of color.

DEFINING POVERTY, NOT ALLOWING POVERTY TO DEFINE

Educators often struggle to talk explicitly about race and see its connections to their work; they tend to be much more comfortable discussing poverty and how it might influence their practices. While numerous studies demonstrate relationships between poverty and other variables, qualitatively, it is less clear just what this connection is. Students' receiving free or reduced-price lunch is the common marker to identify poverty or social class; however, there is much less consistency about how poverty manifests and influences student achievement. Poverty tends to be described and understood based on three measures: (1) the federal government's formula for the poverty line, (2) free and reduced-price lunch formulas that vary, or (3) particular categories and situations people find themselves in because of the amount of monetary and related material capital they have or lack.

Poverty has been found to have lasting effects on social class and psychological well-being,[8] and poverty and socioeconomic status (SES) have

been linked to school size,[9] trust,[10] students' and teachers' sense of community,[11] classroom and school technology use and integration,[12] growth trajectories in literacy among English language learners,[13] public high school
outcomes and college attendance rates,[14] the ability of young children (ages
five through eight) to self-regulate,[15] and course selection and enrollment
in rigorous mathematics.[16]

Indeed, poverty is a serious social problem in the United States and
beyond that has a profound influence on students' experiences in schools.
Understanding the social aspects of students' educational experiences is
essential because academic challenges are closely tied to social and societal
ones.[17] Parents' (especially mothers') educational level and family income
appear to be strong outside-of-school predictors of student performance in
school.[18] Figures I.1 and I.2 demonstrate the relationship between education level and earnings, both annually and over a career span, from 2000
and 2010.

Education level is a strong predictor of most people's earnings and
consequently their ability to acquire material possessions, including their

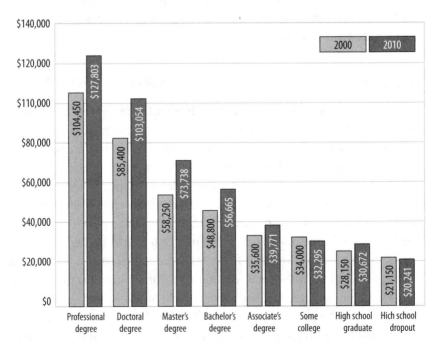

FIGURE I.1   Annual salary based on education level, 2000 and 2010

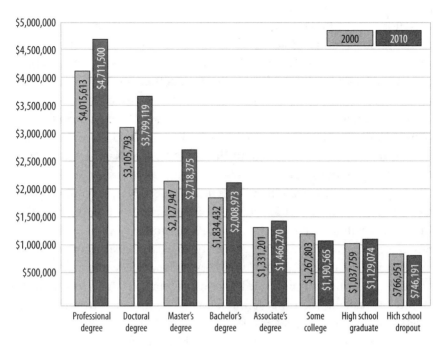

FIGURE I.2 Career salary projections based on education level, 2000 and 2010

homes, which impact where their children attend schools. To illuminate, the home or zip code people are able to "purchase" is of course linked to income and education level; property taxes fund school systems across the United States. Resources can be limited in high-poverty schools, and thus so might student experiences.

It is important to note that just because parents lack the academic degrees of a formal education does not mean they are not intelligent, capable of supporting their children, and concerned about their children's education. To the contrary, many living in poverty care deeply about their children's educational opportunities and life changes for the future. Clearly, people are not "high" or "low," "adequate" or "inadequate," "better" or "worse," but the conditions under which they are placed can be. *Poverty does not and should not define a person or group of people—there is no "culture of poverty"—but it can define a stratified system in which a person or group of people may live.* Moreover, people living in poverty respond to the material conditions of their experience. So those living in oppressive situations due to inadequate and unstable jobs, transportation, or housing, for instance, behave, practice, and act based on those conditions. Thus, understanding how cultural practices are different from culture is an essential aim of this book—one that has the potential to help teachers re-envision what they believe and think they believe about their students.

Burney and Beilke explain that "a family is considered to be poor if its income for a particular year is below the amount deemed necessary to support a family of a certain size."[19] According to the Philanthropy News Digest, the official poverty rate in the United States was 14.5 percent in 2013, down from 15 percent in 2012—the first year-over-year decline since 2006.[20] Consider data from three data points: 2009, 2011, and 2013, respectively (tables I.1, I.2, and I.3), which outline the poverty levels for families and individuals according to the federal government.

In defining and "measuring" poverty, the U.S. Census Bureau uses "a set of money income thresholds that vary by family size and composition to determine who is in poverty. If a family's total income is less than the family's threshold, then that family and every individual in it is considered in poverty. The official poverty thresholds do not vary geographically, but they are updated for inflation . . . The official poverty definition uses money income before taxes and does not include capital gains or noncash benefits (such as public housing, Medicaid, and food stamps)."[21] Excluding

TABLE I.1   2009 U.S. Poverty Guidelines

Persons in family	48 contiguous states and D.C.	Alaska	Hawaii
1	$10,830	$13,530	$12,460
2	14,570	18,210	16,760
3	18,310	22,890	21,060
4	22,050	27,570	25,360
5	25,790	32,250	29,660
6	29,530	36,930	33,960
7	33,270	41,610	38,260
8	37,010	46,290	42,560
For each additional person, add	+ 3,740	+ 4,680	+ 3,740

Source: Federal Register 74, no. 14 (January 23, 2009): 4199–4201.

TABLE I.2   2011 U.S. Poverty Guidelines

Persons in family	48 contiguous states and D.C.	Alaska	Hawaii
1	$10,890	$13,600	$12,540
2	14,710	18,380	16,930
3	18,530	23,160	21,320
4	22,350	27,940	25,710
5	26,170	32,720	30,100
6	29,990	37,500	34,490
7	33,810	42,280	38,880
8	37,630	47,060	43,270
For each additional person, add	3,820	4,780	4,390

Source: Federal Register 76, no. 13 (January 20, 2011): 3637–3638.

TABLE I.3   2013 U.S. Poverty Guidelines

Persons in family	48 contiguous states and D.C.	Alaska	Hawaii
1	$11,490	$14,350	$13,230
2	15,510	19,380	17,850
3	19,530	24,410	22,470
4	23,550	29,440	27,090
5	27,570	34,470	31,710
6	31,590	39,500	36,330
7	35,610	44,530	40,950
8	39,630	49,560	45,570
For each additional person, add	4,020	5,030	4,620

Source: Federal Register 78, no. 16 (January 24, 2013): 5182–5183.

Hawaii and Alaska, in 2009, a family of four earning below $25,360 was considered below the poverty line, whereas in 2011 this threshold was $25,710. The federal government's classification and distinction has important implications for the kinds of resources available to families, such as welfare support, subsidized housing (including section VIII), health-care assistance, Title 1 programs in schools, as well as Head Start opportunities for young children.

These three tables provide some quantitative perspective about poverty; however, poverty in many ways is socially constructed because there is diversity in people's experiences living below the poverty line. Indeed, it is difficult to definitively say what poverty means, and educators should be careful not to pigeonhole or stereotype their "poor" students into a distinct, standardized category. My parents grew up in poverty in the rural Jim Crow South during some seriously challenging times. However, they have told me that they did not even realize they were living below the poverty line because they were well supported at home with family and community; they lived in a safe and caring environment, and their teachers, predesegregation, taught them effectively. Thus, the point is that poverty does not define people, but structural experiences can shape people's experiences and practices living in poverty.

Their teachers, my parents have told me, did not view their worth as based on the clothes they wore nor did they think of them as representatives of their parents' bank accounts. Teachers taught my parents responsibly because they (1) understood them and deliberately sought to learn more about them; (2) expected them to succeed; (3) empathized with them because they were neighbors, attended church with them, and knew firsthand what was happening in the local community; (4) recognized their strengths and drew upon them in curriculum, instructional, and assessment practices; and (5) took into account the broader social contexts of their students' lives beyond their rural community in considering how to respond to and teach them.

My parents' experiences echo what other researchers and social scientists—including James Anderson, Jackie Irvine, Michele Foster, Vanessa Siddle Walker, Gloria Ladson-Billings, Carl Grant, William Tate, Linda Tillman, Jerome Morris, and Derrick Alridge—have uncovered in their research about how educators effectively taught black students (many living in poverty) predesegregation. Clearly, not all students who live in poverty fail, and many live meaningful and productive lives despite the popular perspective that those living in poverty are inferior and need to be "understood" in order to save or "fix" them.[22] In the simplest terms, poverty should not define people, and educators should not allow socioeconomic status to determine their views of the potential of their students.

Although a major point of this book is that poverty should not be the defining framework in how educators shape their work with students, we also cannot escape the fact that the schooling and educational systems have poorly (no pun intended) served students and families living in poverty. Addressing poverty in schools is neither simple nor straightforward. Moreover, the fact that students living in poverty can be successful does not mean teachers will not struggle to teach them. It is difficult to teach students in different social contexts with diverse needs. I have worked with teachers and students in rural, suburban, and urban contexts. There are challenges in *all* contexts, and addressing all of them far exceeds the scope of this book. From a philosophical perspective, poverty is not an absolute state but a relative one, dependent on a wide range of factors beyond a formulaic poverty line or location.

Perhaps the most disturbing reality of living in poverty is the limitations of what low income and its related resources, systems, structures, policies, and practices allow people to do. For instance, it can be difficult for those in poverty to get high-quality health care, to eat healthfully (especially fruits and vegetables, which may be too expensive or unavailable in food "deserts" without adequate transportation), or to experience high-quality schools. Haberman explains that students living in poverty are too often miseducated because they are not prepared to think through complex problems, build on their own creativity, or develop their own consciousness about how to deal with, respond to, and disrupt inequitable situations.[23] He observes that some students who drop out of school are better prepared to function in society than others living in poverty who stay in school for thirteen years. Again, the point here is that the educational system can grossly underserve students living in poverty, and the outcome is that students are not successful.

Offering a policy and legal studies perspective, Burch explains that "citizens residing in affluent districts (overwhelmingly White) are educated to govern, whereas citizens residing in economically disadvantaged districts (overwhelmingly people of color) are educated to be governed."[24] I would revise Burch's language away from "educated" to "schooled." Anyon, Kozol, and Haberman all demonstrate, to an extent, that instructional practices in many high-poverty schools conceive of knowledge as basic skills that students are taught by a teacher (who is the knower) in order to receive a reward, whereas instructional practices in more affluent communities are more iterative and responsive to the nature and needs of the learner, who is seen as a contributor to knowledge.[25]

Thus, it is difficult to concretely define poverty because of the range of people's experiences living in it. Thinking seriously about what it means to live and learn without the necessary resources for success is at the root of this book. It matters more, from my perspective, that we think about causes, outcomes, and consequences for people living in poverty than to settle on a universal definition.

(SOCIAL) CLASS

We are learning more and more about how social class influences students' opportunities to learn.[26] Weis and Dolby explain that class should be understood as "practices of living," not individual traits or categories of people. The researchers expand on practices of living linked to social class:

> The books we read (or if we read at all); our travel destinations (if we have them and what they look like); the clothes we wear; the foods we eat; where and if our children go to school, how far and with what degree of success, with whom, and under what staff expectations and treatment; where and with whom we feel most comfortable; where we live and the nature of our housing; where and if we attend and complete postsecondary education, and under what expectations for success and imagined or taken for granted financing (parents, public/ state/national/federal money, on or off campus job) are all *profoundly* classed experiences, rooted not only in material realities but also in shared culturally based expectations and understandings.[27]

How people interpret these practices of living allow for value judgments about who or what matters more and why. Teachers, for example, may have higher expectations for students whose parents are physicians or other educators because of their perceived social status, which is informed by these groups' practices of living.

Social stratification is omnipresent because there is and will always be a socially constructed and perceived top, middle, and bottom based on some set of classed predeterminants. For instance, Max Weber and others have explained that people's relative power, prestige, and property influence their practices of living, which in turn shape the ways in which people react to them.[28] In classrooms across the country, teachers consciously and subconsciously tier, group, and stratify students based on forms of logic that have been in a sense ingrained into their (our) conceptions of who needs what type of support. Social stratification and the ways in which we have been socialized induce educators to believe there must always be a "top" reading group in elementary school, a "middle" mathematics group in middle school, and a "low" history class in high school. To be clear, this stratification often occurs implicitly and on a classroom level, not necessarily through some form of structural or institutional tracking. These stratified conceptions are classed.

For example, teachers who teach Advanced Placement students or others who are considered "gifted" subconsciously group students in this way, and these students are automatically deemed those who deserve rigor and high expectations, even though Ford has made it explicit that all students benefit from rigorous expectations.[29] Although school policies and programs may place students in a particular group, course, or program for their ability, teachers still tend to tier students even within the established tracked grouping because that is what they are accustomed to doing. We classify and rank—stratify—in society, in school, and in the classroom. The same stratification holds true for students in remedial courses, groups, or programs. I have observed Title 1 reading teachers who "point out" the students who show greater promise than other students—almost creating a tiered system within the broader established system.

It is unclear whether our educational system has an assertive goal of elevating all students to the highest levels regardless of property, power, and prestige. Many argue that the system is meant to maintain the social order and the status quo. Sociologist James Henslin explains several reasons why the United States deliberately and purposely remains a stratified nation.[30] A compelling point is that someone has to assume particular kinds of work in order for society to function. For instance, without a stratified workforce, who would do the socially constructed "menial" jobs in our country, such as janitorial work or garbage collection? Educators in schools assume that certain groups of students will take on particular kinds of jobs, and thus play a role in preparing students for that work. Teachers will overtly stress that "some students just aren't capable of particular types of jobs—especially those that require robust thinking skills." A central problem is that educators fail to understand that skills can be learned and developed over time—they are not finite traits that some people inherently have while others do not.

It is important to note that while social class and income are linked, they are not automatically causal. For example, people tend to socially construct the idea that some positions (such as doctors, lawyers, judges, dentists) are more "important" than others and consequently people tend to earn higher levels of compensation. However, attorneys may or may not be viewed as having high class status. People in the helping professions such as social work and nursing may not earn as much money as physicians, but are often seen as part of a high social class structure. Moreover, while sanitation workers may not be viewed as of a high social class, their levels of compensation can be relatively high. Conversely, clergy may be viewed as high class, but their pay may be low. The idea is supposed to be that people are rewarded (economically) based on their contribution and merit—what they have "rightfully" earned through their perceived hard work, skill, and ability. However, the notion of merit has been strongly contested and seen as a myth because many people are rewarded on the basis of other factors and privileges that far exceed their earned status and contribution.

Anyon provides a compelling example of social stratification and also the social reproduction produced in and through schools. She describes four types of schools where students were stratified and where social and societal privileges were either enabled or suppressed at the expense of students. Students in the low-income schools were taught how to obey orders; they were not taught or encouraged to question authority or to engage in critical thinking about the content or context of various texts they encountered. Teachers made few connections to the real world, and students were not expected to think about inequity or to develop skills to confront or change racist and inequitable policies and practices, either in or out of school. Much of the learning centered around completing worksheets and following directions. The more affluent schools, on the other hand, allowed students to engage in deeply complex activities where they learned how to problem solve, build and convey their positions and arguments, and engage in critical thinking while showcasing their creativity. In this sense, schools were complicit, albeit unknowingly, in replicating and reinforcing the status quo, and guaranteeing that society would remain stratified with particular students assuming particular kinds of work. In Anyon's words, "knowledge and skills leading to social power and reward are made available to the advantaged social groups but are withheld from the working classes, to whom a more 'practical' curriculum is offered."[31]

RACE TO CLASS

Although conscientious educators will aspire to pursue the issues explored in this chapter (race, poverty, social class) individually, throughout this book, I focus mostly on the intersection of race and poverty and call for a renewed focus on them. Substantiated through my own research and the established research literature, the data suggest that it is ineffectual to address poverty or social class without methodically and simultaneously addressing race.

Munin, building from DeNavas-Walt, Proctor, and Smith, provides a contemporary picture of families living below the poverty line by race.[32] Table I.4 demonstrates that white families represent about 9.4 percent of those living in poverty, while black and Hispanic families represent 23.7 percent and 22.3 percent, respectively. Munin clarifies an important point regarding these data:

> Families of color are much more likely to live in poverty and thereby have less access to societal benefits granted to the economically

TABLE I.4   Percentage of U.S. families below poverty line by race

Race/ethnicity	Percentage below poverty line
White	9.4%
Black	23.7%
Hispanic/brown	22.3%
Asian	10.2%

Source: Adapted from A. Munin, *Color by Number: Understanding Racism Through Facts and Stats on Children* (Sterling, VA: Stylus, 2012); and C. DeNavas-Walt, B. D. Proctor, and J. C. Smith, U. S. Census Bureau, Population Reports, P60-236 *Income, Poverty, and Health Insurance Coverage in the United States: 2008* (Washington, DC: U.S. Government Printing Office, 2009), http://www.census.gov/prod/2009pubs/p60-236.pdf.

privileged. However, it is important to point out that this [race and poverty] is not a perfect correlation. Not all people of color are poor, nor are all White people rich. It is very difficult to live in poverty, regardless of one's race.[33]

I am not suggesting (nor is Munin) that people are in poverty because of their race but rather aim to demonstrate how race can be a salient factor in education—and consequently how people experience and inhabit the world. My point is that those of us in education should work to eradicate poverty for all students, not just students of color. However, we need to first understand why a disproportionate number of students of color live in poverty and are from lower social class backgrounds. We should not ignore this reality: proportionally, more people/students of color live in poverty than do white people. Why? Now look at table I.5.

This table demonstrates the disproportionate representation of white, black, and Hispanic (brown) low-income families in the United States. In Munin's words:

> In an equitable society, if Whites constitute 65% of the total population, they should also make up 65% of those in the low-income bracket. But this group is actually 23.6 percentage points lower in representation in the low-income family category. Conversely, Blacks make up a larger percentage than their overall size in the low-income population by 9.8 percentage points. The same is true for Hispanics, who constitute a greater share of the low-income group compared to their population size by 14.6 percentage points.[34]

TABLE I.5   Percentage of low-income U.S. families by race

Race	Percentage of low-income families	Percentage of U.S. population
White	42%	65.6%
Black	22%	12.2%
Hispanic/brown	30%	15.4%
Total percentage for black and brown	52%	27.6%

Source: Adapted from A. Munin, *Color by Number: Understanding Racism Through Facts and Stats on Children* (Sterling, VA: Stylus, 2012); and M. C. Simms, K. Fortuny, and E. Henderson, "Racial and Ethnic Disparities Among Low-Income Families," Urban Institute, 2009.

A consistent question throughout this book is, why? In their study of high-poverty urban schools, Slaughter-Defoe and Carlson explained that "[i]t is important to search for the main effects of race and culture in any study within a society that is as stratified as that of the United States . . . However, not only are they [race and culture] important to society generally, they are also important to education."[35]

In an important analysis, Ladson-Billings and Tate determined that:

> Although both class and gender can and do intersect race, as stand-alone variables they do not explain all of the educational achievement differences apparent between Whites and students of color. Indeed, there is some evidence to suggest that even when we hold constant for class, middle-class African-American students do not achieve at the same level as their White counterparts.[36]

Cooper, Crosnoe, Suizzo, and Pituch wrote: "Although poverty cuts across racial lines, the likelihood of growing up in an impoverished family is much higher for racial-minority children than for White children."[37] Strong racial messages are pervasive in many of the challenges in education, such as patterns in special education[38] and in office referral rates, including students who are subsequently suspended or expelled for misbehavior.[39] Yet, practicing teachers may ignore or at best minimize race, racism, and discrimination as explanations for these patterns.[40] For them, poverty and social class trump race as well as the intersecting nature of them. Still, in a policy brief entitled *The Colors of Poverty: Why Racial and Ethnic Disparities Persist*, Lin and Harris pose some provocative questions. They ask: "Given substantial progress in civil rights and anti-discrimination policies—as well as the increased ethnic diversity of the nation—why is poverty still so colored? Why have racial differences in poverty persisted for so long?"[41]

Simply put, people's experiences are mediated, constructed, and informed by their race. Lareau demonstrated how race shows up in how parents make decisions about their children's outside-of-school practices and experiences. For instance, her study revealed that middle-class black parents monitored the "racial composition of each activity" before enrolling their children so that they were not the only black children in particular activities. What happens to students, and in society in general, is not the consequence of neutral interactions between and among people. Recognizing the intersection of race and social class is essential to improving education, especially for those living in poverty.[42]

Indeed, generally, people of different races living in poverty have analogous but not identical experiences. Ladson-Billings made it clear that although black American and white American experiences may be similar, their experiences are *not* the same because race still matters to the very essence of who people are and how they inhabit society. Thus, due to individual, structural, and systemic forms of racism, black and brown students may experience poverty in ways that are qualitatively (and perhaps quantitatively) different from white students.[43]

SUMMARY

This book rests upon eight interrelated suppositions that guide subsequent chapters:

- *Students are (and should be viewed as) more than mere test scores.* The U.S. obsession with test scores can make it difficult for teachers to focus on teaching that fosters student development and learning to build long-term academic and social success.
- *Racism and inequity are still pervasive in society and in many schools across the United States.* Although some believe that we live in a postracial society and issues of racism and inequity have ended, students still experience racism and inequity in schools and consequently their outcomes are influenced by them. These experiences should not be ignored.
- *Students' academic and social success are deeply connected.* Student development should focus on academic *as well as* social development, as these factors are inextricably linked.
- *Schools must be responsive to the realities their students face outside of school.* It is not enough for educators to focus their attention solely on school issues such as teaching subject matter or handling discipline in a school environment; they must also understand and respond to the material conditions of students' lives and their lived experiences outside of school.

- *Microlevel and macrolevel structures and systems are interrelated and have the potential to enable or stifle student learning and development.* For profound progress to occur for our nation's most vulnerable students, concurrent attention must be placed on both broad and microlevel problems and solutions. Focusing on policy without reforming classroom practice (and vise versa) can do little to systemically redress inequity.
- *Good teachers and teaching can address challenges in education such as poverty, but many additional factors must be considered as well.* Too much attention on teaching and teachers without considering other forces such as resources, school culture, and administrative expertise and support can actually exaggerate what teachers can do in classrooms. Teachers should not be blamed for factors outside of their control.
- *Poverty is not a culture or a descriptor of an individual or group of people; poverty is a condition of a system.* Although some believe that there are inherent or innate cultural characteristics, values, and belief systems of those living below the poverty line, evidence negates these perceptions, as students and their family's beliefs and practices vary. Although we might be able to identify common practices among those living in poverty, these are a direct result of the conditions in which they live. For instance, a practice of crime can be a result of unemployment, discrimination, inadequate housing, and transportation. Thus, poverty is not in the individual or culture; it is in the system.
- *Teacher education programs must be reformed if teachers are to have a fighting chance to adequately support and teach students of color living in poverty.* Teacher education programs need to refocus practices and experiences to support teachers who work with some of the most vulnerable students in U.S. schools. These changes need to take place not only in the programs themselves but also the broader policies that inform how teachers are prepared.
- *Although socioeconomic status and poverty matter to student success, race remains a constant theme in understanding and addressing disparities in education.* Even students of color from middle- and upper-class backgrounds can experience inadequate educational opportunities. Proportionately, more students of color are not reaching their academic

and social potential than white students, and this reality must be addressed to build practices, policies, and interventions that support all students.

While these principles will be addressed throughout the book, the main thesis is that we must emphasize the intersections of race, class, and poverty to meet the needs of students who are perpetually underserved in schools. When schools and districts make these emphases (race and poverty) a priority, they are better able to develop practices that give every student an equitable chance to succeed—something the educational system is currently not designed to provide. Radical reform is essential if we want to improve the educational—and thus life—experiences of all students, and live up to the idea and ideals of a democracy: an educational system where every child has an equal opportunity to succeed because it is not only his or her constitutional right, but also our nation's moral responsibility and imperative.

HOW TERMS AND CONSTRUCTS ARE USED

Throughout this book, I use the term *educators* in some cases and in others, *teachers*. I do this intentionally. I refer to educators when I want to stress points related to a broader audience including teachers, principals, counselors, coaches, social workers, and so forth. In some discussions, I use *teachers* and *other educators* when I am focused on teachers in particular, but other educators are also essential to consider in the discussion. In other words, rather than just using *educators* in those instances I mention teachers in particular. In addition, throughout this book, I use the phrase *students living in poverty* rather than *poor students* or another classification. I agree with Haberman, who maintains that "language is not an innocent reflection of how we think. The terms we use control our perceptions, shape our understanding, and lead us to particular proposals for improvement."[44]

My decision to use particular phrases and terms is in no way meant to minimize or denigrate the people or places analyzed and discussed. The language I use represents my best attempt to maintain coherence as well as the integrity of the literature I review and analyze. Moreover, I attempt to honor the teachers and other educators as well as the students I have learned from and draw from in this book. Therefore, I decided to place the poverty emphasis on students' and families' situations rather than on the individuals themselves. Finally, I variously use the following phrases: *students/children of color living in poverty*; *poverty and race*; *poverty and racism*; and the *connection between poverty and race/racism*. There are no major distinctions or deliberate shifts between these word choices. My point remains regardless of the language: I encourage readers to transform the patterns by which poverty and racism undermine the educational opportunities of too many students across the United States, because every child matters in our educational system. It is time for us—all of us—to act like it.

CHAPTER 1

School- and District-Level Reform for Effective Teaching and Learning

A black person grows up in this country—and in many places—knowing that racism will be as familiar as salt to the tongue. Also, it can be as dangerous as too much salt.

—Maya Angelou

I believe in the law. I think we have a great system of justice. But I do think that system of justice has been corrupted by racism and classism. I think it's difficult for "poor people"—poor white people, brown people—to be treated fairly before the law in the same way that upper-class people are.

—Henry Louis Gates

I N MY WORK AS A SOCIAL SCIENTIST, I have visited dozens of classrooms—surely more than a hundred—and observed, both systematically and informally, exceptional teachers working in various environments across the United States—urban, suburban, and rural. Some of these are places that those on the outside might consider inadequate or substandard. But outstanding teachers are found in almost all contexts. I used to believe these individual teachers could orchestrate the kind of change necessary to overcome the ferocious inequities prevalent in schools in high-poverty urban environments, which include large numbers of black and brown students and those whose first language is not English. In fact, to an extent, I still believe this: individual teachers can and do make a difference in the lives of students. But I also now believe that constructing a deliberate fight against poverty through our educational system requires a much broader, more holistic approach for educational change that is transformative and sustainable.

In my last book, *Start Where You Are, but Don't Stay There: Understanding Diversity, Opportunity Gaps, and Teaching in Today's Classrooms*, I showcased effective teachers who demonstrated their capacity to be transformed and transformative despite the type of structural and institutional circumstances that prevent many students (and teachers) from reaching their full capacity to learn.[1] However, a true reform of schools that honors the essence of who students are and the many assets they bring requires a rethinking of the ways in which schools operate. *Start Where You Are* has helped many educators revise their practices to meet the needs of all students. I consistently receive e-mails from teachers, administrators, and a few superintendents who express the utility of the book. *Start Where You Are* is useful because it highlights teachers in unexpected places doing extraordinary work—building relationships with students, teaching to teachers' and students' strengths, negotiating differences, and envisioning their work through the lens of opportunity rather than through achievement gaps. *Rac(e)ing to Class* continues the emphasis on the necessary reshaping of educators and their practices, but it also expands the scope to include school and district reform. Teachers still matter, of course, but they work in systems—sometimes broken ones—that shape what teachers can do in the classroom.

A PROFESSIONAL DEVELOPMENT QUANDARY

Over the years I have conducted hundreds of professional development sessions with educators across the country. I have conducted these at both the school level—for example, where a principal invited me to talk to a school's faculty—and the district level, where a superintendent invited me to address all district personnel. What many district-level leaders request and expect from my talks is how schools can address the needs of students who are underserved, and they often ask me to talk to teachers, both as individuals and in groups, about how to recenter their minds and hearts as well as how to improve their curriculum, instruction, and assessment practices in their respective classrooms. However, high-level decision makers like principals and superintendents rarely ask how *they* can transform their entire district, the role *they* play as key stakeholders and decision makers, or how *they* might develop and galvanize systems of far-reaching effectiveness. Many of them want and expect teachers to be excellent in their individual classrooms without thinking seriously about what is essential from them, as leaders, to promote, ensure, and sustain teacher effectiveness.

The locus of control and, quite frankly, the onus of creating such transformation is usually placed on individual teachers, or perhaps on school-level administrators like principals and assistant principals, rather than being coordinated on a broader district level. After twelve years of doing professional development work with schools, I have concluded that some district leaders and even some principals are not really committed to reforming their policies and practices for the sake of students living in poverty, primarily because they believe what I once did: that if individual teachers teach more effectively, student learning will improve. Sadly, I have learned that the decision makers in charge of professional development expect me to deliver a pep talk, provide a few specific strategies, and perhaps offer some ideas about what can be done in the classroom to help teachers reach children living in poverty. However, there seldom is much of a commitment to the kind of true reform that will most benefit their students. I am waiting on the phone call from a superintendent or district official who invites me to help them rethink both the broad and more localized policies that need to shift to better support teachers. I yearn for the call that asks about transforming an entire district to embrace, build from, and strengthen the communities it serves while simultaneously building partnerships to foster excellence among students in individual classrooms.

I realize that district-level reform is tough. But reform that better responds to students living in poverty is not impossible. It can be done. Shifting the ethos of a district to one that centers its care around those who are most vulnerable requires leaders to embrace principles that reverberate throughout the entire district, not only through what they say but also what they do and expect of others. The lack of commitment from some leaders is a function of what they have come to know. For instance, if district officials have never themselves lived in poverty, experienced racism or other forms of discrimination, or been part of reforms that deeply benefited those on the margins of teaching and learning, they may struggle to understand how to be transformative. To be sure, I do not believe district or school leaders lack the desire to improve learning opportunities for their students. But they do not understand what it really takes to create a broad system

of excellence. In essence, a fight against poverty in education requires dis-
trict- and school-level leaders who are committed to several fundamental
principles in serving children who are living in poverty and their families.
I address these principles in this chapter and throughout the book. Two
central questions shape the imperative for school and district reform:

1. What happens when a group of students does not have an exceptional teacher?
2. What happens to a group of students that has an exceptional teacher
   in, say, third grade, but has only less effective teachers in subsequent
   grades?

In shaping this book, I struggled to decide how much emphasis to put
on broad-level change, as I wondered how many district leaders would go
beyond just enjoying "feel-good" stories about teachers who beat the odds,
and actually consider my recommendations. I concluded that, even though
district leaders do not often ask how to reform their practices, I should offer
my ideas (drawing from solid evidence) about what I believe has the greatest potential to reform schools for students living in poverty. Therefore, I
have dedicated this chapter to describing some of the steps necessary to
forge such *intentional* reform. Indeed, my eyes, heart, and mind are on the
children who may have ineffective teachers for several years and who lack
the outside support to complement what does (not) happen inside of school.

TOWARD DISTRICT- AND SCHOOL-LEVEL REFORM WITH ALL
DELIBERATE SPEED

A recurrent question is why district leaders do not advocate for the kind of
change with the level of intensity and urgency that would seem essential to
address the suffering of so many students in our nation. While school leaders typically have control over some practices, policies related to resources
tend to be much more contentious, as superintendents do not control state-
level decisions about funding and the distribution of resources. They do
not control federal policies that determine how resources will be allocated
relative to students' success or annual yearly progress. Thus, district leaders
tend to be accustomed to chipping away at small-scale problems and making minor progress, and this incremental change has led them to expect

only minute improvements over time. These leaders are thus complicit in maintaining the status quo that directly affects their students. Critical race theorists, such as Derrick Bell, Gloria Ladson-Billings, and Carl Grant, refer to the slow pace of such change and how people of color are adversely affected by the lack of progress.[2] Districts need to consciously work toward reform for students living in poverty *with all deliberate speed*, to borrow from the language of the 1954 landmark desegregation case, *Brown v. Board of Education*. However, unlike states' abilities to prolong desegregation due to their interpretation of vague language around "deliberate speed" in the court's decision, I stress that by deliberate speed, I mean immediately—right now. Admittedly, this reformation is urgent to me because it is personal. I witness firsthand how our educational systems are underequipped to serve children living in poverty.

My point is that, though teachers can have a huge impact on student learning and development, they cannot succeed alone in reaching every child in every classroom. Therefore I offer recommendations for system-wide reforms that can inform and shape classroom- and school-level work, and can result in more effective teaching and support for students—particularly children of color living in poverty.

I focus on four goals for reform that are drawn from my own research as well as that of others involving students living in poverty:

1. Understand and practice equitable decision making
2. Understand and respond to neighborhood conditions
3. Reduce class size for school-dependent students (i.e., for students who rely heavily on school for their academic, social, emotional, behavioral, and affective development)
4. Rethink and reform the inflexible, narrowed curriculum

Although these reforms are neither simple nor easy, they are possible when and if decision makers are committed to eradicating the inhumane inequities and inadequate educational practices that too many students experience. My point is not to blame those in decision-making positions for issues and situations beyond their control. Rather, I wish to help districts consistently pursue principles and practices that can make a difference. I encourage decision makers to work toward these principles and practices even if they are not able to completely implement them. It is in this light—what is in the control of district leaders—that I offer the following recommendations.

GOAL 1: UNDERSTAND AND PRACTICE EQUITABLE DECISION MAKING

Reforming districts and schools—and, consequently, classrooms—with high concentrations of students of color who live in poverty requires that leaders understand equity and practice it in their decision making. I have observed apparent misunderstanding of the definitions of and relationship between equity and equality when analyzing school resources and funding. Secada describes a major difference between the terms:

> There is a history of using terms like equity and equality of education interchangeably. Though these constructs are related, equality is group-based and quantitative. Equity can be applied to groups or to individuals; it is qualitative in that equity is tied to notions of justice.[3]

Equity, according to Secada, is a judgment as to whether or not a given state of affairs is just. Equity in education means providing students with what they need (and I would add deserve) to succeed, regardless of their racial, ethnic, cultural, or socioeconomic background. Children living in poverty may need and should receive *more* support than those in other communities. Secada explains further:

> The essence of equity lies in our ability to acknowledge that even though our actions are in accord with a set of rules, the results of those actions may still be unjust. Equity goes beyond following the rules . . . equity gauges the results of actions directly against standards of justice.

In this sense, *equity* and *equality* do not have the same meaning. What is necessary for success in one school or district or for one student may look quite different from what is needed elsewhere. *Equality* means sameness, while *equity* means, in the effort to achieve equal results, being responsive to the particulars of the circumstances. The "rules," as Secada describes them, and the policies that govern what happens to children should reflect equity.

A large number of high-need districts that lack sufficient resources often receive the same resources as districts with fewer needs. Some districts institute "equally funded programs into schools regardless of how many students need them. For example, a district might allocate $100,000 to each school with English-language learners, even though one school might have 200 students with limited English proficiency and another—often a more affluent school—might have only 20 [such students]."[4]

Practicing equity sometimes carries over into public and educator views of fairness. Several years ago, for example, a student in a graduate inservice teacher education course I taught was resolute in his position that "his tax dollars" should be used to fund "his own children's schools" and that communities need to "take care of their own." He also stressed that providing one classroom or school with more resources based on need was a form of reverse discrimination, as his children and others who got fewer resources would be "set up to fail," and those who received additional resources would somehow be at an advantage. At the core of this teacher's concerns was competition. The teacher believed that his children were somehow entitled to a "superior" education because he worked and paid taxes (as if parents in underserved communities do not!).

A fight against poverty in education must consider exactly what students need to succeed. Traditional understandings and practices of equality may be easier to accomplish in reform efforts; for example, it is not difficult to provide schools, districts, and states with equal (the same) funding. It is much more complex to develop formulas that address the individual needs of students in schools and districts. Policy experts have methodically examined trends in funding allocations and distributions and made important recommendations, such as the point that "states need to take a greater share of education funding and target more money to the districts with the biggest challenges" and the greatest needs.[5] Moreover, Roza declares that "if public school systems are serious about closing achievement gaps, they must begin to allocate more resources to the students with the greatest needs."[6]

Such positions—where policy makers allocate funds based on need and are responsive to individual schools and districts—may seem antithetical to the very essence of what equity or equality means, or at least should mean, in the United States. Critics of such an approach question how it can be equitable to give one district or school more than another. Again, district administrators must enforce the principles surrounding equity and communicate why equity, over equality, is essential for advancing the life experiences of children living in poverty through schools. Although this is a challenging task, decision makers must help educators and the public interested in education understand that some groups have reaped the benefits of unequal and inequitable structures within and outside schools for many years. Due to these systems of inequality and equity, black and brown people as well as those living in poverty have been adversely affected.

Liu writes that "wealthier, high-spending states receive a disproportionate share of Title I funds, thereby exacerbating the profound differences in education spending from state to state. Title I makes rich states richer and leaves poor states behind."[7] In essence, richer states receive more funding than states with students who are from lower socioeconomic groups or live in poverty. Liu stresses that "high-spending states get more Title I money per poor child than low-spending states. The net effect is that Title I does not reduce, but rather reinforces, inequality among states." For example:

> Maryland . . . had fewer poor children than Arkansas but received 51 percent more Title I aid per poor child. Massachusetts had fewer low-income children than Oklahoma but received more than twice as much Title I aid per poor child. Similarly, Minnesota had fewer poor children than New Mexico but received 27 percent more Title I aid per poor child.

Finally, Liu adds, wealthier states do not necessarily put more energy into providing educational support but have "higher per-pupil spending and thus receive higher Title I aid per poor child."

"Standardized" policies that do not take into account the multiple layers of need and issues in particular contexts often result in inequities and inequalities that can be difficult to control or reverse.[8] One problem is that "district budget documents report how money is spent by category and program rather than by school."[9] The categories and programs are uniform, so it is difficult to determine which areas need additional funding. As is evident in Liu's analysis, the reverse should be true. Richer states should not receive more funding because they spend more per student and, conversely, poorer states probably should receive additional funding to help provide extra support for students in need. Districts tend to take a "one-policy paradigm fits all" approach across the board, and the states, districts, and schools whose students may really need additional support do not necessarily receive it.[10] Roza writes, "More often, the patterns are created in response to pressures to equalize services across all schools. Where earmarked categorical funds such as federal Title I money pay for such extra services as full-day kindergarten or reading specialists in high-need schools, more flexible state and local money is often used to fund the same services in the low-need schools."[11] Indeed, as Ryan declares, from a moral, philosophical, and legalistic perspective, we should be practicing equity in funding because of "basic fairness and decency to innocent children."[12]

Using Resources Properly and Effectively

Increasing funding and resources for schools with a high number of students living in poverty can make a huge difference if adequate, equitable resources are used properly and effectively. However, it is important to note that researchers have found that simply increasing funding without explicit insights and recommendations as to how programs, policies, and practices should be altered can fail to achieve desired outcomes.[13] Noguera and Wells conclude that several million dollars in funds to support high-poverty schools had little impact on student achievement. These researchers found that financial support from several donors and programs, including the Annenberg Foundation, the Bill & Melinda Gates Foundation, and Title 1, have been somewhat innocuous in advancing progress for children living in poverty:

> While it may be unfair to characterize the reform efforts . . . as a total failure, it is accurate to point out that the changes enacted as a result of the grants did not result in the large-scale improvement that was hoped for. It was especially clear that very little progress was made in the poorest communities where school failure was more pervasive.[14]

Even though arguments that increased funding and resources have largely been ineffective in meeting the complex needs of underserved students, one might well ask what the educational experiences would have been for the children who did benefit, had their schools not received increased support. In other words, some gains, albeit not huge, are better than none at all from the increased monetary support.

In *The Opportunity Gap in Education Is Growing*, an eye-opening report on the New York City schools, the largest district in the country, Walker discusses several staggering findings, including the following, which point to the need to give increased attention to equity in our nation's schools and districts:

- A black or Hispanic student is nearly four times more likely than an Asian or white student to be enrolled in one of the city's poorest high schools.
- High-poverty districts have significantly fewer high-quality teachers.
- Students from low-income families have little chance of being tested for gifted and talented programs.
- Any student who is eligible for free or reduced-price meals is likely enrolled in one of the city's lowest-performing high schools.[15]

When increasing funding to their schools, district administrators need to examine which students will benefit most from additional resources, and how racial demographics and increased support correlate with variables such as attendance rates, test scores, graduation rates, and other factors. Districts especially need to consider how *opportunity gaps* such as those listed above are both persistent and pervasive. Serious thought should be given, also, to how increased funding and support programs can provide the most effective, wide-ranging, and scalable benefits for all students. Although poverty transcends race, analyzing which racial/ethnic groups of students receive added support and how their performance improves as a result could provide important information about how to address, and hopefully redress, the disproportionate number of children of color living in poverty. To recap, our goal should of course be to eliminate poverty for all racial groups, but examining how resources are used, for whom, and the outcomes that result could help elucidate why so many more children of color live in poverty.

Generally, due to systemic forms of inequity, discrimination, racism, and other -isms, more material resources and human capital should be provided to schools with a high number of students of color and others who live in poverty. When viewed with a deepened understanding of equity, district- and school-level practices should include the following:

1. Systematically and consistently study the local context to determine how best to utilize additional funds to support children living in poverty.
2. Increase per-pupil expenditure for students in high-poverty schools.
3. Provide additional people (human capital)—school principals, teachers, social workers, counselors, tutors, and community members—to supplement student learning and social development in high-poverty schools (in every classroom), a recommendation Noguera has consistently found to be essential to improve student outcomes.
4. Develop relevant training and support opportunities for the increased human capital and also for educators who are periodically in the school/district, such as substitute teachers, community members serving as mentors, and other school volunteers.
5. Secure ongoing professional development for educators (teachers, librarians, counselors, coaches, leaders) to enhance their instructional capacities and practices.
6. Increase funding and resources to support afterschool and out-of-school programs that advance student learning and social development as well as assist their families.
7. Similar to recommendation number one above, examine the progress of students from various racial and ethnic groups living in poverty in order to pinpoint what forms of support work best and for which groups of students.

GOAL 2: UNDERSTAND AND RESPOND TO NEIGHBORHOOD CONDITIONS

Schools must understand the neighborhoods where their students live in order to work with their families to improve their communities in ways that will advance student learning and social development. State- and district-level policies and practices must be shaped to respond to different types of neighborhood conditions—urban, rural, and/or suburban. Where students live can have a lasting influence on their life experiences and their chances for success inside of school. Districts need to examine the specific needs inherent to these various neighborhoods and strive to provide equitable resources to help families secure jobs, child care, and prenatal care as well as offer parenting classes to assist families. Other educational services might include tutorial programs, health and physical education, and nutrition classes as well as resources to help families afford healthy food items such as fruits and vegetables. Moreover, understanding the neighborhood conditions that students experience when walking to and from school each day can provide insights about why some students are overly anxious when they arrive and/or leave school. Some students walk through gang activity, violence, and overall unsafe conditions, and it is the school's responsibility to understand these realities and provide solutions.

Due to structural and systemic inequities—what Tate calls the "geography of opportunity"—the neighborhood landscape can shape where businesses, transportation, housing, and related resources are located.[16] The jobs students and their families can obtain may be limited by where they live.

In addition, environmental conditions can negatively affect children's health.[17] Munin explains that children of color and others living in poverty are much more likely to be exposed to hazardous environmental conditions that affect their health and consequently their performance at school:

> Families live amid air and water pollution, waste disposal sites, airports, smokestacks, lead paint, car emissions, and countless other environmental hazards . . . However, exposure to these toxins is not shared equally among our population. Studies show that these environmental conditions disproportionately affect people of color and the poor.[18]

These conditions have been shown to increase asthma in children, cause mothers to deliver their babies prematurely and with low birth weights, increase the prevalence of attention deficit hyperactivity disorder diagnoses, and increase student absenteeism. Thus, the environmental conditions where students live can have a profound impact on their performance. It is a district's responsibility to know about these neighborhood conditions and work to improve them. Most of these circumstances fall far beyond the control of students and their families. Why, then, are students and their families punished for issues that they do not control or cause?

Learning about these situations requires a conscious effort. In one district in the Midwest, educators are required to take a bus tour at the beginning of the semester. They ride through the neighborhoods that are home to a majority of their students living in poverty, including two housing projects as well as very low-income housing communities. While I certainly believe this tour provides insights for the educators on the bus, my worry is that such an experience could do more harm than good. For instance, after one bus ride, a teacher told me that she witnessed two men "screaming" at each other on a street corner. She thought at one point they were getting ready to fight (a physical altercation). But after a minute or two, as the bus was stopped at a red light, the two men gave each other "high-fives," laughed, and left in separate directions. She explained that the men were talking about a sporting event and were just "really expressive." The danger of such community tours is that, because educators do not actually get off the bus and talk to the people, and immerse themselves in the community, stereotypes about particular communities may be reinforced rather than dispelled. Moreover, a one-time bus ride hardly gives educators the insights they need to understand, respond to, and hopefully empathize with their students and community members. Thus, the learning I am advocating for here is deep and requires a level of sustained inquiry that extends far beyond a one-day bus tour through a community.

Race, Urban, and Rural Poverty

According to the National Center for Education Statistics (NCES), in 2010–2011, nonwhite students were overwhelmingly represented in the student population of large cities. For instance, American Indian/Alaska Native students numbered 65,149, Asian/Pacific Island students 575,119, black students 2,182,086, and Hispanic students 3,195,522; white students numbered 1,685,694, and mixed-race students 155,477 (see table 1.1).

The point is certainly not that only students of color live in poverty, because this is not true. Rather, because proportionately more students of color than white students live in large cities, educators need to be aware of demographics in relation to poverty.

Although much attention is focused on urban poverty, Cass has found that poverty is sometimes more pronounced in rural areas.[19] In both rural and urban communities, however, those who live in poverty can experience several disheartening realities: housing instability; hunger, health, and nutrition problems; physical, emotional, and psychological abuse due

TABLE 1.1   Total students in large U.S. cities by race, 2010–2011

American Indian /Alaska Native	60,860
Asian/Pacific Islander	592,533
Black	2,140,795
Hispanic	3,047,646
White	1,537,390
Two or more races	155,477
*Total students*ᵃ	7,531,542

Source: Adapted from National Center for Education Statistics, Rural Education in America, Table B.1.b.-1, Fall 2010 data, http://nces.ed.gov/surveys/ruraled/tables_archive.asp.
ᵃ Total excludes 51,637 students with missing race/ethnicity information.

to stress; family instability; and inadequate schools and educational experiences. Of course, students can experience these same challenges outside of poverty, but proportionately, these hardships are intensified when living in poverty.

While many families in the rural communities I have studied live below the poverty line, some do own their homes, usually by inheriting property from deceased family members. However, the value of the homes is extremely low due to the lack of infrastructure, businesses, and related amenities in the area.

Although people living in rural poverty tend to have some land around their homes, those living in poverty in large urban areas often reside in apartment-style homes, typically known as housing projects, which are government supported. Those living in urban poverty experience higher levels of crime than in rural areas, but they do benefit from public transportation and other large-city conveniences. Thus, while families live in poverty in both rural and urban areas, their experiences can be quite different.

Many schools in both contexts have challenges. States, districts, and schools must more deeply understand the root causes of hazardous and troubling living conditions for students they serve. Such conditions can lead directly to distressing practices and realities, including the following:

- Physical, psychological, and/or emotional abuse
- Drug abuse, gambling, or alcoholism

TABLE 1.2   Total students in rural U.S. communities by race, 2010–2011

American Indian/Alaska Native	239,499
Asian/Pacific Islander	260,251
Black	1,203,021
Hispanic	1,541,521
White	8,507,674
Two or more races	239,701
Total students[a]	*12,015,228*

Source: Adapted from National Center for Education Statistics, Rural Education in America, Table B.1.b.-1, Fall 2010 data, http://nces.ed.gov/surveys/ruraled/tables_archive.asp.

[a] Total excludes 51,637 students with missing race/ethnicity information.

- Health and nutrition problems, including high rates of "asthma, ear infections, stomach problems, and speech problems," and poor eating patterns, such as not eating well-balanced meals or missing meals altogether[20]
- Irregular school attendance, frequent tardiness and school changes, and difficulty concentrating on learning and interacting with classmates
- Homelessness

Educators must keep these neighborhood conditions and related practices on their radar and be intentional about responding to them if real reform is to happen. Districts truly committed to helping their children living in poverty cannot take the position that these factors are outside the realm of their work as educators. Again, addressing these concerns requires a broader reach than one effective classroom teacher can have. Holistic reform requires district- and school-level efforts and commitments that seek to improve neighborhoods even as they work to improve the classroom. Educators must work with communities to improve their neighborhoods and the plethora of challenges students may face.

Student and Family Homelessness

Homeless students and their families deserve special attention mainly because their needs are too often left on the margins of reform. During the

Thanksgiving holiday one year, my family and I traveled by car to visit family in Nashville. While we drove, we discussed what we saw from the car. When stopped at a traffic light in Nashville, my three-year-old daughter, Anna, pointed out homeless people she observed on the street corners. Most fascinating for her at one point was a family of four—a mother, father, and two children who appeared to be in their early teens. The mother and children sat on the grass while the father stood at the street corner selling "street newspapers."[21] Anna posed lots of questions about what she observed: "Why is that girl sitting on the ground while it's so cold?" "Isn't she cold?" "Why don't they go inside of their house?" When I saw the unsatisfied look on Anna's face after I responded to her questions, I knew I had done a poor job of answering her. This interaction with my daughter touched my heart in a profound way, and she reminded me of what James Banks, professor and pioneer in multicultural education at the University of Washington, taught me more than a decade ago. At a presentation at the annual meeting of the American Educational Research Association, he declared that we have to engage the work of underserved students with our *heads* and our *hearts*. Sadly, the family we observed on the street that cold day in Nashville reflected what appears to be a growing epidemic in the United States: children suffering from the effects of poverty and homelessness.

Sociologists Lee, Tyler, and Wright wrote that "homeless children suffer from their parents' poverty, as evidenced by more frequent school mobility, absenteeism, and grade retention; lower achievement test scores; and a greater risk of learning disabilities, behavioral disorders, and related problems."[22] Family structure, particularly homelessness, has been shown to influence students' experiences and outcomes at schools. Duffield, who examined the effects of homelessness on students' school attendance, enrollment, and academic success, describes homelessness as "the manifestation of severe poverty and lack of affordable housing; simply put, homeless families are too poor to afford housing."[23] Homelessness can result from "family problems, economic problems, and residential instability" and students can become homeless either with their family or alone.[24] Nooe and Patterson describe the various settings homelessness can take: "Homeless individuals may experience changes in housing status that includes being on the street, shared dwelling, emergency shelter, transitional housing, and permanent . . . hospitalization and incarceration in correctional facilities."[25]

Although most people have at least a surface-level understanding of what homelessness is, the problem is not well defined or categorized either in the scholarly literature or by society. Finley and Diversi stress that the fuzziness in how homelessness is defined, especially from the perspectives of policy makers, results in the false impression that homelessness is a smaller problem than it actually is. This nebulousness essentially lets states, districts, and schools off the hook in terms of addressing the challenges this population faces, and, consequently, the resources available to assist homeless children often are limited. Finley and Diversi argue that the number of homeless individuals and families has been distorted:

> Let us be clear here. Such distortion has profound consequences for actual lives. For instance, families forced into couch surfing with relatives and friends are most often not counted . . . Nor are the families living in tent cities, vehicles, and parks around the country. As a result, thousands of lives and stories are buried under an ideologically self-serving sensation that things aren't as bad as some claim. Or if the housing crisis is as bad as it seems, it is due solely to irresponsible individual choices.[26]

Finley and Diversi make an important point: many believe people are homeless due to an ethos of irresponsibility or bad choices. This inaccurate view also applies to many people who live in poverty. Unfortunately, this perception leads some to believe that people deserve to be in the situations they are.

Mawhinney-Rhoads and Stahler observe that

> homeless children are particularly at risk for poor educational outcomes, which can have lifelong consequences for their future livelihood and economic independence. If school systems do not provide special educational interventions to address the particular educational barriers that these children face, then it is likely that these children will stay marginalized in the lowest economic rung of society.[27]

Mawhinney-Rhoads and Stahler have identified several educational barriers that homeless students face at school that should be addressed through policy and practice. One barrier is a residency requirement; homeless students and their families who lack a permanent residence or perhaps are living out of a car are challenged to produce proof of residency, which "can block some students from attending certain schools or maintaining their status in their current school."

A second barrier is what these researchers called "guardianship"; that is, "homeless children often reside with a family member who is not a legal guardian" and consequently may be denied access to school or be subject to a stressful process.[28] Another barrier is proof of medical records, which are required by schools before a child can enroll. Transient students and their families often lack or lose these documents. The authors explain that transportation and transience are related problems: "[B]ecause homeless families are so often transient, a homeless child attending school and residing in a temporary shelter within a given school district might move 30 days later to another shelter outside the district boundaries." This can make it difficult to get to school on time or to attend school at all, particularly if the family does not have a car or access to public transportation. A final barrier they identify is socioemotional challenges—homeless students tend to have a difficult time interacting with peers and teachers. They may find it difficult to get along with others because they have low self-esteem and are worried about their home situation, or perhaps because they are suffering from a lack of sleep. Mawhinney-Rhoads and Stahler conclude that school reform policies must be able to meet the evolving needs of the homeless students they serve.

Of course, it is important to note there are also students living below the poverty line and homeless students who beat the odds, who persevere and succeed in spite of difficult neighborhood conditions and related issues. Thus, the story of homeless students should not end with the idea that they only experience turmoil; some of them, whether they classify themselves as homeless or not, succeed amid challenging situations.

Students who live in poverty and/or are homeless are often misunderstood, ignored, or relegated to the margins in broader policy and reform movements at the state, district, and school levels. We must address this marginalization and end it. We also must be mindful of how racism and other forms of discrimination contribute to students' experiences, as well as to policy makers' responses to them. Policy makers need to consider several questions: What are the demographic patterns of homeless children and youth? How might racial discrimination and other forms of oppression and marginalization (such as classism against white students) perpetuate homelessness and poverty? Mawhinney-Rhoads and Stahler note that "today, a significant proportion of the homeless population is comprised of minority, single-mother households with multiple children" and that black people represent about 40 percent of the homeless population.[29]

According to the *2011 Annual Homeless Assessment Report to Congress*, there were 636,017 homeless people, 22.1 percent of them (140,560) under the age of eighteen.[30] Table 1.3 provides a snapshot of homeless children by ethnicity.

To achieve real reform, I contend that states, districts, and schools must work toward these goals:

1. Be more aware of how neighborhood conditions influence students and their families.
2. Develop partnerships with community organizations, such as churches, synagogues, recreation centers, community councils, and so forth, to support students and their families outside and inside of school.
3. Recruit and prepare local community members—such as social workers, counselors, clergy, and coaches—to assume the role of educator in both traditional and nontraditional capacities, including through afterschool programs. This means that initiatives should be developed to recruit these individuals into teaching.

TABLE 1.3　Number of homeless children by ethnicity, January 2011

American Indian / Alaska Native (4.0%)	5,622
Native Hawaiian / Pacific Islander (0.8%)	1,124
Asian (0.7%)	984
African American (38.1%)	53,553
Hispanic (8.9%)	12,510
White (39.5%)	55,521
Two or more races (7.9%)	11,104
Total children (99.9% reported by ethnicity)	*140,419*

Source: Adapted from *2011 Annual Homeless Assessment Report to Congress*, November 2012, U.S. Department of Housing and Urban Development, Office of Community Planning and Development, https://www.hudexchange.info/resources/documents/2011AHAR_FinalReport.pdf.

4. Partner with communities and work to elect political officials, including school board members, who will address the real-life concerns of neighborhoods and schools.

5. Demand that policy makers and decision makers address harmful environmental conditions, such as hazardous wastes that contaminate water and cause health concerns. (Indeed, educators are political advocates whether they admit it or not).

6. Develop partnerships with health-care providers to support students who experience unhealthy living conditions and work to prevent health challenges by providing dental and health support for children.

In sum, I am suggesting that states, districts, and schools would do well (better) to consider making some radical shifts in the way they think about the purview of their responsibility, as it is clear that students find it difficult to learn when they are burdened by the challenges discussed above. Teachers cannot teach when students are not ready to learn because of ecological factors. States, districts, and schools must begin to see themselves as more than mere educational institutions concerned only with classroom teaching and learning, and strive to respond to neighborhood conditions. Seriously reforming districts and schools will require that school and district leaders understand and embrace the *political nature of their work*, as the type of school transformation I am advancing here is political, economic, and radical.[31]

GOAL 3: REDUCE CLASS SIZE FOR SCHOOL-DEPENDENT STUDENTS

So far, I have emphasized two goals for broad reform, involving equitable decision making and responses to neighborhood conditions. Next, I stress the importance of reducing class size for school-dependent students.

Meaning of School Dependence

Before discussing class size reduction, I want to define what I mean by school dependence. Being school dependent can mean students rely on school for basic needs such as breakfast and lunch, nutritious snacks, and academic support, as well as exposure to museums and other learning centers outside the traditional classroom. Research has shown that students from lower socioeconomic backgrounds, including those living in poverty, depend on school more than their more-affluent classmates to help them understand, navigate, and function in school.[32] To be clear, all students attending school—public, private, independent, poor, affluent, rural, suburban, urban—depend on the school institution to some degree to achieve academic and social success. However, although most parents are involved to some extent in their children's educational experiences, students living in poverty may rely on their schools to meet myriad needs that other student populations fulfill elsewhere.[33] For instance, because parents living in poverty may work low-wage jobs during the evenings or even during graveyard shifts (midnight–8 a.m.), students may rely more heavily on schools to support them.[34]

In addition, in previous research I have conducted, I learned that a reasonable number of middle and high school students living below the poverty line work part-time jobs (babysitting, mowing lawns, working at fast-food restaurants) to support their families. Many of these students are motivated to learn and aspire to earn good grades. A large number of them plan to attend either a two- or four-year institution of higher education. However, they struggle to complete homework assignments after school and on weekends, when they usually work long hours.

Schools that attempt to respond to the intricate and perhaps idiosyncratic nature of their students should insist that all members of the school community reflect on the following types of questions:

- Which of my students' needs are not being met at home?
- How can I learn more about my students' assets in order to draw from and build on their strengths inside the classroom?
- How can I discover which of my students depend most on school for academic, social, emotional, behavioral, and affective support?
- In what ways is the school already meeting the needs of school-dependent students, and how do I know? How can we build on this success?
- What else can the school do to address the needs of school-dependent students, and who else inside and outside of school should be involved in this effort?

It is important that conversations about meeting the needs of school-dependent students (1) acknowledge the fact that some students' needs are being met at home while others may not be and (2) take place within a space of possibility, optimism, and hope, as they could easily regress into a negative focus on the deficits of students and their families. For instance, although some students living below the poverty line may be working part-time jobs and unable to dedicate long hours to homework, recognizing the level of responsibility associated with part-time work allows educators to see these students from a strength-based orientation. Serving school-dependent students requires an approach that involves both the head and the heart, as teachers, administrators, counselors, and other school personnel play a critical role in the social, emotional, behavioral, and cognitive development and demands of these students.

Konstantopoulos has found that "in early grades, teacher effects in one grade lead to higher academic achievement in the following grade. This finding supports the notion that effective teachers can increase achievement significantly for all students."[35] In other words, teachers can make *the* critical difference in whether or not highly school-dependent students succeed. However, it can be difficult for teachers to meet the multitude of student needs in large classes. Moreover, although some teachers succeed in this arduous task, systemic and structural involvement can only help. So, districts need to pay careful attention to the numbers of students—especially heavily school-dependent students—teachers have to serve. Put simply, class size matters, and it can shape a teacher's ability to be responsive to students.

Unfairly, school decision makers place large numbers (proportionately and otherwise) of school-dependent students with teachers who show success with these students. Effective teachers are then seemingly punished for their achievement by being assigned even more students with high needs. This practice is especially prevalent in elementary and middle school environments. The overreliance on particular teachers to serve students whose needs are highest leads to teacher burnout. These teachers become emotionally drained because of the taxing needs of their students. This is not fair but is pervasive in schools across the country. Class size matters for both optimal student support and teacher workload. Thus all educators need to be prepared to support the most vulnerable students, and then classroom settings need to be restructured to address intricate needs of students.

Teaching and Class Size Reduction

Conventional wisdom might suggest that smaller classes would almost automatically raise student test scores. However, results are mixed. Although researchers have persistently explored the benefits of smaller class size for students living in poverty, and states and even the federal government have paid increased attention over the past twenty years to the effect of smaller class size, some evidence suggests that reducing class size has little direct impact on the achievement scores of students living in poverty.[36] The debate continues, but there has not been a concerted national movement to reduce class size for those most vulnerable to ineffective educational practices, particularly those living in poverty.

Based on my observations and experience, I can confidently stress that smaller classes provide greater opportunities for academic, social, and other student development that may never show up on a standardized exam. In short, smaller classes can influence students' decisions and experiences, both inside and outside of school. In classrooms with fewer students, I have seen the following benefits:

- Teachers are able to communicate more directly with individual students, about not only academic matters but also family circumstances and other out-of-school situations.
- Teachers are able to address students' specific needs in terms of learning the curriculum (providing additional instructional time on multiplication); making the curriculum relevant (finding literature that helps a student deal with family issues or other problems); and learning unrelated to the formal curriculum (advising an underage student who wants to move out of his parents' home).
- Teachers learn about individual and collective student needs to help shape the curriculum and create instructional synergy.
- Because teachers have the time to address more than academic needs, students are able to build social skills they need to function within and beyond the classroom and school.

- Students are able to work more cooperatively with each other (through group learning/work) in order to complete academic projects.
- There is a greater sense of community in the classroom for teachers and students alike because there are fewer people to get to know. Relationship building is more authentic and sustainable.

Middle and high school teachers I have worked with over the years have commented that they find it difficult or even impossible to address their students' needs—not only academic but also social, psychological, and emotional—because they have too many students in a class. For instance, one middle school teacher told me that in two of her classes, she needed either a teaching assistant or fewer students, because she was worried that several of her students would otherwise not get the attention they deserved.

Based on my observations, this teacher did have too many students in those two classes (twenty-seven in one and thirty-one in the other), which made it impossible for her to make the kind of connections with students essential for their learning and development. It was unfortunate that the school's administrators were either unaware of the need to reduce class size or unable to do so due to factors beyond their control, such as a lack of money, space, or a qualified teacher to teach an additional class. Either way, the students were the ones who suffered. It appeared that most of the students had "checked out" because what occurred daily in the classroom can best be described as chaos: students did not find the class useful; they continually talked to each other about matters other than schoolwork; they did not bring their books and other materials to class or complete homework; and they refused to participate in the learning activities. Meanwhile, the teacher tried to control the students, but she was frustrated and often sent students out to stand in the hallway or to the office, which students did not protest because they did not desire to be in the classroom. What I observed and what the teacher shared with me was consistent with what Haberman classified several decades ago as a "pedagogy of poverty."[37]

Though Haberman's discussion was not related to class size per se, it did shed light on the complex challenges faced in urban schools and classrooms. I do believe the teacher I mention here aspired to help her students succeed, but she did not have the tools to do so in such large classes, where many students needed individualized attention. Moreover, she spent a great deal of time simply trying to manage the students. The teacher had good intentions but neither the knowledge nor the skill to work with so many students with an inordinate range of needs. In conversations I had with students in her classes, some said they "felt sorry" for the teacher and were frustrated by the lack of order and learning in the classroom. Some students corrected other students themselves and told them to "shut up." However, these efforts and those of the teacher were insufficient—with so many students, what was this teacher to do?

I have heard other teachers express concern about not being able to build the relationships necessary to be successful with their students. One teacher relayed this story:

> Several of my girls are struggling this year unlike anything I've ever seen in the past. I suspect some are being bullied by classmates, and one of my girls was living with her boyfriend and his parents. Rumor has it that the parents were allowing them to sleep together. And, well, when the kid got pregnant the parents put her out. And she hates her own mother and grandmother but she had to go back home. What is she supposed to do? She is so sad every day. She mouths off and puts her head on the desk most days. I know it is a plea for help and attention. I wish I had more time to connect with her, but when you have 30 kids staring at you and expecting you to teach them science, then you have to teach to the masses. Most days when I drive home, I say to myself, "Did you touch [Anisha] today?" She needs help, but I'm afraid I'm not helping much.

Research has shown that some students will not learn from teachers with whom they do not have a meaningful relationship, yet it is difficult to develop such connections in large classrooms, where as many as thirty students have nuanced, individual (often traumatic), and complex needs.[38] Students rely on the school, and the school is not well equipped to support this reliance.

Jepsen and Rivkin have studied the effects of reduced class size on student test scores in California, specifically in mathematics and reading. They looked at this development:

> In the summer of 1996, California enacted the most expensive state level education reform in U.S. history. The state's class-size-reduction . . . program reduced K-3 class sizes throughout the state by roughly

ten students per class, from 30 to 20, at an annual cost that exceeds one billion dollars.[39]

Recognizing the complexity of studying the effects of reduced class size and its interplay with teacher quality and student achievement, Jepsen and Rivkin concluded that smaller class size did raise math and reading achievement. However, these results were not straightforward. They reported that "although the results show that smaller classes raised mathematics and reading achievement, they also show that the increase in the share of teachers with neither prior experience nor full certification dampened the benefits of smaller classes, particularly in schools with high shares of economically disadvantaged, minority students." Jepsen and Rivkin did of course argue that competing factors, such as variations in teacher quality and experience, made it difficult to determine the effect of smaller class size; for instance, was improved student achievement a result of the quality of the teacher or the reduction in class size? The researchers also questioned whether the impact of reducing class size was worth the cost.

Although critics might suggest that reducing class size plays only a small role in raising student test scores, it is unreasonable to suggest that class size does not matter from a broader, more holistic perspective—especially for school-dependent students. While researchers may not have found significant links between reduced class size and student test scores, my research has revealed that smaller class size can have a profound influence on the sociology of the classroom, especially among school populations that include large percentages of students living in poverty and highly school-dependent students—that is, students who rely on the school and its employees to assist them in their academic, social, emotional, behavioral, and affective development. Thus, reducing class size can provide a foundation for the type of student-teacher connections necessary for success, especially for school-dependent students.[40]

It is essential to point out that reducing class size alone cannot provide the kinds of curriculum reform, instructional innovation, and teacher-student connections discussed earlier. Graue, Hatch, Rao, and Oen conducted a qualitative study with nine high-poverty schools to investigate a statewide class size reduction initiative that required changes in staffing, instructional strategies, and space allocations, and lowered the student-teacher ratio. The results of the study were mixed, yet they led the researchers to conclude that reforms were necessary both programmatically and instructionally. For instance, *if teachers persist with the same curriculum development and instructional practices they use with larger classes, reducing the number of students may not have a lasting influence on test scores or in other areas.*[41] In essence, these researchers found that what teachers actually do with the curriculum is paramount to the success, or lack thereof, of class size reduction. They stress the importance of professional development in helping both individual teachers and schools' collective teaching staff to transform their pedagogical practices to take full advantage of smaller classes.

When I began teaching at Vanderbilt University after earning my doctorate at The Ohio State University, I had to learn how to teach smaller classes. As a graduate teaching associate at Ohio State, I usually had large classes, and my teaching practices had to reflect that. I tended to lecture using overhead slides, engage in some general activities, and then put students into small groups to discuss the complex issues I had introduced. At Vanderbilt, however, my smaller classes forced me to drastically shift the nature of what I taught and how I taught it. With smaller classes, I was able to hear more students and respond to their comments. I also had time to engage one-on-one with students during and after classes.

In smaller classes and especially with school-dependent students, I encourage teachers to do the following:

- *Meet with students individually.* The idea is that smaller classes enable teachers to get to know students, which helps teachers decide what to teach and how to teach. To fulfill this idea, teachers should meet individually with their students and ask questions that will help them learn about student interests, needs, and expectations.
- *Teach individual students.* As teachers learn about their students, they should aim to teach to the broad interests and strengths of both the group and individual students. Some school districts have begun to develop Individual Education Plans (IEPs) for all students, not only those classified as having special needs. With fewer students, teachers will find it easier to develop IEPs and to tailor their curriculum and instruction to students' specific learning and development needs.
- *Develop a learning agreement.* Smaller classes allow teachers to negotiate with students about the nature of the teaching and learning

exchange, draw on students' assets, and address the challenges they encounter. Learner agreements or "contracts" may be structured like IEPs or be developed at the district, school, or classroom level. The point is to create contractual agreements that are responsive to students' varied needs. Students should be involved in these agreements, which might address behavior, learning, or forms of assessment.

- *Encourage creativity and innovation.* In small classes, teachers are able to move beyond traditional pedagogical practices and allow students to engage in activities that build on their own creativity, such as drawing, music, and other forms of art and expression.

- *Develop meaningful and relevant assessments.* Teachers and students together can develop varied assessments that allow students to demonstrate their development, learning, and overall progress through music or other forms of popular culture or the arts that are consistent with their interests. It is important to note that these assessments should not replace traditional tests, but rather help to gauge what students know and have gleaned from instruction. Because the system is set up to test students by any means necessary, teachers and students alike could suffer if students are not prepared for traditional assessments—unfortunately.

- *Construct innovative projects and assignments.* Teachers should allow students to have some input into developing the projects and assignments they are expected to complete, providing that they address the standards and curriculum that must be covered. Projects that allow students to build on their strengths and interests can have a lasting influence on what they learn, retain, and can transfer to other settings. Moreover, engaging in these projects could pique students' interests and foster a love for a particular domain.

GOAL 4: RETHINK AND REFORM THE INFLEXIBLE, NARROWED CURRICULUM

Some see the curriculum as a static entity that teachers can point to on a board, read from a pacing guide, or copy from a Web site, without giving serious attention to the students' lived experiences. Curriculum can generally be defined as what students have the opportunity to learn in school, but student learning involves much more than what shows up in a school's official written curriculum. Further, standards are not the curriculum. Students experience learning opportunities all the time and in various locations. Students learn (a curriculum) in their homes with their families, with their friends in the park or the playground, on the street, on the bus ride to school, on the sidewalk while walking to school, and in other spaces, such as churches, synagogues, and recreation centers. Students have learning experiences in the school building where they see materials on the walls and even on the playground.

Eisner presents several important forms of curriculum students encounter:[42]

1. The *explicit* curriculum concerns intended student learning opportunities that are taught overtly from printed documents, policies, and guidelines, such as course syllabi, the Common Core Standards, or a school Web site.

2. The *implicit* curriculum is intended or unintended, but it is not overtly expressed or written down, though it is part of what students have the opportunity to learn. Take, for instance, a situation where a school administrator asks over the intercom for a teacher to send a "young man" to the office to pick up a box of books and take it back to a classroom. An implicit gender role message is inherent in what students may learn in this situation—perhaps that a "young woman" is not capable of delivering the box.

3. The *null* curriculum deals with what students do not have the opportunity to learn. From my perspective, this is the most fascinating of Eisner's forms of curriculum. Information and knowledge that are not available to students are also a form of curriculum, in that students are learning something based on what is overlooked, not emphasized, or not taught. What students do not experience in the curriculum thus becomes a message. For example, if educators do not empower students to question, critique, or critically examine power structures, students may be learning that it is not essential for them to critique the world in order to improve it. From Eisner's perspective, what is absent from the curriculum is still present in student learning.

Inflexibility

A curriculum that is narrowly scripted may help teachers decide what to teach and when, and even what to say in the classroom at a particular time, but it stops short of concretely helping teachers know *how* to teach. Many teachers are expected to follow a predetermined set of steps. I have spoken with teachers, especially those in rural and urban schools that have a large number of students of color who live in poverty, who report that when administrators visit their classrooms, they expect the teachers to be teaching specific, predetermined content at that particular time—sometimes even on a certain page! The idea of curriculum inflexibility is that a scripted curriculum will ensure that all students are exposed to the same material regardless of where they live, their needs, or their teachers' skillset. However, inflexible guidelines for what can be taught make it challenging for teachers to exercise their professional judgment in supporting student learning.

Although a scripted curriculum has some benefits, especially for new teachers or those who have been trained in fast-track teacher education programs, it can also be detrimental for teachers and students alike because it disregards the complex nature of teaching in relation to student needs. If teachers have not been trained well and/or are new to the field, a narrow, scripted curriculum gives them a tool to draw from in the classroom, protects them from being overwhelmed by a broad curriculum, and even tells them what to cover, almost word for word. While this may sound ideal, especially for traditionally underserved student populations, Ede writes that "the diverse ethnic and cultural makeup of today's classrooms makes it unlikely that one single curriculum will meet the needs and interests of all students."[43] King and Zucker maintain that the impetus to narrow the curriculum stems in part from the need for teachers to focus on what will most likely be tested in any given year.[44] Not allowing teachers the autonomy and professional judgment to develop their own curriculum can leave them, and the public, feeling that teachers are incapable of making effective choices on their own. Scripted curricula can effectively de-skill teachers and force students to learn from a curriculum that is inflexible, not attuned to their interests, and disconnected from their lived experiences, both individually and collectively. To be clear, my point is not to critique all aspects of curriculum narrowing and scripting. There are some benefits to such narrowing along with the real problems—points I will expand on throughout this book.

A scripted curriculum can be advantageous for teachers who need framing guides to help them cover information that could benefit students. However, teachers must have the skills to be able to interpret the script in implementing it with *real* students, with *real* life situations. In essence, administration has to allow teachers freedom to make instructional decisions that make sense for their students. A scripted curriculum, along with other bureaucratic controls, can make it difficult or even impossible for teachers to respond to the context and realities of their work environment. Again, what students in a suburban district need for success might look very different from what students in a rural or urban context need.

Narrowing

The overemphasis on reading and math to the exclusion of other content areas, such as social studies, art, music, and physical education, narrows the scope of student learning. A report published by the Center on Education Policy states that "many educators reported that their efforts to align curriculum to standards and focus on tested material in reading and mathematics have diminished the class time available for social studies, science, and other subjects or activities."[45] Jerald concludes that

> some schools might well need to expand instructional time in reading to enable students to become fluent readers. But educators should be made aware that cutting too deeply into social studies, science, and the arts imposes significant long-term costs on students, hampers reading comprehension and thinking skills, increases inequity, and makes the job of secondary level teachers that much harder. Only when teachers and administrators are fully aware of the tradeoffs can they make good decisions about whether, how, and for whom to narrow the curriculum—one educational strategy that should *never* be considered lightly.[46]

Cawelti argues another important critique; he stresses the content and learning opportunities students will miss when narrowing the curriculum forces teachers to focus only on math and language arts/reading in the hope of preparing students for standard examinations.[47]

A scripted, standardized curriculum can make it difficult for teachers to understand and respond to the sociological composition of their classroom, school, or community, especially in schools where resources are scarce. In other professions, employees are expected to learn from the particulars of their working conditions and their clientele and to use their professional judgment in responding to problems they encounter. A scripted curriculum makes it difficult for teaching professionals to do this. In examining the language arts curriculum in one school district, Smagorinsky, Lakly, and Johnson found that district officials expect teachers to use the same curriculum materials across the diverse district, in the same order, and even at the same time of day.[48] They explained that

> [curriculum] uniformity meant that all students, whether living in an affluent suburb, in the inner city, or on a farm on the fringe of the county would receive the same [curriculum] at the same time . . . The curriculum [was] further tied to standardized county-wide tests that assessed students after each unit, further pressuring teachers to follow the curriculum guide faithfully.[49]

Crocco and Costigan provide a compelling perspective on curriculum narrowing:

> Under the curricular and pedagogical impositions of scripted lessons and mandated curriculum, patterns associated nationwide with high-stakes testing, the No Child Left Behind Act of 2001, and the phenomenon known as the "narrowing of curriculum," new teachers in New York City (NYC) find their personal and professional identity thwarted, creativity and autonomy undermined, and ability to forge relationships with students diminished—all critical factors in their expressed job satisfaction. These indirect consequences of accountability regimen as it operates in NYC may exacerbate new teacher attrition, especially from schools serving low-income students. The data reported here suggest a mixed picture of frustration and anger, alongside determination, resistance, and resilience in the face of these impositions.[50]

Clearly, teaching a narrowed curriculum can make it difficult for teachers who are committed to developing a curriculum that is responsive to their students' day-to-day experiences, particularly those who live in precarious circumstances.

In a qualitative study of third-grade students, Dutro investigated the extent to which students living in poverty were able to connect with a district-mandated reading curriculum. She found that the mandated curriculum portrayed "economic struggle as a temporary condition, located only in historical or national disaster contexts."[51] She explains that the teacher's edition for the curriculum, which teachers used as a classroom guide for learning, included language that did not support students' critical thinking about the relationship between themselves and poverty. This study demonstrates how the curriculum can be disconnected from students' lived experiences and framed in a way that does not encourage students to think about matters in their own communities that might help them understand more fully how the world works, for whom, and what they can do to challenge and change inequity.[52]

I agree with Dutro's finding that the range of curriculum materials should "allow children to see themselves, access experiences that differ from their own, and foster talk about issues of equity and social justice."[53] Some teachers may believe, however, that focusing on matters of inequity or social justice is disadvantageous, inappropriate, or irrelevant to the "real" curriculum, and thus they avoid such emphases.[54] But students suffer from such omissions, as a focus on race and poverty can help them examine their own lives, make connections, draw conclusion about inconsistencies, and think about the direction of their lives as they interact with others. Narrowing the curriculum away from emphases on race and poverty does little to prepare students to understand and respond to situations in which they might find themselves.

The research suggests that, to advance the fight against poverty, curriculum should be relevant and responsive to students.[55] Much of my earlier work suggests that curriculum relevance and responsiveness is really a microlevel classroom issue that teachers can address without any real support from broader systems or structures. However, I now believe that a movement for a curriculum that is relevant and responsive to students goes far beyond what classroom teachers alone can accomplish because of the broader policy emphasis on narrowing the curriculum. The evidence suggests that when teachers do deviate from the scripted or narrowed curriculum, they can be punished, and severely. Therefore, rethinking a narrowed curriculum must be done at the state, district, and school levels. Teachers must be taught how to construct curriculum and instructional practices that are responsive to students, and districts and schools must support teachers in this work. I am not suggesting teachers should be given the liberty to construct their curriculum without any structure, accountability, or input from those outside their classroom. What I am stressing is that teachers should be able to examine and adapt curriculum standards and guidelines to make them appropriate for their own students. In sum, the curriculum should "fit" the students it is designed to serve.[56]

Gloria Ladson-Billings, Geneva Gay, Carol Lee, Tyrone Howard, and others have stressed the importance of developing responsive and relevant curriculum materials and instructional practices. As schools attempt to do this, states and districts should all aim to develop educators in ways that allow them to do the following:

- *Locate curriculum sites* that relate to students and get them excited about the content being covered (and excited about learning in general).
- *Explicitly relate the curriculum* to students' life experiences in ways they understand and are able to place in a past, current, or future context.
- *Select a curriculum that speaks from the point of view* of students, their communities, and their families.
- Expose students to a curriculum that has *some references outside the students' own* worldview, cultural experiences, and belief systems and, simultaneously, help them draw connections to both the familiar and the unfamiliar.
- View *students themselves as curriculum texts* and use them as sites for developing and making connections to the curriculum.

Leading thinkers about reforming the curriculum for students of color who live in poverty have stressed the importance of the curriculum's flexibility, relevance, and responsiveness in mathematics, science, social studies, and language arts. However, teachers must be well skilled to work with this flexibility. I call this type of practice curriculum agility—where teachers are able to stretch and modify the curriculum and curriculum practices in ways that transform student thinking. Hinton and Berry explain that the curriculum should reflect "children's needs as well as who they are."[57] Tatum finds a need to select texts for teaching African American males that help to "shape a positive life trajectory and provide a roadmap that can help students resist nonproductive behaviors."[58] Clearly, given the right curriculum and curriculum practices, students have the best chance of building knowledge and skill for success. The curriculum also can be a vehicle for these students to understand how to negotiate difficult situations and make meaningful contributions to their own communities and the broader society. But the scope of these possibilities lies in state, district, and school involvement and improvement. Teachers cannot achieve these reforms without administrative support and leadership at various organizational levels, from superintendent to building school principals.

CULTURAL AND ORGANIZATIONAL SHIFTS

In this chapter, I have outlined four interrelated goals that are necessary in reforming state, district, and schoolwide policies, programs, interventions, and practices to meet the needs of students living in poverty: understand and practice equitable decision making; understand and respond to neighborhood conditions; reduce class size for school-dependent students; and rethink and reform the inflexible, narrow curriculum. I have stressed that several additional state, district, and school-level reforms are also essential, but those I elaborate on in this chapter are the ones that emerge consistently in my study of states, schools, and districts that are more effective in meeting the needs of all students. While these four goals have implications that extend far beyond a school or classroom, they directly relate to what teachers are able to do and what students are able to learn inside the classroom. I stress that it is impossible to fight poverty in a district or school if the overall ethos is counter to collective efforts to address reform. In other words, the culture has to shift in both the district and the school, and there must be a collective commitment among those "in charge" to bring about true transformation. This change does not necessarily mean that the people (teachers, principals, superintendents) must change; organizational and cultural shifts are possible with the same people. In some instances, the people may have to change for the kind of reform necessary to support students for success. However, significant shifts must occur, and change can be difficult. I have found that cultural shifts start with individual mind-set shifts. In short, leaders at the district level must set the tone through their vision and principles that translate into practice for the kind of reforms needed to fight poverty in schools. School leaders must empower, support, and hold teachers accountable for the kind of reforms outlined herein that can have a long-term impact on students of color who are living in poverty. But administrators should lead the efforts through their work, words, and actions in helping to cultivate a culture that can ensure change and improvement.

A school's or district's pervasive belief systems, goals, missions, philosophies, and discourses—essentially the overall culture and organization—can prevent positive, effective change; thus educational institutions must be prepared to address these challenges. Clearly, the culture and climate of a district or school have important bearing on the experiences and practices of classroom teachers and other educators. Teachers' willingness to engage and try new practices is shaped by the overall school environment, which is often created by school, district, and even state-level officials. The district and school climate is far from trivial in the overall scheme of transformation. For instance, Cook and Amatucci discovered in their study of Kristi—a teacher in the early stage of her career who aspired to implement principles of multicultural education that she had learned in her teacher-training program to meet the needs of underserved students—that several important cultural and organizational structures contributed to her success. They learned that the social context of her teaching experience played a meaningful role in her ability to construct literacy instruction through a multicultural lens and with a multicultural emphasis.[59] This approach likely made a huge difference in the learning opportunities and identity development of her students and what this teacher decided to emphasize in her work. The context and culture of the district and school matter! They can either stifle or enable the kinds of practices, programs, and policies that could deeply transform the lives of youth. Yet at time teachers—even those with good intentions—become ultimate pessimists and can even be antagonists against reform. Counterproductive discourses, practices, and mind-sets of teachers as they choose to participate in or disrupt cultural and organizational shifts can originate, for instance, from (1) unproductive bureaucratic structures evolved from state, district, and school policies and leadership; (2) interpretations and experiences of unsuccessful reform efforts in the past; and (3) apathy and laziness of educators who do not wish to expend the effort necessary for transformation. Moreover, teachers may become frustrated by the moving targets of reform. With school and district leaders changing so rapidly bringing in different reform efforts, it can become tiring for teachers to make shifts when they believe they are temporary—in place only until the next leader shows up.

While district and school culture can propel a teacher's success, conversely, it can also produce obstacles. The support, or lack thereof, of colleagues, parents in the community, and/or the school administration can determine just how far reform can actually go in helping students and their families. Although it could be argued that a small minority of teachers do succeed in making deep, structural reform in their particular classrooms without the support or buy-in of colleagues or the school administration, research suggests that reformers (educators) must be prepared to negotiate, balance, and combat pervasive counterproductive discourses and practices that already exist and that might work against reform.[60] With this in mind, states, districts, and schools committed to educational transformation for the fight against poverty must also make the cultural and organizational shifts necessary for transformation.

CHAPTER 2

Focus on Instruction

Certainly we can end racism with love.

—bell hooks

If we talk about the environment, for example, we have to talk about environmental racism—about the fact that kids in South Central Los Angeles have a third of the lung capacity of kids in Santa Monica.

—Danny Glover

T HIS CHAPTER IS ABOUT INSTRUCTION—instruction in the individual classroom and also as the cornerstone of a school's collective efforts to promote and support student and teacher learning. Teachers, administrators, counselors, and other adults are not the only knowers in school; students, too, are knowers—especially of their own life experiences—and teachers need to work in environments that encourage and cultivate their own learning as well as that of students. So far in this book I have stressed that teachers and other educators must be aware of how experiences and realities outside of school, broader policies, and reform efforts mediate what happens, and what should happen, inside of school for students living in poverty. I have also emphasized that the role and salience of race cannot be ignored in discussions about how to meet the needs of those living in poverty. I have stressed that classroom teachers alone cannot solve the multilayered challenges students encounter, and that state-, district-, and school-level structures, policies, and institutions must play a central and interrelated role in addressing myriad issues facing some students, their families, and communities. But how do teachers teach while straddling two worlds—home and school—in a way that effectively benefits students? Moreover, how do teachers teach when negotiating multiple roles and worlds, including policy and reform "worlds" to which they may have little or no input. Research has revealed important insights about the inter-section of home and school (illustrated by figure 2.1).[1]

I have observed that teachers often struggle to determine what respon-sibility they have, if any, to try to understand students' experiences outside of school. Many teachers I have worked with believe they should concern themselves only with what happens at school, particularly in their own classrooms. They often question whether they can or should do anything to address students' home lives. Understanding students' experiences out-side of school can guide in-school decision making, such as what subjects to teach and how to get students engaged, and help educators respond to the intersection of home and school, and is thus essential in meeting the needs of students living in poverty.

To be effective educators, it is critical for teachers and other school personnel to center their practices at the intersection of students' home and school lives. In so doing, they are responding both to the school's expectations, such as raising test scores and applying the Common Core Standards (or other standards if a state has not adopted the Common Core) to the curriculum and instructional practices, and to students' realities outside of school, such as financial hardship, divorce, family sickness, and

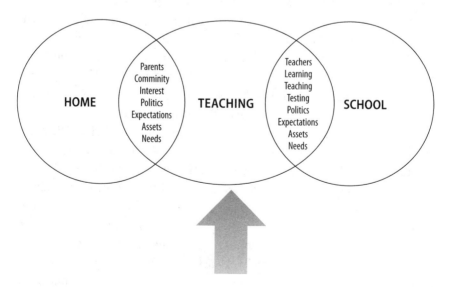

FIGURE 2.1   Teaching to the middle

a declining job market. Teachers should also notice the positive experiences students and their families have outside of school. For instance, community volunteerism, family unity, altruistic acts of kindness, and parental involvement in school should all have a bearing on how teachers think about their students, their families, and their communities; what teachers teach; and how they teach it. In terms of positive features and acts, families living in poverty can have really strong family connections and ties, and they may support each other and their communities by passing down clothing items from other children to younger ones, cooking and sharing meals with family and friends in need, inviting family and friends to work on start-up businesses that may not yield much financial gain initially, and showing up at school to support their students even after they have worked long hours. Surely, educators can find assets embedded in these and similar outside-of-school practices. However, how do teachers use these assets as sites for instructional building in the classroom?

In short, the intersection of students' home and school experiences should inform curriculum, instruction, and assessment. As figure 2-1 suggests and Gutierrez, Baquedano-Lopez, and Tejeda report, teachers have to teach to the middle of school expectations and home realities.[2] All students and their families have assets; the challenge is to help teachers and other educators recognize them. Understanding students' life experiences enables teachers to teach to students' strengths and work to redress negative situations that shape their life changes. An essential component of this kind of instruction—which teaches to what students, their families, and communities actually bring into the learning environment as well as addresses student challenges—is to listen to the voices of students.

LISTENING TO THE VOICES OF STUDENTS

Although school personnel—principals, counselors, teachers, and coaches—generally have good intentions and work diligently to meet their students' needs, they rarely talk directly *to* or learn *from* their students. In fact, most schools have no systematic way for educators to hear what students have to say. For instance, teachers may never ask students if there are ways they can better support them or improve their practices to more effectively meet student needs. Over the years, I have worked with students in high-poverty environments, typically African American and

Latino students in elementary, middle, and high school. At other times I have interacted with white Appalachian youth, especially adolescents living below the poverty line. My work has focused on many areas, from instructional enhancement and tutoring in language arts, to motivational speeches, to workshops on building study and social skills. I once even worked directly with a group of eighteen middle school students to help them pass the state language arts exam in Tennessee.

In my experience, I have found that we—researchers, teachers, principals, counselors, parents, policy makers—often spend time talking *about* students and not enough time talking and listening *to* them. When I work with students, I typically ask them three questions that I believe can shed light on aspects of teachers' work that can inform their teaching. Schools and educators could use these questions, revising them as appropriate, in their schools or classrooms to foster a form of dialogue between students and adults. One point that needs to be stressed here is that students from elementary through high school could benefit from this type of interactive learning, with students sharing and educators listening. Some believe that when students turn seventeen or eighteen, they are somehow mini-adults. However, developmentally, students are still children, even in later adolescent years. Moreover, even when students' physical bodies might suggest that they are older than their age, educators can still learn from them because indeed they are still children and should be supported as students who are developing rather than adults. Thus, having students respond to these questions provides insights for teachers but also creates the type of environment that encourages students to be active participants in the kind of education they receive, deserve, and aspire to experience. Perhaps most important, students feel like they matter and that their voices are germane to the educational process.

1. What can teachers do to better meet your [the students'] needs?
2. What can you do to improve academically?
3. What do you aspire to do in your life and how will you accomplish that goal?

For the purposes of this discussion, I elaborate on the first question only. Following are responses from students in elementary through high school to the first question, What can teachers do to better meet your needs?

Interestingly, I have received both oral and written feedback from hundreds of students living in poverty, and the focus of their responses is pretty consistent. Four general themes have emerged. Although my focus is students living in poverty, I believe these insights will be relevant in other contexts.

- *Teachers need to be patient with students and motivate them to learn, as learning is a developmental process.* This comment seems to stem from students' belief that when they make mistakes, their teachers at times become frustrated. Students say they hope their teachers will not give up on them.
- *Teachers need to increase the rigor of their classes and their expectations of students.* Students consistently report that they want and need "more" to help them succeed.
- *Teachers need to dedicate themselves to their work, to plan and put forth effort, and to find joy in what they do.* Students report that many of their teachers seem upset and angry, and they wonder if the teachers even like them and/or their chosen profession.
- *Teachers need to communicate more often, more openly, and more directly with their students.* Students yearn for their teachers to talk to them and get to know them. They consistently report that teachers need to talk more *to* them and less *about* them.

These four themes provide valuable insights as to what individual classroom teachers, as well as districts and schools, can do to improve their students' school experience.

The need for teachers to be patient with students and motivate them to learn is perhaps the most consistent response I hear from students. Interestingly, they rarely say they do not want their teachers to have high expectations of them or that they want teachers to give them days off from doing classwork or other learning. A few students have said that they need their teachers to "ease up" on them academically and not to be so "tough" on them when they misbehave. However, the vast majority ask that teachers push them toward excellence. What is interesting about this finding is that students often feel they are not being challenged as much as they should be, which they blame on their teachers' "laziness." Here are some direct comments from elementary, middle, and high school students:

- "One thing I would like my teacher to do is have extra homework and afternoon work so I can get better."
- "Teachers should give us time before and after class to finish our homework because I work late hours at [my job] after school. I don't want to lose points for not finishing the homework."
- "[Teachers can] stay after school and teach better."
- "[Teachers can] explain the homework better so I am not up all night trying to figure it out especially my math teacher."
- "[Teachers can] make things more interesting by doing their [own] homework and being prepared to teach every day."
- "[Teachers can] explain work better and not be lazy."
- "[Teachers should not] be lazy and sit down all period."

It is important to note that while some students expressed wanting "more" homework to "help [them] get better," others talked about how difficult homework could be for them—especially high school students who worked long hours after school and on the weekends. Some students requested that teachers give them time to finish their homework right before the start of class or at the end of class because they found it difficult to complete their homework after school. But even the students who worked long hours at jobs and did not want "more" homework seemed to want the teacher to do "more" to help them improve. Although some of these requests were tied to grades—"give me more assignments, including homework, to pull up my grade average in the class"—the overall point was they wanted to "get it," to learn and develop.

Still, when teachers assign homework, we must ask ourselves just whose work is being developed and evaluated. For instance, a mother who is a chemist probably has the ability to help her child with chemistry homework in ways that most people cannot. And even if that parent is unable to help with homework because she is too busy, she may be able to hire a tutor. In both scenarios the student is at an advantage because of opportunities that many children living in poverty do not have. These advantages are a direct result of affordances—frankly, privileges—that are far beyond the control of the students themselves. The assigning of, expectations for, and assessment of homework, then, are equity issues that are not trivial by any means.

We should be looking at the ways homework further perpetuates inequity. Although I agree that homework can potentially enhance in-class learning, questions about the uneven distribution of resources to assist students should be at the very heart of our philosophies and practices in deciding on assignments. Teachers and administrators should be mindful that not all students have access to people and resources (computers, Internet) to help them reach their full learning capacity after school. Also, because some students work part-time jobs, it is difficult for them to complete homework tasks, even when they want to. Thus, student voices seem to point to the need to complement learning and student development but not to use homework exclusively as the mechanism to do so.

Another consistent theme concerns teachers' interactions and "moods," which students interpret as disinterest in teaching. Because they sometimes perceive teachers as too tense, students consistently report they believe their teachers "do not like" them or do not "want to teach." Asked what they would like to say to teachers, they offered the following:

- "Stop being mad all the time."
- "Loosen up."
- "Don't be in a bad mood every day."
- "Find a different job if you don't like children and don't want to be here."

In considering students' perceptions of their teachers' moods, it is important to note that teachers do tend to be under an enormous amount of pressure from work expectations. Moreover, students may not understand that teachers are working hard to help them learn and are themselves grappling with challenges outside of school as well. The teachers whom the students tend to describe are likely experiencing multiple layers of pressure at school (and at home), and they have to work through those realities.

Additionally, students at all levels (elementary through high school) overwhelmingly point to the need for teachers to communicate more effectively, to get to know them and empathize with them:

- "I wish they would let me know when I am failing and give me makeup work [even homework] and not wait until report cards come out."
- "[I wish they would] just have time to talk to me."

- "[Teachers should] put themselves in our shoes and try to understand how hard it is and what we have to go through."
- "[Teachers should] communicate better with me and learn who I am."
- "[I wish they would] give more attention to me individually."
- "[I wish they would] listen more."

I have included these quotes for a couple of reasons. First, students can help us identify areas that need to be addressed in ways that people outside their situation cannot. Students know their experiences better than anyone else. In addition, these students speak to common attitudes, practices, and experiences that can influence student learning and social development. Moreover, the posing of questions to students provides a space for students to have voice and to exert it. Asking students to shed light on their views is an important step toward excellence in a school. The question is, will teachers—who must of course work within their educational system—listen and transform their practices accordingly?

BEYOND A CULTURE OF POVERTY

Educational consultant Ruby Payne and her staff conduct numerous professional development seminars for school districts across the country on teaching students living in poverty. In fact, I have heard from dozens of educators who rely on Payne's work in supporting these students. Payne's self-published book, *A Framework for Understanding Poverty*, outlines her ideas. The framework, which includes twelve principles, is intended to challenge educators to rethink what they know about the nexus of poverty, learning, and teaching. Payne describes her core ideas:

> Poverty is relative. Poverty occurs in all races. Generational and situational poverty are different. This work is based on patterns. All patterns have exceptions. Schools operate from middle-class norms and values. Individuals bring with them the hidden rules of the class in which they were raised. There are cultural differences in poverty. This study is cross-cultural and focuses on economics. We must neither excuse them nor scold them. We must teach them. We must teach them [students] that there are two sets of rules. To move from poverty to middle class, one must give up (for a period of time) relationships

for achievement. Two things that help one move out of poverty are: education and relationships. Four reasons one leaves poverty are: "too painful to stay, vision or goal, key relationship, and special talent/skill."[3]

Criticism of Payne's work is extensive.[4] Gorski, for instance, found that Payne's approach and message fail to critique systemic barriers and inequities in schools, and that she relies on cultural deficit models in explaining her fixed categories.[5] Her book also relies on research that is too thin to support her claims, and her work includes little critical analysis of racism, discrimination, and oppression. Unlike many other frameworks and conceptual analyses, Payne does address "the elephant in the room"—race. However, her framework seems to do more to reinforce racial stereotypes than to address the systemic racism that prevents many students living in poverty from succeeding. That is, by suggesting that students and families of color, in particular, do not understand how to operate in the white, mainstream "culture," Payne does more harm than good because she operates from a deficit perspective that reveals her shallow understanding of race and of the intersection of race and poverty. Moreover, Payne suggests that families living below the poverty line often do not value education, which again, is a problematic conjecture that can lead teachers to believe they have little or no control over students' academic success and development. The onus, in many ways, is on families and students themselves, as Payne describes.

Educators tend to appreciate the book because it lets them off the hook and verifies what they have believed, or at least suspected, all along. Teachers have a resource that does not challenge them to improve but confirms that they are working with people who just do not get it. The book validates what educators hoped for: it is the parents' and students' fault that they are not succeeding, not the poor instructional quality students receive, the inadequate administrative practices that set the tone in a school, or the lack of or inequitable funding that prevent students living below the poverty line from succeeding.

The work of Oscar Lewis, in which he uses the term "culture of poverty" to describe the lives of Mexican and Puerto Rican families living in San Juan and New York, parallels Payne's position of blaming poor children and their families for not understanding how to operate within mainstream culture (note that I am not suggesting there is one mainstream culture).[6]

He identifies several behaviors that paint poor families as inferior, deficient, and substandard. From an anthropological perspective, *poverty is not a culture*, although Lewis and Payne classify it as such.[7] According to Osei-Kofi, Lewis and Payne pathologize those living in poverty.[8] However, it is important to note that, although Lewis had a deficit perspective of the communities he studied, he attributed the behaviors and practices of poor families to the structural conditions and consequences of poverty. It is essential for educators to understand that culture and cultural practices are not the same, a point that will be addressed later.

Misunderstanding Meritocracy

Unfortunately, because of the reach of Payne's framework, schools tend to rely on a set of assumptions that allow them to avoid responsibility for their role in supporting students to reach their capacity, socially and academically. Sadly, teachers may believe they are teaching to a "culture of poverty" that they cannot change. It is interesting and quite ironic that, although many schools and districts rely on Ruby Payne as the "expert" in addressing poverty with their students, they still struggle to make any real strides or improvement with this most underserved and vulnerable group of students and families.

In addition to misunderstanding a culture of poverty, educators can also misunderstand meritocracy. I have found that many readily identify socioeconomic status as the reason some students are underprepared to succeed in school.[9] Teachers feel quite confident that socioeconomic status and certainly not race is the most important determinant of student success. Further, I have learned that educators often embrace the idea that the success and status of their students and students' parents, and even their own success, have been earned. They may believe that school failure is a result of students' bad decisions, such as not trying in class. Payne explained some "myths" and "facts" about poverty and wealth:

Myth: "Poverty is caused almost totally by the system and exploitation."

Payne's Fact: "In addition to systemic and exploitation causes, poverty is also caused by individual choices, addiction, illness, war, lack of education, lack of employment, mindsets, disabilities, and thinking."[10]

What Payne fails to acknowledge is the "fact" that individual choices and such are strongly correlated with "the system and exploitation."

Many educators believe their own success is merited because they have worked hard, obeyed the law, and made good individual decisions. They have little conception of how class and socioeconomic privilege manifest, and how unearned opportunities and outcomes are passed from one generation to the next. For instance, wealthy and middle-class teachers of any racial background can fail to recognize their privileged status and the unearned advantages and opportunities it affords them.[11] Moreover, they remain unaware that people who grow up in poverty or those with lower SES generally do not start their educational or life experiences in a fair, equal, or equitable position.[12]

Opportunity is at the center of meritocracy (the argument that people are rewarded and succeed based on their *own* individual merit of hard work, intellect, knowledge, and skill) for student success. Although U.S. society is ideologically structured around the idea that all people are created equal, all people do not have the same opportunities for success, nor are all educational practices and opportunities equitable.[13] There is in fact enormous variation in students' social, economic, political, and educational opportunities, which contrasts starkly with the "American dream." Nevertheless, many educators believe that if their students simply work hard enough, and have what it takes "in them," they will achieve and be rewarded. This view fails to recognize systemic barriers that prevent even hard-working students from achieving success.

I do not support Lewis's and Payne's concept of a culture of poverty.[14] I suggest instead that students and families living in poverty may sometimes engage in *cultural practices* as a reaction to the material conditions and structural inequities that can be devastating for them. Gutierrez and Rogoff caution against generalizing people's practices based on individual traits, and they encourage researchers, theoreticians, and practitioners to understand the "importance and benefits of knowing about the histories and valued practices of cultural groups rather than trying to teach prescriptively according to broad, under-examined generalities about groups."[15] The instructional practices outlined here are meant to help teachers understand and develop responsiveness to students' experiences, and to use them as guides to create a more equitable curriculum. The evidence reviewed for this chapter suggests that curriculum and instructional practices should be tailored to help teachers and students recognize that oppression, discrimination, and marginalization are the central reasons why many people, particularly, proportionately, people of color, live in poverty and consequently may behave in ways that seem counterproductive. People are reacting to their lived and perceived reality.

Culture can be defined as the deep-rooted values, beliefs, languages, customs, and norms of a group of people. However, it is not a static "category for conveniently sorting people according to expected values, beliefs, and behaviors," but a dynamic concept that encompasses racial and ethnic identity, class, economic status, and gender.[16] Whereas culture has to do with shared values, beliefs, and worldviews, cultural *practices* are reactions to situations in which people find themselves. It is essential that teachers understand the distinctions between culture and cultural practices. For instance, robbing a convenient store for money is a practice that might be shared by a group of people—perhaps a group living below the poverty line. However, it is not their culture but a practice based on the lived realities of those who commit the crime. Educators' roles and responsibilities are to deeply understand culture and cultural practice, respond to them, and concurrently shape and build a new shared culture and cultural practices that are cultivated by all involved.

SCHOOL- AND CLASSROOM-LEVEL INSTRUCTIONAL REFORMS

In this section, I focus on what I call instructional reforms. I use this term for the changes in teaching practices I advocate because the word *reform* has a more intense emphasis. I am calling for deep shifts in not only what individual teachers do (instructionally) in a class but also what can and should happen in an entire school. I outline the following instruction-focused reforms, which schools and teachers should consider adopting:

- Infuse language arts across the curriculum
- Build and sustain meaningful relationships
- Develop teachers' knowledge and skills beyond academic content
- Teach and cultivate student social, organizational, and study skills

The reform recommendations discussed here are based on what I have observed in "successful" and "improving" schools and districts across the United States in addition to the research literature on practices that support instructional reforms to meet the needs of students living below the poverty line. I use the term *successful* carefully here. I understand that success emerges in schools in different ways, and I am against relying solely (or even mostly) on student test scores as the metric to gauge student and teacher success. The term *improving* feels more aligned with what I hope to demonstrate in terms of the influence of the proposed instructional reforms. Still, improvement is relative. I focus on schools that get better, perhaps on tests but also in other areas such as student attendance, a decrease in confrontations and fights, and an increase in overall student and adult morale. It is also important to note that the four practices I discuss were used in combination with other changes that go beyond the scope and space of this chapter. I offer these insights as the most essential aspects of success and improvement.

Infuse Language Arts Across the Curriculum

A first instructional reform I recommend is to include language arts across the entire school curriculum, led by the language arts staff or by others interested in and capable of heading such an effort. Building language arts synergy across different content areas is the goal. If a language arts teacher is struggling to help students learn from context clues, this could be communicated to other faculty in other content areas who can provide tools and strategies to assist students. Language arts have the potential to contribute to other subjects, such as social studies, music, art, mathematics, and science; *every* teacher in a school should be a language arts teacher.[17]

Language and literacy is a foundational subject area that has connections to and is transferable to other content areas (a point I make throughout this chapter). Teaching across subject matter areas requires teachers to (1) understand the basics of the language arts standards, content, and expectations, and (2) meet with colleagues regularly to conceptualize what topics and themes will be taught, when, for how long, why (and perhaps even how). Elementary teachers tend to engage in this type of cross-disciplinary collaboration and teaching more seamlessly than middle and high school teachers because they are expected to be knowledgeable across different subjects. However, some content areas are given limited instructional time if they fall outside a teacher's realm of interest or expertise. Indeed, many elementary teachers who teach in self-contained classrooms—that is, teachers teach all subjects in one classroom; students don't change classes or have different teachers to cover the curriculum—have told me that they spend as little time as possible covering mathematics because they are "not good at it." This of course is problematic and can leave some students underprepared in this and/or other areas.

Nevertheless, benefits of teaching language arts across the curriculum include the following:

- Students are able to gain reading, thinking, and writing skills, which are essential elements to most other disciplines (science, social studies, art).
- Students begin to see the relevance and connections between what they learn in language arts and other disciplines.
- Students are better able to master skills such as vocabulary, reading comprehension, phonics, or whole language because they are reinforced in other classrooms.
- Students are able to construct narratives and conceptual schemas that help them think about what they are learning in language arts and make appropriate linkages with other content.

Language and literacy researchers would argue that reading is a core competency needed to transcend poverty.[18] Edmondson and Shannon surmise that literacy education, learning to read in particular, can help people to "prevent or overcome poverty."[19] Adler and Fisher stress that "children who do not learn to read fluently and independently in the early grades have few opportunities to catch up to, and virtually no chance to surpass, their peers who are reading on grade level."[20] In sharing their synthesis of the research on effective language and literacy instruction for all students, they explain that "instruction that provides opportunities [for students] to master concepts of print, the alphabetic principle, word recognition skills, and phonemic awareness and that affords engagement and interest in reading through a wide range of materials in the context of developmentally appropriate instruction" is essential.

An interdisciplinary perspective would suggest that teachers from different content area backgrounds should build skills that have some relevance to language and literacy development. In this sense, language arts teachers must become leaders in helping their colleagues in other disciplines learn to assist in the teaching of language arts across the curriculum.

Of course, having the time to learn from each other is essential for this type of teaching to occur across the curriculum, and districts must commit to providing such time. Based on their interpretation of student needs and the expectations associated with standards, teachers must decide how to make literacy development germane to student learning across the curriculum. Using a developmental framework, teachers might start by integrating basic language arts learning opportunities and moving gradually into more complex ones. At a minimum, there should be agreed-upon practices that are reinforced and addressed in the instructional fabric of schools committed to supporting students whose needs have not necessarily been met through our educational system.

In their case study of a high-poverty school that beat the odds, Adler and Fisher identify several qualities and practices of a successful literacy program: a strong focus on language and literacy student outcomes, multiple reading programs in every classroom, shared responsibility for student success, strong leadership at the school and classroom level, and a knowledgeable, committed veteran faculty and staff.[21]

In sum, the research suggests that a movement to develop literacy across the school curriculum could empower students to strengthen their academic skills, perform better in other subjects, read the world more critically and analytically (both inside and outside of school), and move out of poverty. It is essential that teachers build a pervasive, schoolwide narrative that helps students make connections between different aspects of the curriculum. In the next chapter, I provide insights into how teachers can use a common student/community experience—a robbery committed by high school students—to teach across disciplines in middle school.

Going Beyond Books Alone

Ladson-Billings has found that many students are in fact interested in reading.[22] However, they may not be interested in reading what is required of them in school if the readings seem irrelevant to them and dull. Therefore, language arts teachers should consider carefully constructing learning opportunities that go beyond what is traditionally required by state, district, and school standards. Although it can be difficult to teach beyond the traditional, that does not mean it should not be done. But again, teachers need assistance from those in power to be able to move outside of the tradition. Providing student access to high-quality literature beyond the canon can promote student interest in reading rather than merely providing spaces where students lose their interest in reading altogether.

However, if we are not able to change what students are required to read, we must then change how we engage them in reading.[23] Language and literacy scholars such as David Kirkland, Maisha Wynn, Ernest Morrell, Valerie Kinloch, Jeffrey Duncan-Andrade, Yolanda Sealy-Ruiz, Alfred Tatum, and Carol Lee advocate for thinking beyond traditional texts or at least for reshaping how they are taught. Therefore, teaching language arts across the curriculum requires teachers to conceptualize a practice that goes beyond books alone.

For one, students, teachers, and others are themselves "texts" that are "read" and interpreted. The social world, too, is a text that people read (in the classroom, community, and broader society). Students are actively involved with literacy and language throughout the day, even if they do not realize or internalize it. They actively engage at a very early age with letter recognitions on signs, colors of traffic lights, and patterns and shapes they see on newspapers, magazines, and books. Older students today often are engaged with Facebook, text messaging, Internet surfing, and so forth; yet, many teachers view students' engagement with these media as peripheral to their literacy development. Rather than building on students' literacy engagement outside of school, teachers often view these technologies as an enemy to "real" learning—the prescribed or scripted curriculum—saying that they "get in the way" of the literacy and language skills they want their students to master. Moreover, although some teachers do integrate various forms of technology into their teaching and, when incorporated effectively, students benefit, many schools have not kept up with students' use of and interest in technology.

In teaching language arts across the curriculum, there seems to be value in drawing on some technologies. For instance, teachers could use text messaging as an opportunity for students to code switch from conversational language to academic language, and vice versa.[24] Consider one such learning opportunity I observed in a fourth-grade classroom:

Text message: R U Ready 4 ur apptment . . .

Translation: Are you ready for your appointment?

Using this example, the teacher helped her students "switch" the text message into language they might use in a composition paper for class or on an essay exam. The teacher did not criticize the text message language; instead she *overtly* explained to students that they need to be able to communicate and write in both academic and conversational "text message" language.[25] Importantly, the teacher did not assume the students were aware of the different ways of communicating in different formats. She helped the students think through a "standard" way of communication, and explained various other elements of the texted sentence that could be useful to students in other experiences, such as case structure, the use of the ellipsis, and punctuation. The students saw the relevance of this activity and found humor in the teacher's decision to use a text message in a lesson. They shared additional text messages that the class then translated and "switched," both from conversational to academic and from academic to conversational. This experience was especially effective because the teacher chose to complement her students' existing literacy skills rather than to criticize them. This type of lesson requires teachers to make a cultural shift that enables them to construct such learning opportunities across different content areas and to recognize the assets students already have and build on them. Whereas students tend to be resentful and oppositional when teachers take away from their written language, this teacher *added to*—that is, complemented—what her students already knew in a way that was relevant to their everyday lives.[26]

Teachers should be aware of the following powerful out-of-school activities as they construct language arts opportunities across the curriculum:

- The average child begins consuming online media regularly at age eight.
- Even though Facebook's minimum age requirement is thirteen, it has about five million users under the age of ten.
- Children aged eight to eighteen spend about ten hours and forty-five minutes per day online.
- Twenty-five percent of teens log on to social media more than ten times per day.
- Fifty-one percent of kids say they've been bullied online, and 49 percent say they have been the online bully.

- Only 50 percent of parents have installed parental controls to regulate their kids' online interactions, although 72 percent say they worry that their kids will reveal inappropriate information online.
- Eighty-eight percent of teens say they value social media because it helps them keep in touch with friends they don't see often.[27]

Literary Elements

By drawing on students' existing language and literacy interest, skills, and tools, several literary elements can help them see links between academic expectations and the real world, and grow their expertise in different content areas by drawing from their language arts skills. I have found the following literary elements particularly transferable across content domains, though others are relevant as well:

- *Character.* The characters in passages from books, song lyrics, news articles, and so forth can get students to think about the complex, evolving, and dynamic nature of people, perhaps in their social studies, geography, or even science classes. For instance, having students research leading mathematical thinkers at particular moments throughout history could be germane to their understanding of character and context. Moreover, students' interactions and experiences in the classroom can help them understand character as a literary element.
- *Theme.* Focusing on the main point of particular reading passages, music lyrics, or mathematical or science concepts can help students transfer this type of analytical thinking into other contexts.
- *Thesis statement.* The thesis statement communicates the focus of a piece of writing, a song, or even a social interaction. Helping students build writing skills, from a five-paragraph essay to a poem, also helps them identify the main focus of a piece of writing or oral interaction they construct or read. There tend to be main focal areas even within conversations students have or from short news reports on the radio.
- *Conflict.* The internal and external tension, struggle, and hardship experienced by characters in a narrative can supplement traditional learning that occurs in a classroom. Conflict can occur in mathematical thinking, in a history lesson, and even in a required reading, but teachers may not classify the experience as conflict. Because students are "texts" themselves, helping students identify elements of conflict

among themselves also holds promise. Being explicit about the nature of conflict can help students build connections between content they are learning and constructs that are being covered.

- *Figurative language.* Teachers and students regularly engage with metaphorical and symbolic language that teachers can draw from when teaching other subjects. This may help students sharpen their ability to identify and develop figurative language across content and contexts. Engaging in figurative language and supporting students in thinking metaphorically allows students to engage high(er)-level thinking because a level of abstraction is required to communicate in this way.
- *Onomatopoeia.* "Mrs. Officer," a popular rap song by Little Wayne, is an example of how onomatopoeia is used and can be identified across genres. Using such sources to help students see links between their schoolwork and pop culture has the potential to break down barriers between teachers and students, an important step toward students' academic success.
- *Plot.* By supporting students in identifying the development of events that shape a story, teachers are also showing students how to identify and construct a story line of their own lives as well as content themes across disciplines. Developmental features are prevalent in science, mathematics, art, social studies, and others.
- *Setting.* The social context and the time and place in which experiences and events unfold have the potential to help students understand, contextualize, and historicize what they are learning and why within a particular domain. Setting is often addressed in language arts and history, but less so in science and mathematics. However, every disciplinary area, including physical education, music, and art, has a social context that should be explored, understood, and incorporated through learning opportunities across the curriculum.
- *Rhyme.* Many students are actively engaged in popular culture such as hip hop, country music, R&B, and other art forms that have a rhyme scheme. Rhyme can also be used to build connections with students through the music they enjoy listening to and by having them write songs and raps that have purpose—academic and even socially conscious.
- *Imagery.* Helping students develop mental pictures in their schoolwork can help them build conceptual and cognitive understanding and insights into and across different subject matter.

Vocabulary

Vocabulary development, spelling, word meaning, syntax, pronunciation, and other language and literacy skills are logical sites for language arts teaching and learning across the curriculum at all grade levels. Although many of these skills are addressed across disciplines, pronunciation is not always one of them. Pronunciation—speaking ability—carries deep social-class implications because dialect and diction often lead people to make assumptions about the intellectual and social capacity of others, usually inaccurately and unfairly. I was raised in the rural Southeast, and I often have been negatively judged by my southern accent by people who assumed that, because the way I spoke was not as "sophisticated" or perhaps "northern" as others, I was not socially adept, intelligent, or capable of thriving in a large northern city or in my particular profession.

As a parent to very young twin daughters, I am already aware of the ways in which they pronounce particular words and construct their language. They spent their first three years of life in Nashville, Tennessee, and I noticed how they pronounced words like *can't*, *bike*, or even *toy*. Their pronunciation of these words carries a regionalism related not only to social class and ability but also to race. Lisa Delpit and Joanne Kilgur Dowdy poignantly describe the confluence of race and language as "the skin that we speak."[28] To illustrate, I share the following personal story:

> Our daughters were in a very racially diverse daycare in Tennessee, but their gymnastics class outside of the daycare center was not racially diverse at all. Our two daughters were typically two of four or five black or brown children in the gymnastics class of twenty. One Saturday, I dropped my daughters and my wife off at the front door and drove to find parking. When I walked into the gymnastics class, one of my daughters, Elise, yelled across the room in her most excited voice, "Daddy here, Daddy here!" Parents chuckled and one of the teachers said quite loudly, "Yes, darling, Daddy IS here."

Although the gymnastics teacher likely did not mean any malice with her comment, my wife and I pointed to a subtle *skin speaking* that possibly assumed that our, at that time, two-year-old black daughter did not know any "better" and, even worse, perhaps would not be taught any differently because her black parents would not know better. We will probably teach our daughters what is expected of them within the white, mainstream norms, but we will also help them understand the racism and discrimination that black and brown people experience due to the ways they verbally express themselves. Drawing from Freire, we will help Elise and Anna learn to speak the *word* and the *world*, while teaching them to critique, challenge, and *change* the word and world they (will) live in.[29] The issue that the gymnastics teacher pointed out was certainly not one of meaning or understanding: Elise's exclamation of "Daddy here!" was clearly understood by those in the facility. Yet, she was "corrected" even at the age of two.

When I taught high school English in South Carolina, I regularly used pronunciation exchanges—almost as a game as the students and I talked with each other, correcting pronunciation patterns. The exchanges helped students negotiate, understand, and ultimately fight to participate in and to change what Delpit calls the culture of power.[30] We had developed relationships that allowed us to listen intently to the way each of us pronounced particular words, and we talked about how and when to use them and in which context. As I did to my students, they corrected me when I "misspoke" or pronounced a word in a way that would suggest a particular interpretation of my cognitive or linguistic ability. This type of vocabulary enrichment and pronunciation development can be done across different subjects. For example, teachers can post examples of vocabulary and pronunciation on word and vocabulary walls in the classroom and throughout the entire school (such as in the hallway, gymnasium, cafeteria, or even restrooms). However, to be broadly effective, the school must make a cultural *shift*, as discussed previously, that includes vocabulary and expected pronunciations that are shared throughout the school or district. To be clear, vocabulary is commonly taught in schools, while pronunciation can be an afterthought. Common Core Standards call for increased attention on speaking, and pronunciation is an essential element to addressing this recommendation.

In my language arts classroom my students and I explored hundreds of words throughout the school year. To do this across the curriculum requires teachers to communicate the following to help students contextualize vocabulary and pronunciation development: (1) people *should* be able to pronounce words in any way they choose, regardless of accent or dialect; (2) we live in a society that makes assumptions and judgments about others based on how they pronounce and enunciate words; (3) the goal of vocabulary and pronunciation development is to *add to*—complement, not take away from—students' ability to navigate and participate in multiple worlds; (4) developing broader vocabulary and pronunciation enables students to contribute to and participate in discussions they otherwise might not be able to, including changing power structures that judge people based on how they speak.

Word pronunciation across different subject areas can include words specific to and outside of the discipline being covered, from elementary through secondary grades. Common words that can shed light on variation in diction and region include *police, ambulance, street, ask, sword, Illinois,* and so forth. Looking at word pronunciation in this way also deepens the meanings of the words themselves, while helping students gain access to a power structure that they might not otherwise have.[31]

Writing

Writing development is another important and potentially beneficial element of classroom instruction across different subject areas. Indeed, students need to have the ability to communicate well in writing in any class. They must be able to express themselves in ways that are organized and grammatically acceptable, and that convey the content and character of a particular writing genre. In too many schools that serve students living in poverty and students of color, teachers use writing as a form of punishment, which I am strongly against. I have observed the following written on a board in an elementary school:

> *Copy 100 times:* I will not talk while others are talking.
>
> *Copy 50 times:* I will keep my hands to myself when walking to the lunchroom.
>
> *Copy 50 times:* I will raise my hand before answering a question.

How can students develop an appreciation and love for writing when it is used to punish or correct them? Schools should be cultivating creativity and various forms of expression among their students.

In a study conducted by Applebee and Langer and published in an important policy brief by the National Council of Teachers of English (NCTE) in 2011 called *Reading and Writing Across the Curriculum,* eighth-grade students reported doing weekly writing in 46 percent of social studies classes, 32 percent of science classes, and 13 percent of mathematics classes.[32] However, by 2007, these numbers had declined to about 44 percent and 30 percent for social studies and science, respectively, with mathematics remaining the same. Twelfth-grade students in 2002 reported writing engagement in 40 percent of social studies classes, 20 percent in science, and 8 percent in math. In 2007 the numbers were 42 percent, 21 percent, and 8 percent, respectively.[33]

Although the Common Core Standards movement stresses a uniform and consistent curriculum with teachers sharing responsibility for content development and delivery, teachers outside of language arts often resist teaching writing. They may fail to see the relationship to writing of their content areas, especially in math and science, and students thus typically receive little guidance and few opportunities to build their writing skills in these areas. Teachers' concerns about incorporating writing into their content areas likely stem from feeling they have neither the training to teach it nor the time to grade student writing. They also may see the emphasis on writing as peripheral to the kinds of learning opportunities they should construct in their particular subject areas.

As a former high school language arts teacher, I know that the time it takes to grade essays and to acquaint oneself with novels and other forms of literature can be overwhelming. Teachers outside of language arts may find these tasks even more challenging. Some good news for these teachers is that the NCTE has found that learning can be enhanced with short writing assignments that ask students to (1) explain key concepts, (2) summarize arguments on a given topic, and (3) outline a procedure.[34] Drawing from Keys's work in science education, the NCTE recommends several strategies that address teachers' concerns about the amount of time needed to help students develop writing skills, even outside of English language arts classes:[35]

- *Peer responses to writing.* Teach students how to understand peers' writing and provide feedback. Modeling is essential in this type of exercise. For instance, students may not understand how to provide substantive feedback to their peers on writing, and it is teachers' responsibility to teach them. Students actually learn from the process of providing feedback.
- *Whole-class discussion of student writing samples.* Provide examples of excellent writing and explain the various elements of a successful essay,

including topic sentences, supporting evidence, thesis statements, transition words and phrases, vocabulary usage, and so forth.

- *Students' reflection on their own writing.* Empower students to see the value of writing development by having them examine their own work and discuss ways to improve it.
- *One-on-one conferences about writing.* Teachers can set up times to talk with students about a particular aspect of a paper, such as the introductory or concluding paragraphs, rather than providing feedback on the entire assignment.[36]

The idea is that students have the potential to become better writers and readers when they write regularly in ways that foster learning across different courses and receive some form of feedback. Writing in different subject areas should be standard practice at schools that are committed to students' language arts development, which can enhance their success in different disciplines. For example, students can learn to write descriptively and persuasively in science as they conduct lab experiments or in mathematics as they "talk through" their mathematical and conceptual thinking. This means that teachers and, consequently, students will move away from total reliance on textbooks.

Thus, writing across the curriculum means that students have numerous and varied opportunities to write. Today some schools are developing successful student-initiated blogs, Web pages, and newsletters that are part of their courses, not extracurricular activities. In science, for example, students might blog about the growth of molecules over time or contributions of black and brown people in the sciences. In social studies, they might develop an informative Web page about religious customs inside and outside the United States and their relationship to community advancement and empowerment. The point is that writing across the curriculum, similar to vocabulary and pronunciation across the curriculum, is essential to a broader language-arts-across-the-curriculum movement.

What Teachers Can Do to Help Students Learn to Write and Write to Learn

Teachers can use numerous activities to support the development of student writing across the curriculum; some examples follow. These writing opportunities can be as simple or complex as teachers and students find appropriate in the beginning but hopefully will intensify in intricacy over time.

- *Class/content summaries.* At the end of a class session, lesson, or unit, allow students time to capture, in writing, different elements of the content covered by focusing on main ideas, transitions, and supporting evidence based on claims. These summaries should have a particular aim; for instance, it may be more important for students to be able to understand and summarize the content rather than follow a set of mechanics related to grammar. Being explicit about how students' writing should be focused and how it will be evaluated are important as students develop these written documents. Encouraging students to identify, define, and underline in their own written assignments the different constructs/vocabulary words that were covered is a logical way to summarize content across different disciplines as well as build writing skills and understanding of particular content.

- *Prewriting/prethinking activity.* Allow students to write what they believe they already know, will learn, or want to know about a topic being explored across different content areas or in a particular class. Prompting students with phrases like "I think . . . I feel . . . I believe . . . I am concerned about . . . " may be useful. Helping students differentiate between thinking, feeling, and believing can also help them shape their thoughts and build their prewriting. For example, students in a social studies class could write about what they *think* or *believe* they know about the Bill of Rights, the Fifth Amendment to the Constitution, the Preamble to the Constitution, or even the different branches of government and how they *feel* about the implementation of them historically and currently.

- *Writing postcards.* Ask students to write down three or four new ideas they learned from a day's lesson, some areas where they are confused, and a burning question about the lesson or the topic being explored. This short activity requires only a small amount of time, five to ten minutes at the end of class, but it allows students to think about the content covered and to write about it.

- *Journals and learning logs.* Require reflective opportunities for students to delve within themselves to see how classroom content is relevant to their own lives. If students do not see the classroom content as relevant, this is an important data point for the teacher, and students could write about this as well. The point is for students to consistently reflect on, and make connections to, what they are learning and their own life experiences. Encouraging students to develop the ability, habits, and intentional practices of reflecting and writing are the central goals of this type of journaling, which can be done through social media such as blogs as well.

- *Quick writes.* Each day, allow students to spontaneously capture their thoughts on a particular topic for a specified amount of time. These quick writes can occur at the beginning, middle, or end of the class period or day. For instance, to check for learning, teachers may pause their instruction for a quick write about the topic just covered. Or, students in a math class might write a brief explanation of how to solve a new equation.

- *Writing for evaluation.* Include some form of essay on examinations across different content areas. Indeed, as a school attempts to transform the entire culture, writing must be a central aspect of student assessment across disciplines. This means that math teachers would require students to construct word problems or write about their thinking to solve a complex math problem. An art teacher might ask younger students to identify and write about color patterns in a picture, while older students might be expected to research and write about the artistic period of a painting. In this way, every subject would require some form of writing, perhaps culminating with a five-paragraph essay capturing the essence of the content being covered—depending on grade level and ability. If the entire school culture is focused on writing, students will over time develop skills that strongly influence their capacity to write.

- *Global pen pal partner.* Teachers could also develop relationships with schools in other countries by initiating a writing partnership program where students write letters to their peers. The focus of these letters could be related to student interests as well as a subject being covered and communication could occur through various mediums.

In general, it is important for teachers to model what they expect in the written documents, especially in content areas that traditionally have required little writing, such as math and science. Modeling, a common marker in the field of science, requires that teachers make expectations explicit and build student skills over time. For instance, a science teacher might begin by having students keep a journal and underline key concepts, themes, or ideas in their writing as they define the concepts. What I have found most useful in my own work helping college students develop their writing is sharing with the entire class both strengths and areas needing improvement I have observed across all their papers. This type of analysis requires teachers to carefully study students' writing for consistencies and inconsistencies and provide insights into themes that emerge across different papers.

Consider the feedback I shared after grading a set of essays for a recent course I taught on the social context of education. After reading through the papers, I carefully examined some common strengths and weaknesses. Subsequently, in a PowerPoint presentation, I discussed the following points with the entire class:

- Strong, innovative, and excellent ideas across the papers. Grammatically solid papers.
- There were some tense concerns (what does APA require?). Be consistent.
- Some essays were not well organized. There were no thesis statements.
- Do not abbreviate or use contractions.
- Edit carefully.
- Substantiate, cite, reference, build a case for points made (does not always have to be citations . . . consider qualifiers like *sometimes, often, I have found*).
- What needs to be cited and referenced?
- Update references/citations.
- Epistemology: how do you know what you claim?
- Awkward wording.
- Definitional work/unpack complex constructs.
- To whom are you speaking and why?

After sharing these general findings with the class, I observed significant improvements across student papers. At a minimum, in future assignments, students tended not to make the errors I shared with the entire class. I found this approach of sharing themes across papers and discussing those themes with the entire class to be more effective for improving student writing than simply writing my comments on individual papers, expecting students to improve their writing. Pulling these themes together required that I study not only each individual student's work but also challenges across all the different papers.

Regardless of the intensity of the cultural shifts schools must make to develop literacy across the curriculum environment, schools need to decide on the essential areas related to literacy that every teacher/classroom will address. This consistency allows students to build skills that are reinforced throughout the school and throughout the day. This means that janitorial staff, cafeteria workers, teachers' assistants—all school personnel—are on the same page in terms of the literacy skills being stressed. Every person in the school matters and building common language arts patterns can be a difference maker for students.

Build and Sustain Meaningful Relationships

Another instructional reform that has a real impact on students living in poverty is centralizing relationships. I stress that relationship building is an instructional approach, not a tangential social interaction, which can have a lasting influence on student outcomes. Although few, if any, would argue against the importance of building and sustaining relationships with students, how many districts and schools across the country have actually developed a movement to focus on them? There is compelling evidence that relationship building can be an essential element to teacher and student success.[37] After educators (teachers, principals, superintendents, counselors, and coaches) read my book *Start Where You Are*, they consistently pointed to sections that highlighted the salience of relationship building for student academic and social success. However, many readers wanted more insights and strategies in building such relationships. I address that request in this section.

Surely, students should be at the center of relationships that are developed and cultivated in schools. In its simplest form, effective teaching of students living in poverty has at its core the ability of those in schools (perhaps as a result of district expectations) to build community-centered relationships with family, community, colleagues, and students (see figure 2.2).

In fact, building and sustaining relationships can make a huge difference for teachers working with those living in poverty and students of color. Factor analyses were used to study a thousand African American and 260 Latino third graders' perceptions of their school environment.[38] The researchers, through their analyses of the twenty-four-item measure, found

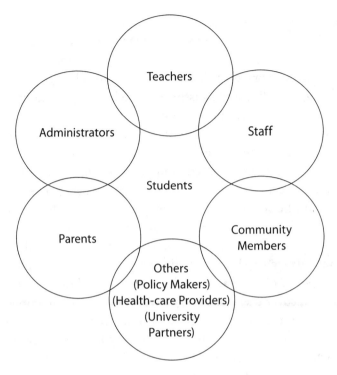

FIGURE 2.2   Community-centered relationships

that African American students viewed their relationships with teachers to be most important in evaluating the school context. These relationships focused on both schoolwork and personal concerns that the African American students wanted to discuss with their teachers. Latino students stressed that notions of fairness, care, and praise for putting forth effort were most important in their interactions with teachers. This study suggests that building and sustaining relationships can influence how welcome students feel in an environment and also help them construct positive attitudes about school—and consequently put forth more effort in their schoolwork. Later in this chapter, I provide specific strategies and insights on how teachers and other educators can build and sustain relationships with students.

Thinking About Parental Involvement, Race, and Poverty

Parental and family involvement goes beyond showing up at Parent Teacher Association (PTA) meetings. For instance, it can mean that parents (or other family members) engage in a variety of activities such as ensuring that homework is completed, monitoring student progress and improvement through school visits and in the home, talking over the phone to teachers and administrators, planning activities for the school, participating in fund-raising, attending and assisting with field trips, attending extracurricular activities such as sporting events and plays, staffing concession stands, volunteering in the classroom, and serving on advisory boards.[39]

When I was growing up, my father worked as a forklift driver at General Motors. We lived in a rural community about forty-five miles from his job. He left home around 4:45 each morning in order to make it through the Atlanta traffic before his workday began at 6:00 a.m. He returned home around 5:30 or 6:00 p.m. He rarely was able to make it to organized parent-teacher conferences. However, he was very actively involved with my education: he talked extensively and overtly to my siblings and me about college and the importance and value of education. He read the local newspaper from cover to cover every day and talked to me about the importance of being able to read and understand what was occurring in the world. He made sure we had financial support necessary for me to have a tutor in reading when I was in elementary school. He made sure I was actively involved in sports and other extracurricular activities such as church events. Despite his schedule, my father was very engaged in my education. However, traditional notions of parental involvement might suggest that he was not, simply because he was not able to attend parent-teacher conferences or show up physically at the school on any given day.

My mother worked as a beautician in our small town. She owned a salon and her day often intensified when her clientele got off work at around 4:30 or 5:00 p.m. This meant that my older siblings—especially my sister—had to assume certain roles and responsibilities to make sure our household functioned. My sister acted, in some ways, as a parent. Because it is sometimes an older sibling, grandparent, aunt, uncle, or even a family friend who supports students in their development, it is essential for schools to broaden conversations about parental involvement to include family and community members. In other words, family and community members can make huge contributions to the social and academic development of students.

In their study of parental involvement among different racial and ethnic groups living in poverty, Cooper et al. found that low-income African

American, Hispanic, and white students experienced more academic problems than students from more affluent families.[40] However, the researchers found no difference between low-SES and high-SES Asian students—an important finding. Both groups of Asian students (low and high SES) tended to perform well on academic measures. The researchers also found that both "poor" and "non-poor" African American students participated in organized extracurricular activities. Unfortunately, the researchers determined that this organized activity did not necessarily correlate with higher achievement for these students, although other research suggests that organized activities supplement students' in-school learning and consequently their performance on tests.

Although out-of-school activities can have an influence on students, and those living in poverty can potentially benefit, this was not the case for African American students in the Cooper et al. study. Cooper et al. determined that the families of both the low- and high-SES Asian students had strong values and high expectations, which resulted in the academic success of students from both groups.

A common idea across the literature is that students from higher SES outperform those from lower SES. Another persistent narrative is that white students outperform other racial groups of students in both high and low SES groups. For instance, whiteness is normalized and other racial groups are compared to that norm; even when Asian students outperform other racial/ethnic groups, they are still often compared to white students.[41] It is important to note that the Cooper et al. study has to be read in context. For instance, readers must be careful not to assume that black and white parents living in poverty do not value education. To the contrary, black and brown parents do indeed care about and value education. The Cooper et al. study suggested that both high and lower socioeconomic Asian parents place a high value on education. It also found that black parents consciously and deliberately provide their children with supplemental opportunities outside of school to enhance their lives. Unfortunately, too many do not focus on the benefits of such extracurricular activities beyond how they translate on a test.

In their study of African American families living in poverty, Gutman and McLoyd examined the management and involvement of parents both in and out of school. In their qualitative study, they learned that parents of high achievers used particular strategies in assisting their children with homework and had supportive conversations with them about their potential. Outside of school, parents of high achievers had their children actively engaged in the community through extracurricular activities—including religious activities.[42] This story line might counter discourses suggesting that (1) students living in poverty cannot be high achievers, and/or (2) parents do not have specific, deliberate practices to keep their children involved, engaged, and successful in and out of school. For instance, do black parents show up for PTA meetings? If not, it is important to ask why. Do these parents work during the meeting times? Are there problems with transportation? Moreover, do these parents feel that their needs and interests are being addressed at the meetings? Who decides the agenda? Teachers sometimes have negative images of parents living in poverty who do not take part in school activities to the degree teachers believe is appropriate. Understanding why parents participate rarely or not at all is key to address the reasons and possibly increase participation. Clearly, for instance, if parents are working graveyard shifts, juggling two or three jobs, or caring for other children when the meetings are held, it can be very difficult for these parents to show up.

Studies have examined not only parents' expectations and values for their children but also their expectations of teachers. While parental and family involvement seem to be a critical aspect of students' academic and social success in school, research has found that parents also value their children's teachers, though for different reasons. Jacob and Lefgren discovered that parents in high-poverty contexts "strongly" value the effectiveness and ability of teachers to raise their children's test scores. Contrarily, those from higher SES, according to the study, place more emphasis on teachers' ability to keep their children "happy." The researchers wrote:

> Because academic resources are relatively scarce in higher-poverty schools, parents in these schools seek teachers skilled at improving achievement even if this comes at the cost of student satisfaction . . . In higher-income schools, parents are likely to oppose measures that increase the focus on standardized test scores at the cost of student satisfaction.[43]

Again, because students living in poverty may be more *school dependent* (as discussed earlier), parents may rely on teachers and the school to do the heavy test prep work. Those from more affluent backgrounds may have the means to supplement school programs with the home tutoring necessary for test score success.

Milne and Plourde conducted another study that focused on race, poverty, and families.[44] They identified essential elements of success that assisted high-achieving students living in poverty. Parents in the qualitative study of six second-grade high-poverty high achievers had educational materials in the home, such as books and other written materials. Parents were deliberate in spending quality time with their children to ensure they (as parents) were aware of student needs and the school's expectations. They had dinner together regularly, talked extensively to their children, and served as a strong support system. Through talk in the home, parents also stressed the importance of education because they, indeed, valued education themselves. The Milne and Plourde narrative helps to counter conceptions that families living in poverty (black families in this case) do not value education or that they do not help their children develop academic and social skills in the home that are transferable to school.

Unfortunately, parental involvement typically declines as students get older and move from elementary to high school.[45] Yet, peer pressure can increase as students get older. Younger students often want their families to show up at school and participate, but older students sometimes resist parental input. In addition, parental involvement can be more complicated, though not impossible, for single parents or for parents who are employed outside of the home, live far away from school, work long hours, or do not have reliable transportation to get to schools. Just about all families care about their children, but families sometimes struggle to understand how to help their children succeed and what role they should play.[46] Overwhelmingly, teachers and administrators see the value in parental/family involvement in school. Thus, parental/family partnerships with schools are built *on purpose*, not by accident.

With all this in mind regarding parents, families, communities, and students, on a classroom level, building meaningful relationships rests upon several suppositions, including the following:

- Teachers understand that it "takes a village" to educate students and that they as teachers cannot succeed without the assistance of others: parents, family, health-care workers, and community members are critical partners in students' learning and social development.

- Teachers should develop and display empathetic dispositions with students and others involved in their students' lives.
- Teachers identify influential partners in their students' lives (such as older siblings, cousins, friends, clergy, or grandparents) and work with them to support student development and success.
- Teachers draw from community resources to establish relationships that can benefit students academically as well as socially.

The general point is that teachers understand that there are individuals and organizations that may serve as critical partners in supporting students. Of course, teachers should be careful to make sure individuals are screened to work with young people and are approved through the district and school.

Possible community partners may include professional coaches and athletes, local political officials/leaders, organizations (such as the Boys and Girls Club, the United Way, and the 100 Black Men), and entertainers. It might also be helpful to develop a list of past graduates at the elementary, middle, and high school levels—particularly those who have succeeded and perhaps worked through challenging situation—who can visit students and schools to talk about their experiences and serve as role models and mentors. But this involvement from community members and organizations should be sustained, not a one-time appearance. Put simply, students need to "see" folks who have excelled despite obstacles and have opportunities to converse with them about their own possibilities.

Because teachers and other educators can sometimes unintentionally marginalize parents, other family members, and community members, teachers must be vigilant in their efforts to build partnerships *with* them. For instance, in general, some parents may feel intimidated by teachers and the school as an institution. These feelings may result from their own experiences as students or even the discourse, the language patterns inherent in a school (we tend to use lots of acronyms and "code" language in schools). I recall listening to a special education teacher use three acronyms to describe to a group of parents the diagnostic exams and policies she was administering. They looked baffled by all the jargon, and teachers must be conscious of this. Moreover, parents may not see school/academic engagement as their primary or central role. Rather, parents may see themselves as a financial resource more than an academic one—to pay the bills, put food on the table, clothes on their children's back, shoes on their feet. For many parents, it takes extraordinary effort to accomplish goals and expectations beyond trying to provide for their children—especially when they are working multiple jobs just to survive. The pressure and stress these parents experience cannot be overstated, and teachers must be mindful of this in their work, expectations, requests, and interactions with parents. Whatever the source of contention, educators must work with parents and others to build relationships because their ability to do so can shape what happens to students themselves, how much effort students put into learning, and the resulting outcomes.

To connect with parents, teachers should consider (1) developing explicit suggestions for how they can support their children at home (this can be essential for early childhood and elementary school teachers as they develop tools to help parents support their children's learning and development); (2) explicitly sharing in writing four or five things they expect or need from parents. These expectations could be written on an index card and given (or mailed) to parents at the beginning of the year. For instance, teachers might expect parents to help their children with homework, provide updated contact information, and so forth. Schools assume parents already know what is needed and expected, but this may not be the case. Expectations are typically focused on students, but it is also important for schools to tell families what they need from them and perhaps provide some framing about why. While there are tensions embedded in the practice, some charter schools even have parents sign contracts that outline an interrelated set of shared responsibilities between home and school. Similarly, parents should express to teachers their expectations and needs as well, and teachers should listen. Keeping these lines of communication open can be an essential element in supporting students. But how often are the parents of children living in poverty asked for input from schools on how to improve? The assumption is that schools already know the needs and expectations of these families which is not necessarily the case.

To be clear, while the suggestions in this section have focused mostly on what individual teachers can do, my point is that building relationships should be an important part of district concerns about transforming schools to better meet the needs of students living in poverty. Careful, deliberate attention is needed to support teachers and other educators in building and sustaining relationships. District- and school-level practices that could potentially enhance these relationships might include (1) making positive phone calls to parents rather than calling only when there is a problem; (2) using various forms of communication, such as newsletters, phone trees, and e-mails, to communicate with parents and the community (some teachers even text the parents); and (3) sharing challenging experiences they have had with their own children to prevent parents from feeling uneasy about their ability to support and parent their children/students.

Develop Teachers' Knowledge and Skills Beyond Academic Content

To meet the complex needs of students, teachers need to know a range of information that far exceeds their academic content discipline, from how to organize their classroom to maximize student learning to how to best handle discipline problems. In addition, teachers need to understand and be able to respond to the contextual idiosyncrasies and nuances that present themselves as they teach their subject matter, whether it is mathematics, science, art, language arts, or history. Shulman's work points to the need for teachers to develop content knowledge as well as pedagogical knowledge.[47] He also stresses the convergence of the two: the knowledge teachers have of their content and how they teach that content to their students. But what else must teachers need to know to provide students with what they need to succeed, academically and socially?

I can recall experiences as a student in high school and college when it was clear that although some teachers possessed a wide and deep knowledge of their particular subject, they could not effectively convey that content to students. As an undergraduate in college, I had several higher-level mathematics and history professors who were well-respected experts in their respective fields, but they struggled to engage students, to explain and illuminate complex mathematical ideas or historical movements, or to reflect on why their students were not succeeding and then adjust their practices. The point here is that having deep subject matter knowledge does not necessarily mean strong teaching skills.

Additional knowledge and skills teachers must develop include the ability to

- build relationships with students
- develop classroom management strategies and skills

- understand and build on the historical context of a community and school
- understand and negotiate the sociopolitical landscape of an environment
- develop partnerships with family members of their students, the community, and other stakeholders
- work collaboratively with their colleagues and administrators for student success
- develop culturally relevant and responsive instructional materials and practices
- understand psychological, traumatic, and socioemotional needs of students
- determine and address basic needs of students such as hunger, nutrition, and health
- gauge and address students' socioeconomic and language development needs
- understand racism, sexism, homophobia, xenophobia, and other forms of discrimination
- understand the role of popular culture (including music, videos, television, video games) in students' lives
- understand and negotiate policy and reform movements on both local and national levels
- negotiate the political landscape of a school and community
- build on and from the interests, expectations, and needs of students and the community
- develop professional identities to make appropriate decisions for student learning
- identify and build on the assets of all students, the community, their colleagues, and themselves (as teachers)
- understand how to contextualize and transform standards in ways that are instructionally innovative, appropriate, and potentially transformative for students

Teach and Cultivate Student Social, Organizational, and Study Skills

The final recommendation for instructional reform is to teach students social and study skills. I have discussed the importance of understanding what factors are essential for student success beyond traditional academic development. However, it is perhaps equally critical that teachers focus on student development that directly influences their academic success, such as social development and study skills. I have found that in some cases, districts and schools serving students living in poverty and students of color fail to help students understand how to function within systems (both outside and inside of the classroom)—even when those systems need to change. Put simply, students need to learn how to "do" school. Similar to instruction that meets at the intersection of home and school, students' ability to function within systems must be developed with out-of-school experience in mind as well. Both through the formal curriculum and in supplemental ways in all classes and beyond, schools should help students foster the skills to succeed socially and academically.

Social Skills

Even as the curriculum is being streamlined away from subjects such as social studies, Banks has made it clear that social studies can be a critical path to shepherd students into social justice-minded citizens who can solve complicated problems for their communities and beyond.[48] He maintains that "the world's greatest problems do not result from people being unable to read and write. They result from people in the world—from different cultures, races, religions and nations—being unable to get along and to work together to solve the world's intractable problems such as global warming, the AIDS epidemic, poverty, racism, sexism, and war." Yet, we are allowing reforms to minimize social studies, and as a result social skills—that is, students' ability to work and live with others—diminish a bit, too. The point is that social skills (and therefore social studies) are essential for student learning and their ability to empathize with others in schools and society.

Consider the following experience:

> Several years ago, a teacher in an urban, high-poverty school who was new to the field invited me to visit her classroom to help identify problems she had with "classroom management" so that she could improve her practices and ultimately student test scores. She reported that her students would not engage in her lessons and she felt that she lacked control over the learning opportunities available in the class. The teacher reported that her boys, in particular, seemed to be disengaged

and were "challenging" for her. I visited several times and saw that much of what the teacher had shared with me about the climate and interactions of her classroom was true. Not much learning was occurring in the class, and the problems seemed to be more related to her (as the teacher) and her inability—especially with her male students—to resolve conflict. The students argued a lot; they brought conflicts from the corridors into the classroom. They did not communicate well with each other. In one class session, the male students argued about the outcome of a football game they had watched the previous evening. Some of their disagreement was a result of sheer excitement in making their point and making sure they were heard and "respected" by their classmates, while other comments suggested that they were not hearing each other at all but were talking over their classmates. In short, the teacher needed to teach some social skills concurrently with the academic curriculum.

What I saw in this teacher's classroom is prevalent in other classes as well. Students (not only in high-poverty schools) sometimes need to be taught social skills—the rules and expectations necessary for learning to take place. I explained to this teacher that the students needed to understand how to *social code switch* in order to function interdependently in the classroom. (By social code switch, I simply mean that they needed to learn how to adjust their interactions in the different social context.)

The following social skills may need to be developed to help students respond and behave in ways that will be advantageous for them. Note these skills are essential for all students, not just those living in poverty:

- *Conflict resolution.* Students need to be taught how to resolve conflict with each other amicably—understanding that they will sometimes agree to disagree and at other times they will have to "let go" of the issue—to choose their battles wisely. The point is to make students aware that at times in life we all have to negotiate. Sometimes we lose and other times we win, but aggression and violence are not the answers. Moreover, students (even those in middle and high school) must be taught to self-regulate and to manage conflict themselves without involving an adult, such as a teacher.
- *Communication.* Another social skill that needs to be explicitly taught is communication, whether in the classroom, hallways, cafeteria, or

bus yard. As a person who grew up in a relatively large family with a host of aunts, uncles, and cousins, I had to learn how to communicate in school because my communication style at home was quite different from what was expected in the classroom. At home, one had to sometimes raise his or her voice to be heard, or just chime in when one had an opportunity, and this meant that the subject might shift based on the speaker's priorities. In school also, the communication style might change depending on the person, and this type of teaching can help students communicate appropriately both in and out of the classroom.

- *Collaboration.* In too many schools, students are not encouraged to learn with and talk to each other, especially regarding their academic expectations. Although collaboration—a skill related to conflict resolution—is useful for both learning and development, teachers often refuse or are unable to foster this type of learning in their classrooms. Students need to learn how to collaborate with others and how to participate on a team as a leader as well as a follower. Helping students understand how to navigate relationships with both friends and classmates is essential to learning to work with others outside of the school environment, in a part-time job situation or even with their siblings at home.

- *Adaptability.* Students also need to learn how to adapt, though not necessarily assimilate, to situations when things do not go as planned. Many students, even older ones, benefit from set routines and procedures in a classroom. However, when those regular procedures or routines shift (for instance, because a teacher is absent and students have a substitute teacher), students need to be able to adjust and function effectively; this is a lesson from which students will benefit throughout life.

There are additional social skills that surely can benefit student development, but the ones outlined here seem most pertinent to assist teachers and students from elementary through high school.

Study Skills

When I first began my work as a professor, an affluent Catholic school invited me to work with a group of their students to help them build study skills during an intersession. At first, I was reluctant to accept the invitation: I had not conducted any research on study skill development or the effects of study skills on student success. And perhaps most important, I wondered why this school was interested in helping their students develop study skills. Naively, I assumed these students somehow understood how to study and be successful in school. Most of the students lived in two-parent "nuclear" households, had financial resources, and attended a school that was well known in the community as academically sound. In fact, students' parents paid tuition for them to attend this private school even though most of them lived in "good" districts that would allow them to attend strong schools. What I learned from my work with the twenty-one students, however, was that although many of them were intellectually sophisticated, many also lacked basic understandings about how to take notes and organize them, what was essential for them to study, how to read a textbook, and/or how to interact with their teachers to get the best results from their courses. It became clear to me while working with those students that educators cannot assume students understand how to "do" school in any sociopolitical context—not even in an affluent community. What was also illuminating about my experience was that, as the school gained insight and perspective, it took responsibility for helping their students build the skills to be successful and did not assume that students would build their study skills outside of the school.

So, in addition to social skills, I suggest that study skills courses, which help students develop organizational skills, are also essential. The idea is for districts and schools to develop opportunities for students to learn these skills—starting early in their development, because students will be able to transfer them to different environments. Study skills can be taught as a separate course throughout a district or school, and/or every teacher could learn how to help students develop these skills in their classes. How many students are taught how to take effective notes? How many of them are taught how to read and interpret a textbook? How many students learn how to organize their notes and related materials before they take tests? How many are truly taught how to study (not necessary to pass a test) and consequently succeed? Students need support on how to study for rigorous courses, and they need to understand how to use the resources available to them (human, print, electronic, and so forth) to maximize their own learning and development both outside and inside of the classroom. Several central areas of focus are necessary to help students build study skills for academic success:

- *Time and task management.* Students need to learn how best to manage their time on various tasks. Helping students understand and prioritize their time can have a lasting influence on what they learn and are able to produce.
- *Study strategies and skills in the disciplines.* Because every discipline is different and requires different levels of intensity and focus, schools are encouraged to provide tutorial and training opportunities that build students' skills between and across disciplines. For instance, study strategies in language arts might look different from those in mathematics but there also may be points of intersection.
- *Note-taking and test-taking skills/strategies.* An important general study strategy is how to capture and organize notes from various classes. Students need guidance on what to focus on in texts and how to effectively read texts to learn from them. Moreover, students need to understand what is worth capturing in notes during lectures, how, by what medium (computer versus handwritten), and so forth. Students need to learn how to listen in class and how to build on what teachers present so that they are able to access the information later.
- *Critical and analytical thinking.* Students also need to understand how to critically examine the information they are exposed to. The goal is to help students evaluate information not only from their teachers and traditional texts but also from electronic and other sources including from other people. Especially because students are actively engaging various forms of technology, students need to understand that what they read may be inaccurate and certainly in need of critical analysis.
- *Problem-solving skills.* Students need to understand how to work through difficult content in order to make rational decisions. They need to learn how to make educated guesses and work through complexity in logical, well-informed ways.
- *Strategies to build a successful future.* Although study skills typically focus on student learning, development, and ability to "do" school in a particular subject area, I have found that helping students think methodically and strategically about their next phases of life can also be advantageous. For instance, I have had conversations with students

who aspire to become doctors but have not enrolled in even the most fundamental math and science courses in high school. Helping students understand prerequisites for further academic work is necessary and can be captured in study-skills courses along with helping them build resumes, develop cover letters for afterschool or summer jobs, and write essays for college.

Whether this skill development is infused throughout an actual academic course or taught as a separate set of learning experiences, the range of student work should focus on academic and social success. This skill development also provides students with the opportunity to engage in some forms of "data" or information gathering where students talk with others about their own academic and professional journeys. For instance, students might conduct a short interview with someone in their career interest area. How did these individuals study? What courses did they take in high school? How did they sharpen their knowledge and skills to be qualified for the profession? Moreover, how did they negotiate tense social interactions? These interviews could be conducted with a college student in their area of interest or someone actually working in the field. It is never too early to help students think about their futures. Students need to be exposed to social and study skills to promote their learning and development. We cannot assume students will automatically know or acquire these skills. Moreover, we cannot assume they will receive them elsewhere. In short, students need to be encouraged to visualize life beyond their current situations and steps necessary to progress.

CONCLUSION

In this chapter, I have focused on the importance of instruction—teaching practices—for students living in poverty. In particular, I stressed that teachers, with the support of their schools and districts, must: (1) infuse language arts across the curriculum; (2) build and sustain meaningful relationships; (3) develop knowledge and skill beyond academic content; and (4) teach and cultivate student social, organizational, and study skills. Noguera and Wells were resolute and unyielding in their critique of what they call a No Excuses Reform Movement, where decision makers in support of it proclaim that poverty is not and should not be an obstacle, or serve as an excuse, in meeting the needs of students. This No Excuses Movement would suggest that, on a microlevel, "a combination of hard work, good teaching, and accountability are all that are needed to produce a greater degree of educational success."[49] While I agree that many factors can hinder progress when teachers are working with students living in poverty, there is evidence to suggest that teachers can be more responsive to students' needs. Unfortunately, too many are not. District and school expectations and practices, ineffective preparation of those in preservice teacher education programs, and the lack of support inservice teachers receive are all reasons for teachers' inability to teach effectively. Moreover, although I believe teachers can be change agents for students, sustainable effectiveness requires that attention be placed on instruction more broadly—that is, not only in a particular classroom but also on an entire district level. The following list captures many of the points I illuminate throughout this chapter regarding what teachers do to meet the needs of their students living in poverty:

- *Adopt learner lenses:* Teachers do not assume that they know everything; they seek to learn about the life experiences of their students.
- *Engage in critical self-examination and reflection:* Teachers engage in introspection that brings to the fore their own strengths, weaknesses, privileges, and issues. Teachers encourage students to engage in self-reflection as well; both groups work to examine how they contribute to disharmony in the classroom, attempting to avoid blaming the other.
- *Make their expectations explicit:* Teachers do not assume that students implicitly understand expectation and rules; teachers make the power structure explicit to students.
- *Use accessible, relevant language:* Teachers do not complicate expectations by using unclear and inaccessible language with students and/or community members.
- *Display caring and empathetic attitudes and dispositions:* Teachers attempt to understand their students and work with them to solve problems rather than seeing students as the enemy.
- *Reject deficit thinking:* Teachers believe that students and families are in fact knowledgeable and bring a wealth of knowledge and expertise into the classrooms; they see students as assets, not as liabilities.
- *Cultivate cultural and racial awareness and understanding:* Teachers understand that students' experiences are shaped historically, socially,

and politically; they attempt to connect to students' cultural and racial heritage.

- *Avoid color-blind ideologies:* Teachers recognize and acknowledge students' race as a central dimension of who students are; they attempt to know students as complete beings, not just fragmented ones.
- *Develop and maintain trust:* Teachers create a trusting environment for students by demonstrating care, by establishing bonds with students through the ways in which they treat students and convey expectations, and by building classroom community.
- *Develop parental and community partnerships:* Teachers recognize that there is strength in having partnerships with parents and the community; teachers work hard to develop partnerships with parents to both understand and scaffold learning and behavior in the classroom.
- *Provide multiple opportunities:* Teachers understand that students are often learning a new culture in schools and will need multiple chances to succeed; they do not give up on students quickly or easily. Teachers realize that many students are not used to experiencing success and work to help them "see the other side."
- *Avoid placing students' destiny in the hands of others:* Teachers realize that they likely know the student better than anyone else in the school and refuse to place the students' future in the hands of another (e.g., principal, resource officer).
- *Develop and maintain high expectations:* Teachers realize that they must push students to reach success because the stakes are so high once students are in the real world. Teachers refuse to water down the curriculum because they feel sorry for their students; they are on a mission to help their students succeed.
- *Realize that each student is an individual:* Teachers reject the idea that "equal" means the same and realize that each student brings a different set of needs into the classroom that must be met.
- *Are stern and fair:* Teachers make it clear that they expect excellence and, at the same time, keep in mind that they must be fair to each student.

What if an entire district worked to build these practices and habits among teachers—from elementary through high school?

Imagine the possibilities if teachers and principals were supported across an entire district and/or school to transform instruction in the ways discussed herein. A main point of this chapter is that such an emphasis has to focus on instruction—teaching! State and schoolwide initiatives tend to focus on policy and accountability (testing). *Rarely do state and schoolwide initiatives focus on instruction. There is power in how teachers teach the curriculum.* Thus, we need a reform movement that focuses on teaching to address the challenges students living in poverty face as well as recognizes the many assets these students bring into the learning environment. The pedagogical is both political and ideological, in this sense.[50]

CHAPTER 3

Case Studies of Practice: Life in Schools and Classrooms

I N THIS CHAPTER, I share case studies that I have constructed based on observations, experiences, and conversations I have had with students, educators, parents, and colleagues. I develop these cases so readers can situate themselves within the stories, critique the particulars of the cases, find points of convergence with their own experiences, and reflect on their own practices and how they might handle similar situations. I provide some insights and suggestions on the issues, and I also make some recommendations about how one might potentially resolve them. However, an important charge to educators is to draw from the discussions in previous chapters of this book to discern what the *real* issues are and how they might be addressed. My point in sharing these vignettes is not to generalize or to stereotype those living in poverty (or educators). Rather, the discussions are meant to help educators visualize "real" matters and think about how to address the myriad obstacles these cases illustrate. As has been discussed throughout this book, there is no one definitive way to work through the complexities of poverty (or race) as they manifest inside and outside of schools. The reality is that students' lives are not scripted (and very rarely predictable), and teachers have to be able to adjust their thinking, beliefs, and practices to address situations as they present themselves.

Thus, I invite readers to identify the layers of nuanced challenges embedded in the cases throughout this chapter. I especially encourage readers to think about specific ways to approach (and to a lesser degree solve) the problems identified in the scenarios. That is, what are the pertinent issues embedded in the case for all involved (teachers, parents, students, administration, and so forth)? What response is necessary to address the situation? For instance, can the issues be handled on a classroom level, or are other entities, institutions, or stakeholders essential to resolving a particular case?

Clearly, it is difficult if not impossible for any book in education to tell readers exactly what they should do in any given situation, because teaching and learning (and education generally) are iterative, evolving, emergent, and somewhat unpredictable. While I have done my best to provide explicit examples and information about what educators and especially teachers can do to better meet the needs of students of color living in poverty, some will still likely complain because they want more. But educators are professionals who should be able to draw from established and new frameworks, professional knowledge, and practice as they handle challenges in teaching. In examining the particulars of each case, I suggest readers consider the four focus areas described in chapter 1: understanding and practicing equitable decision making, understanding and responding to neighborhood conditions, reducing class size, and rethinking and reforming inflexible and narrowed curricula. In addition, on a classroom level, determine how appropriate, responsive, and applicable the following practices would be: infusing language arts across the curriculum, building and sustaining meaningful relationships, developing teachers' knowledge and skills beyond academic content, and teaching and cultivating student social and study skills.

CASE STUDY #1 (PRESCHOOL): "JAMAL, USE YOUR INSIDE VOICE."

I visited almost two dozen preschool facilities searching for the best fit for my four-year-old twin daughters. During one visit, I witnessed a group of five students (one black male, three white males, and one white female) playing together in a classroom. As I watched, the preschool teacher, a white, middle-class woman with fourteen years' experience, told "Jamal," the black student: "You are too loud. Let's use our indoor voice, please." The teacher turned back to me and went on answering my questions. Soon, she turned again to the five youngsters, but once more focused her words on one: "Jamal, you are too loud. I'm going to have to ask you to take a seat if you keep it up."

I was stunned. What I observed was a group of five students yelling and not using their "indoor" voices. Yet this teacher heard one student, Jamal. I wondered what this singling out did to Jamal's self-concept, voice, and identity. What messages is Jamal receiving from this experience and in what ways might he internalize notions that his voice and play were wrong? What can this teacher do to recognize her behavior—an action she was likely not consciously aware of—and ensure it does not happen in the future? I doubt seriously this teacher had any idea she was singling out Jamal and overlooking the voices/behaviors of the other students. Are the issues embedded in this case ones that this teacher could and should address on her own, or should others be involved? Moreover, how would this teacher ever realize what she was doing unless someone brought the situation to her attention?

Recently, U.S. Secretary of Education Arne Duncan released the 2011–2012 Civil Rights Data Collection, which allows online visitors to examine disparities between more-privileged students and those whose first language is not English, students of color, those who live in poverty, and those with disabilities. For the first time since 2000, the database provides current information on approximately 16,500 school districts, 97,000 schools, and 49 million students.[1]

One of the most profound findings from the data is that, although African American students represent about 18 percent of preschool enrollment, in the 2011–2012 school year they made up 42 percent of the preschool students who were suspended once and 48 percent of those suspended more than once.[2]

CASE STUDY #2 (ELEMENTARY SCHOOL): "LAURENCE, I'M TAKING AWAY YOUR RECESS."

Mrs. Turner, a white, middle-class teacher of thirteen years, had been teaching third grade for six years, after having taught fourth grade for seven years. She worked hard and seemed committed to making sure her students performed well on "their tests." She prided herself on creating a classroom culture that was on target, "focused," and allowed students to maximize their time. She shared that for the last several years, her students had outperformed their peers in other classes on the state exam. The students were actively engaged in a classroom activity from bell to bell. Although her students typically gave her a big hug in the mornings as they entered the classroom, she was no-nonsense when it came to her expectations for all her students. Although all the students in her class received free or reduced-price lunch, she told me she was particularly "concerned" about her black male students. She explained that many of them underperformed in comparison to her white students, and she struggled to build the kinds of relationships with them that she was able to garner with her white male and female students.

One day, I visited her classroom and observed a group of three males playing—or in her words, "engaging" in "center time"—before going outside to the playground for recess. Two white males and one black male were in the center, and each child had been assigned responsibility for completing one of the center tasks. At one point the black student, Laurence, had an argument with one of the white students, Jason. Laurence apparently got upset with Jason for cutting the triangles from the construction paper, because cutting the construction paper was Laurence's preassigned task. Laurence stood up and took the construction paper out of Jason's hands, demanding next that Jason also hand over the scissors. It was clear that the conflict between the students was due to a disagreement over instructional tasks, not because of any other challenge. The students were trying to complete the assignment so they could go outside.

Initially, Mrs. Turner rushed to the center area and reprimanded both of the students: "I am very disappointed with this misbehavior, boys. You know I don't tolerate this type of behavior." The boys immediately calmed down as she corrected them. Then, Mrs. Turner turned and faced Laurence: "Stand up," she demanded. "I will not tolerate this behavior from you any longer. You put your hands on another student in *my* classroom and that is unacceptable. You have no right to touch Jason or any other student in my classroom. Do you understand me?!" Laurence's attempts to explain both that Jason had taken over his assigned responsibility and that he had not, in fact, "touched" Jason at all were not heard by Mrs. Turner. "This is not the first time you have had problems keeping your hands to yourself. In my classroom, you will use your words and not be violent. Do you understand me?" She continued by explaining to Laurence that he would not be allowed to have recess with his classmates due to the conflict: "Laurence, I'm taking away your recess," she stated. Laurence was livid. Standing up for himself and not backing down to Mrs. Turner, Laurence continued to state his case. Soon, however, Mrs. Turner declared that one more word, and he'd be sent to the principal's office.

Jason, on the other hand, would be given another chance because he had not had similar "conflicts" in the past and because he had "kept his hands to himself," according to Mrs. Turner. Laurence was deeply hurt because he was looking forward to recess and felt that he had been misunderstood.

After this interaction, I had a conversation with Mrs. Turner about what I observed. I said that Laurence had not in fact "touched" Jason, but that he did take the paper away from Jason and demanded the scissors. Mrs. Turner seemed offended by my observation. I also mentioned that I was surprised at her decision to take away Laurence's recess time since the situation seemed to have subsided after Mrs. Turner spoke to them. Although fortunately for Laurence, he calmed down before being sent to the principal's office, chances are at some point in the future he will be sent to the office because Mrs. Turner made it clear that she would not tolerate any more of his "nonsense." She believed that if she did not follow through in the future it could set a bad precedent. Because Mrs. Turner likely does not understand why Laurence reacted the way he did, how can she be supported to maintain high expectations and at the same time empathize with Laurence's situation? Did she make the right decision to address Laurence individually and to take away his recess? How might Mrs. Turner and Laurence be supported to better communicate and build their connections? Moreover, was Mrs. Turner being equitable in her approach?

CASE STUDY #3 (MIDDLE SCHOOL): "I JUST WANT TO GET MY STUDENTS EXCITED ABOUT MATH AND NOT DEAL WITH ALL THESE OTHER ISSUES!"

Mr. Sears was a black, upper-middle-class math teacher in his first year of teaching at the very middle school he had attended as a student. He had always dreamed of teaching math, even as a middle school student. Although he generally seemed to be "getting through" his math lessons in most of his classes, his Latino students living in poverty seemed to really struggle to grasp the mathematical content. Frustrated, Mr. Sears commented that his Latino students did not even "put forth effort," while he worked diligently to prepare them for the standardized examination they would be expected to pass at the end of the academic year. Although his school was racially diverse, most of the students lived close or below the poverty line, but unlike the African American, white, and few Asian students in his classes, the Latino students seemed, from Mr. Sear's perspective, to "give up" or simply not engage at all in his class.

After a few weeks, Mr. Sears pulled aside four of the Latino students (one male and three females) and asked why they did not make any effort in his class. He alerted them to the dangers ahead of them academically if they did not engage, beginning with a warning that they would fail his class and eventually the state test. He talked about how hard he was working to prepare them, how he wanted them to succeed, and he even reminded the students that he was holding tutorial sessions twice a week for "struggling students" before and after school. He told them how disappointed he was that they never showed up for those sessions, although he was pretty "confident" the students did not understand much of the content and could benefit from the tutorials. One of the students explained:

> I am tired most days because I help my dad with his lawn care business after school. Most days, I can barely wake up in the mornings because I'm so tired. Don't take it personal.

Another student told him:

> And I can't stay after school for the tutorials because I have to get home to help my mom with my younger brothers and sisters.

Another student expressed that she was still learning English and did not understand much of what was being covered in math. She told Mr. Sears that he was indeed moving too quickly through the textbook, and she struggled to understand the lessons and content. She explained that there were times when she wanted to ask for clarification, but was embarrassed and did not want to hamper the progress of the class. She promised Mr. Sears that she did in fact put forth much more effort in her English language arts class because her teacher spoke Spanish and was able to communicate with her in her first language in ways that helped her understand the subject matter.

After hearing this feedback, Mr. Sears seemed to understand, to a degree, that these students faced some pretty complex challenges—many of which he had been unaware. However, he persisted:

> These are not acceptable excuses. No excuses, in fact, will be acceptable. I can't allow you guys to sit in my classroom day after day with

your heads down on the desk. I find it rude and disrespectful, and I won't tolerate it. You have to take personal responsibility for your own learning. The next time I see your heads down, I will have to send you to the office. Period. You must understand that my expectations for you are high, so I can't give you a "pass" and allow you not to engage. It's not fair to your classmates. You'll thank me for this later.

Frustrated, Mr. Sears wondered if he had chosen the right approach with these students. Should Mr. Sears expect things to get better after his stern conversation? Was he demonstrating high expectations with his "no excuses" approach? How did his words and practices convey his high expectations? Are the problems Mr. Sears encountered beyond the scope of his skillset and the classroom itself? In other words, does he need other entities (parents, community members, district officials) and personnel to help address the challenges embedded in this situation? How was he supposed to handle the language barrier in the classroom? Was it his responsibility to work with the student who worked late hours with his father in the lawn business? As a new teacher, what was Mr. Sears to do? Although he realized the demography of the school had shifted pretty dramatically since he was a student at the middle school, he seemed clueless about the best way to handle these situations. In Mr. Sears's words, "I just want to get my students excited about math and not deal with all these other issues!"

CASE STUDY #4 (HIGH SCHOOL): "THE BLACK GIRLS JUST WON'T BEHAVE!"

Mrs. Foreman, a white, middle-class high school language arts teacher of twenty-eight years, has complained about persistent issues she encounters with her female African American students. She says they are "disrespectful" and "mouthy." This year, in particular, she believes students are "harder" to teach. Her sixth-period class, the last one of the day, is proving to be the most challenging, with twenty-three students (7 African American, 4 Latino/a, 1 Asian American, and 11 white students).

One Friday afternoon in this class, two of her African American students, Tonya and Kimberly, sat in the back of the classroom and talked to each other while Mrs. Foreman was standing in the front of the classroom near the smart board, attempting to cover the day's lesson. Mrs. Foreman tried to redirect their attention several times, drawing from instructional techniques she had learned in her teacher education program and professional development, as well as from her experience as a veteran teacher. She walked close to the students during their chatter—moving away from the front of the classroom—as she talked to demonstrate her presence and awareness of their disruption. She stood right next to their desks, tapping her pencil gently on them at one point, directing them to look to the front board where she was describing some literary elements in a story they had read the previous day. She made a general announcement, too, reminding the class that they should not be talking when she was teaching. However, as soon as Mrs. Foreman walked away from the girls' desks, Tonya and Kimberly began (or continued) their sidebar conversation which, frankly, infuriated Mrs. Foreman.

Fed up, about halfway through the lesson, Mrs. Foreman yelled out to these students: "Say another word, and you are out of here!" All eyes in the class moved to Tonya and Kimberly. Mrs. Foreman was clearly upset. And the girls were upset as well after Mrs. Foreman "called them out." Tonya jumped up from her seat and yelled back to Mrs. Foreman: "I wasn't talking—stop trying to embarrass us!" she exclaimed. Kimberly followed Tonya with, "Me either—I was NOT talking."

"Get yourselves together and stop being so loud, rude, and disrespectful," Mrs. Foreman declared. Furious, Tonya spoke her mind in front of the entire class:

> You make me sick. Every time I turn around you are in my face. You just don't like me. Other people in this class talk all the time, and you don't have anything to say to them. I'm sick of it. You always picking on me. Just yesterday, the boys in the corner up there were talking while you were "teaching" and you didn't say nothing to them. It's not fair!

Appalled by Tonya and Kimberly's reaction and especially Tonya's words and tone, Mrs. Foreman drafted a detailed disciplinary form and shepherded the students out the door, down one flight of stairs to the principal's office.

Later, Mrs. Foreman explained to me that Tonya and Kimberly were perfect examples of the hostility, rudeness, and disrespect she experienced with many of her African American female students. "They are just so carelessly disrespectful," she said. In our conversation she wondered just what the girls were referring to when Tonya and Kimberly had pointed to white students in the class who supposedly "talked" during instruction without being reprimanded. Mrs. Foreman also mentioned how insulted she felt when Tonya suggested that she did not "like" her, and complained that whenever she "got on to" these two girls and many other African American students—especially her black females—they "played" the "you don't get us" or the "you don't like us" card.

Mrs. Foreman admitted that she was so aggravated by the girls' blatant disrespect and general loudness that she wished they would drop out of school because they clearly "do not care about their education." She wondered if their parents "value" education because "of course" the type of behavior Tonya and Kimberly portrayed "starts at home." She explained that she no longer wanted to deal with these students and that teachers in general should not have to tolerate such unnecessary disruption because it makes life and learning miserable for other students in the classroom who deserve an education. Teachers should be able to teach, and students should do what they are "supposed" to do—"learn." Alternatively, at the very least, Mrs. Foreman said that she wished the girls would be assigned to a different English language arts course. Basically, she did not want to deal with them; she wanted them to "go away." She wanted them pushed out of her classroom or even school!

How might Mrs. Foreman have better handled the situation with these students? Or did she handle the situation appropriately? Why or why not? Are there any issues of race and socioeconomic status that potentially contributed to the actions and reactions of this teacher and these two students? What, if anything, should this teacher have done to prevent sending the students to the office? From Mrs. Foreman's perspective, she cared about all her students and treated them "all the same." However, many of her students did not see it in this way. They perceived her practices and interactions with them as discriminatory.

DISCIPLINARY PRACTICES FOR STUDENTS OF COLOR AND STUDENTS LIVING IN POVERTY

The preceding case studies all deal with issues of student "misbehavior," classroom management, disciplinary infractions, race, and socioeconomic status. Black and brown students as well as those living in poverty are referred to the office and consequently suspended and expelled more frequently than white and middle- to upper-class students.[3] The cases illuminate how conflicts in the classroom can lead teachers to refer students to the office, which can ultimately result in in-school suspension, out-of-school suspension, or even expulsion. In-school suspension in many instances is just as detrimental as out-of-school suspension because very little learning takes place in the cell-like environments, where students complete worksheets and other menial tasks to pass the day. The adult in the in-school suspension room is often not a certified teacher or one equipped to support student learning and development, especially in the content domains. What I have observed, sadly, is that although students are in school space during in-school suspension, they are learning very little and could likely stay home for the kinds of instruction and developmental interactions they receive. In-school suspension mirrors a prison cell more than a classroom because it excludes students from "regular" society, just as the prison system is designed to do.

Skiba and colleagues found from their document analysis of hundreds of teacher referral records that students living in poverty and/or African American or Latino students were sent to the office for more *subjective* infractions, while white students were referred to the office for more *objective* ones.[4] For instance:

Subjective office referral: A teacher perceives a (Latino) student's response as "too loud" or "disrespectful" or "rude." (Consider the example of Tonya and Kimberly.)

Objective office referral: A teacher refers a (white) student to the office because she has been tardy to class four times, having documented the exact time she arrives.

The cases above are typical of conflicts that emerge in classrooms and, in particular, how teachers subjectively respond to student behavior. I do not mean to suggest that teachers handled the situations poorly or that the students were right. The point is to help educators carefully examine the nature of the situations presented and consider how they would (or perhaps should) handle similar situations.

Overwhelmingly, the findings in the research literature are straightforward, confirming that most disciplinary referrals originate in the classroom and, more times than not, are for students of color and students from low socioeconomic backgrounds. Teachers have the power to refer students to the office. Administrators—typically disciplinary assistant principals—have the power to suspend or expel students based on (1) their *interpretation* of the misbehavior described by the teachers and (2) their *interpretation* of rules and policy violation. Educators' views of student behavior can be racially and culturally shaped, which means teachers' interpretations of student behavior can be misinformed and unnecessary conflicts can result. Student discipline is often counterproductive, because if students are removed from the classroom, they do not benefit from in-class instruction that shapes their learning and outcomes. Thus, student referral and suspension is correlational (not necessarily causal) with their academic performance. *How can we expect students to succeed on academic measures when disciplinary practices cause them to miss learning opportunities?*

But what about the consequences for teachers who overwhelmingly refer children of color and those living in poverty to the office for disciplinary problems?

What rarely gets addressed in discussions about referral decisions and disciplinary practices are consequences for teachers who make choices that are unfairly disadvantageous for students. For instance, what if teachers have implicit racist beliefs and biases that show up in referrals for particular groups of students? Teachers have the power to make disciplinary decisions that can clearly harm students, without any serious ramifications. Why is it acceptable for teachers to make unfair decisions or judgments based on their own, socially constructed interpretations of behavior? Why are teachers and principals not penalized, corrected, or reprimanded for inaccurate subjective practices that negatively impact particular groups of students? More appropriately, as should be the case with students who make mistakes, why are teachers not supported through professional development to improve their practices in future situations?

The story line in the empirical literature is consistent: students of color (particularly black and brown students) and those from lower socioeconomic backgrounds are disproportionately punished and receive harsher exclusionary punishment than white and wealthy students.[5] *Why?*

REASONS FOR EXCLUSIONARY PRACTICES

Although the answers to the preceding questions are complex, some compelling evidence sheds light on reasons for the disciplinary practices that
refer and punish students of color and those living in poverty more often
and more harshly. It is problematic that although we understand what some
of the challenges are, we refuse to address them and reverse these practices
that prevent students from receiving the educational opportunities they so
desperately deserve. Following are several micro- and macrolevel reasons
for the uneven, frequent, and harsh disciplinary practices for students of
color and students living in poverty:

1. *Teacher and administrative fear.* Teachers and administrators may
   indeed be afraid of their African American and Latino students
   and consequently be less willing to work with them to improve,
   which would be developmentally appropriate for students in preK–
   12 schools, in order to keep them in the classroom. Skiba et al. argue:

   > Fear may . . . contribute to over-referral [of students of color].
   > Teachers who are prone to accepting stereotypes of adolescent
   > African American males as threatening or dangerous may over-
   > react to relatively minor threats to authority, especially if their
   > anxiety is paired with a misunderstanding of cultural norms of
   > social interaction.[6]

2. *Institutional and individual racism.* In the midst of pervasive (and
   inappropriate) postracial discourses and belief systems, institutional
   policies on the district and school level (such as zero tolerance) can
   be rife with racism, especially when they follow a white norm that
   excludes the behavioral and interactional styles of nonwhite people.
   In their study, Skiba, Peterson, and Williams found that office referrals were not a consequence of a threat of safety but "those that indi-
   cate noncompliance [insubordination] or disrespect . . . about 40%
   of all students receive at least one office referral in the middle school
   during the school year." The researchers found a pattern of disproportionality "in the administration of school discipline based on
   race, SES, gender and disability."[7] Yet teachers can be fearful of students and act accordingly, even though no serious threats are present. They may fear the bodies of students—their physical makeup,
   not the students themselves.

3. *Underpreparation in teacher education.* Teacher education programs, both traditional and nontraditional, often fail to prepare teachers to support *all* preK–12 students (a point that will be more thoroughly addressed in chapter 4). Some teacher education programs do not see the need to even offer courses on "classroom management," "race," or "poverty," and teachers are left to figure out (or not) how to work with students with a range of needs. Even when a course in teacher preparation provides an experience (or, more frequently, a few sections in a general-education course) in classroom management, it typically does not consider the relevance of race, racism, discrimiation, and/or poverty. The research literature on classroom management has not well addressed the issues of race and poverty.[8] And the literature on diversity and classroom practices has focused limited attention on classroom management. Teachers are not often taught how to handle their students' various ways of behaving in the classroom, nor are they provided professional development to build knowledge and skill through inservice once they are teaching. In short, students suffer because many teacher education programs do not prepare teachers to teach them effectively.[9]

4. *Cultural conflict.* Delpit stresses how dissonance between teachers and students can haphazardly shape what teachers teach, why they teach what they do, and how they react to their students.[10] When teachers misinterpret their students' behaviors—if we agree that behavior interpretation is culturally and socially constructed—conflict emerges that can make it almost impossible for learning to take place. In discussing discriminatory practices of teachers toward students of color, in particular, Weinstein, Curran, and Tomlinson-Clarke write:

> Such discrimination occurs when teachers do not recognize that behavior is culturally influenced; when they devalue, censure, and punish the behaviors of non-mainstream groups; and when they fail to see that their management practices alienate and marginalize some students, while privileging others.[11]

5. *Ineffective leadership.* State, district, and school leadership also play a role in exclusionary practices that suggest that particular groups of students are better served outside of the regular classroom setting.

On a school level, when teachers send students out of the classroom, administrators have several options. They can (1) attempt to resolve the conflict between the teacher and student and get the student back into the classroom; (2) partner with parents and family members to build synergy and collaboration with the teacher and student; (3) send the student to in-school suspension; (4) assign the student some type of punishment before, during (such as lunchtime), or after school such as detention or cleanup duty; (5) suspend the student; or (6) expel the student. Absent from this outline is how teachers might learn from a disagreement or behavioral disruption. Typically, leaders do not provide learning opportunities for teachers to develop, mature, and grow from disciplinary conflict, which places most, if not all, of the onus on the student. Quite frankly, though students usually play a role in conflicts that emerge in the classroom, they are not alone, as teachers typically have a part as well. However, students are expected to comply while teachers, more often than not, are let off the hook.

6. *Inadequate counseling and psychological services.* What does not happen often enough in student discipline under the control of teachers and school leaders is student referrals to counseling and psychological services. Counseling services can be critical for students who are grappling with difficult circumstances outside and inside of school. Student misbehavior is often a consequence of other factors—far outside what teachers are prepared to address and far more difficult than any one student might be prepared to handle without support. Moreover, the roots of student misbehavior include, but are certainly not limited to, the following circumstances: (a) students are grappling with their parents being unemployed or underemployed; (b) students are dealing with the death of a parent, friend, brother, or sister; (c) students sometimes witness tragic murders themselves; (d) students are grappling with various forms of abuse; (e) students are coming to terms with divorce; (f) students are working through conflicts and bullying; (g) students are working part-time jobs to support their families; and (h) students are dealing with conflicts and pressures of friends to do drugs, steal, and have sex. Indeed, getting to the root of student problems and finding ways to address them is a task that schools should support through counseling and

psychological services. The same is true for teachers. How often do teachers have access to counseling and psychological services when challenging experiences arise? I have found that teachers sometimes take their frustrations out on students when in essence they need to see their own therapist: they are hostile, rude, and abrupt with students because they are struggling with home situations and interactions. McGee and Caldwell et al. have stressed the importance of mental health in addressing the social and academic needs of both students and teachers.[12] Both groups likely need affective, psychological, and emotional support but, sadly, are expected to receive such support elsewhere or to work through these challenges themselves.

While this list of reasons for exclusionary practices is incomplete, it certainly speaks to the complex issues that need confronting to better support students and teachers. My point is not to suggest that educators do not care about students or that teachers are at fault for the conflicts discussed in the cases above. Rather, the goal is for educators to reflect on what they do have control over—that is, to critically examine their own mind-sets, beliefs, dispositions, attitudes, mental states, and practices that may hinder academic and social success.

We must consider the price we all pay for disciplinary decisions that exclude students from the learning environment. The fact that many teachers are not aware of their own role in escalating conflict is problematic. Indeed, disciplinary practices that exclude students can result in numerous undesirable outcomes:

- Increased student dropout and pushout rates
- Increased referrals to special education due to behavioral "disorders"
- A decrease in student learning (and, accordingly, lower test scores)
- Increased student absenteeism

Noguera's research suggests that the very disciplinary measures schools and teachers employ in the classroom may be producing and perpetuating what he calls "prison-like" schools and classrooms.[13] The "get tough" approaches that many classrooms and schools have adopted dehumanize students, in his view, and consequently produce mistrust and resistance.

All students are developing—even adolescents. They should be treated as developmental beings, not adults. Noguera also writes:

> [D]isciplinary practices in schools often bear a striking similarity to the strategies used to punish adults in society. Typically, schools rely on some form of exclusion or ostracism to control the behavior of students . . . the assumption is that safety and order can be achieved by removing "bad" individuals and keeping them away from others who are presumed to be "good" and law abiding. Not surprisingly, those most frequently targeted for punishment in school often look—in terms of race, gender, and socioeconomic status—a lot like smaller versions of the adults who are most likely to be targeted for incarceration in society.[14]

Although rationale-minded educators and others should recognize how these exclusionary practices perpetuate an inequitable status quo, the practices and consequences persist. In this way, school disciplinary practices can actually reinforce, perpetuate, and maintain prison occupancy in broader society.

Noguera declares:

> Students who get into trouble frequently are typically not passive victims; many of them understand that the consequences for violating school rules can be severe, particularly as they grow older. However, as they internalize the labels that have been affixed to them, and as they begin to realize that the trajectory their education has placed them on is leading to nowhere, many simply lose the incentive to adhere to school norms.[15]

Further, many students have already "checked out" and feel rewarded when they are sent out of the classroom or school. They do not want to be there because classrooms are not welcoming spaces for them. Some classrooms are not places where students feel connected. In this way, exclusionary practices actually give students what they want—to disassociate with and physically leave contexts that neither honor nor nurture their identity and strengths.

Although I doubt if most teachers would consciously discriminate against any individual or group of students, subconsciously, teachers make decisions that can have lasting negative effects on students. Gross-man explains that

> teachers praise African-American students less and criticize them more than European American students. The praise they give them is more likely to be routine, rather than feedback for a particular achievement or behavior. And when teachers praise them for specific behavior, it is more likely to be qualified ("Your work is almost good enough to be put on the board") or, in the case of females, more likely to be for good behavior than for academic work.[16]

While these practices are likely not deliberate, there are no mechanisms in place to help teachers identify these patterns. So, in too many instances, these behaviors go underdetected and students—in this case African Americans and females—suffer.

CASE STUDY #5: ROBBERY IN THE PERRY COMMUNITY

Several months ago, I was conducting research in an urban, high-poverty middle school when I learned that three high school students had committed an armed robbery at a "mom and pop" convenience store less than one mile from this middle school. One of the robbers had attended this middle school herself. The incident made national news because the store clerk died from the gunshot wound. My work with the middle school was focused mostly on the nature of teachers' classroom practices that were relevant and responsive to students' needs. About a week after the robbery, I returned to the school eager to learn about how the teachers and school broadly responded to the situation and how students dealt with all the media attention and community discourse concerning the robbery.

As a common practice, I arrived before school started so I could interact with teachers and students before classes began. On this day my practices were similar. When I greeted familiar students in the bus yard, they asked: "Did you hear about the robbery?" Students talked mostly to each other as they entered the building. Their questions and conversations continued: "I wonder where they got the gun." "How much time will they get?" "What were they thinking!?"

The same conversations persisted in hallways throughout the day. In the classroom and during lunch, students also talked about the particulars of the robbery. During class they passed private notes that I suspect had something to do with the robbery. Their conversations focused not only on those who had committed the robbery. Because the convenience store was one that many of the middle school students visited on their walks to and from school, some also wondered about the store clerk and his family—people whom they had come to know when purchasing items in the store. They had established an informal relationship with the store owners because the husband and wife opened and closed the store together each day. I heard a student comment about how kind "that man," the store clerk, was to them and how he always told "funny jokes."

But while the students talked extensively about the robbery, there were no lessons or conversations led by teachers. They vigorously avoided the topic of the robbery in the classroom and beyond. When interacting with their students, teachers at the middle school acted as if the robbery had not even taken place in the community and, perhaps most important, as if the students were not affected by, having conversations about, or thinking about it.

As reciprocity—that is, to show some appreciation to and contribute to the many teachers who helped me learn about their practices with their students—I periodically conducted professional development sessions with the teachers, staff, and administration. The general theme of those sessions was "culture and teaching." The purpose was to help teachers critically examine what they were teaching and the various assets and needs of their students, thereby reconstruct their practices to improve the quality of their teaching.

The week after my visit when the students talked about the robbery but the teachers ignored it, I conducted a professional development session with the teachers at the middle school. I began the session by asking teachers why they had not addressed—either instructionally or discursively—the robbery with their students. In their respective classes, I explained how surprised I was that they had not considered the robbery as a site of curriculum development and instruction, especially because students seemed to care so deeply about it. Through unyielding and unapologetic responses, both individually and in unison, teachers informed me of why it was completely inappropriate for them to address the robbery "with these kids."

They seemed offended and aggravated that I would even suggest such an emphasis in their practices. Why should they consider a robbery as a site for thinking about student learning? Teachers had several vocal replies to my query of why the robbery was not "taken up" with their students:

- "The robbery doesn't have anything to do with student learning."
- "Why would we glorify violence?"
- "Our students wouldn't be able to handle a mature conversation about the robbery."
- "Focusing on the robbery might encourage students to do the same thing."
- "Bringing up the robbery might encourage our students to commit such a crime to get attention."
- "Parents probably wouldn't appreciate a lesson about something as pathetic and violent as that robbery."

Additional teacher comments focused on concerns about their skillset and ability to address student responses and needs:

- "As teachers, we are not prepared to deal with students' reactions to the violence they see in these communities."
- "I am not a counselor, therapist, psychologist, or social worker. Students sometimes feel sad when these events of violence take place in this community, and I'm not trained as a counselor or psychologist to work with my students in this way. I am trained and paid to teach, not to lead a therapy session."
- "As teachers, we are not compensated enough to deal with helping kids address their feelings about a robbery."
- "One of the shooters has a cousin in our school; we don't want to cross the lines of having the student feel uncomfortable."
- "There is gang activity in this middle school. Focusing on a robbery could potentially aggravate the gang members."
- "One of the students attended this school. Is this the type of student we want our kids to emulate?"

Two lines of responses, though, were really illuminating and seemed pervasive—that is, most of the teachers in the room agreed with the following statements and could not understand why I would even think of proposing an emphasis on a robbery in a classroom with middle school students, focusing on their feelings about it, linking it to the curriculum, or scaffolding learning opportunities:

- "If we don't focus on the robbery, eventually student concerns and interest will go away, and we can get back to 'normal' until the next act of violence. We are under pressure to teach a 'real' curriculum here, you know?"
- "Why would we focus on a robbery when it doesn't have anything to do with raising our students' test scores?"

Unfortunately, most troubling about these comments was how teachers conceptualized why it was inappropriate and outside of their professional purview to address the robbery. The idea that student concerns, pain, and connectedness to the armed robbery in their community would dissipate, without adult support, over time was troubling. The teachers in this school, however, all seemed to agree that their practices had been to avoid any explicit discussions about violence in the community and expect students to deal with their questions and concerns regarding violence by "waiting it out." "Time heals all wounds," a teacher explained to me.

Sadly, when I mentioned to the teachers that several students were actually grieving the loss of the store clerk who was killed, they were shocked. "I don't know why the kids would be upset about the cashier," one teacher explained. "They didn't know that man." I learned of the grief of some of the students because I actually asked them how they were doing. Based on the reactions I received, it seemed that none or few of the teachers had taken time during a classroom session, before or after school, or throughout the day to ask students how they were handling what was happening.

Several researchers, including Pedro Noguera, Jeff Duncan-Andrade, Ebony McGee, and Leon Caldwell, discuss the ways in which the educational system confronts what Duncan-Andrade calls the trauma of many students in urban environments.[17] In an important lecture he gave at the Harvard Education Alumni Association, he declared that many students who witness or experience some form of violence are actually suffering from post-traumatic stress syndrome in that they are dealing with the overwhelming psychological strain of working through death and violence in their local communities. McGee extends Andrade's point related to mental health conditions of youth by suggesting that students are not having "post" traumatic experiences but "continuous" traumatic stress syndrome because no person or entity is working to decrease the stress; they cannot dispel the psychological tension because services are not in place to assist them.[18] What if students' parents are not able to provide the kinds of mental health support necessary for students to understand and navigate difficult situations such as violence, abuse, or peer pressure? Whose job is it to fill the mental health gaps that need to be addressed to help students concentrate on learning?

A serious problem is that teachers and other educators in schools are underprepared to both diagnose and treat these challenges. Unfairly, we expect teachers to serve in roles that few of them signed up to assume, such as parent, friend, guardian, counselor, and psychologist. Duncan-Andrade also stresses that many students who have experienced serious violence in their communities are too often diagnosed with attention deficit disorder or some other type of special education label that is not the correct diagnosis as students are actually experiencing post-traumatic stress. Indeed, most schools have little support for students who need resources to address their trauma.

Duncan-Andrade makes a profound point about how students in urban communities with large populations of those living in poverty, English language learners, and black and brown students are undertreated in comparison to those in more affluent, suburban communities. He points us to the Columbine school shootings that occurred many years ago and the significant level of support those students received from counselors, psychologists, social workers, and psychiatrists, even for many years after the Columbine incident.[19] The big question here is, why do we find it appropriate to provide supports to wealthy, white, and middle- to upper-class students but deny them to students in urban communities? The CRDC data reveals that nationwide, one in five high schools across the country lacks a school counselor.[20]

Another sad and persistent response from the teachers was their concerns that focusing on a robbery would not help their students score higher on their standardized tests. They were—as are so many teachers across the United States—obsessed with student test scores because of accountability structures that pressure teachers to get the highest scores possible, sometimes seemingly by any means necessary. Never mind the psychological and emotional stress students likely felt about the robbery; what the teachers seemed to care most about was how "addressing," "thinking about," or "using" the robbery in the classroom could help them increase student test scores.

One white male teacher was even more frustrated than the others with my questioning during the professional development session. He posed a question that seemed to resonate with his colleagues, especially other math and science teachers:

> "Not only doesn't it make sense for us to talk about some robbery with *these* kids, I teach math and science. What in the world does a robbery have to do with teaching and learning math and science?"

Unfortunately, not only did this teacher (and apparently his colleagues) find it inappropriate to discuss the robbery for the socioemotional well-being of students, he also did not see how "some robbery" could or should play a role in the curriculum.

The teachers wanted me, as the professional development coordinator, to answer the question and tell them what to do, which is problematic because teachers should have the ability to make professional judgments for and with their students to promote student learning and development. Still, I provided the following examples. Math teachers could pull up Google Maps and work with students to guesstimate the amount of time it would take for the police to arrive at the robbery site driving at different speeds. I also suggested that students could examine the number of liquor stores and gun shops in their neighborhood compared to other communities and develop hypotheses, predictions, and correlations with violence. For instance, are more crimes committed in communities with large numbers of gun shops or liquor stores? Tate discusses similar types of learning opportunities for students in communities where resources are meager and students begin to notice inequity in action.[21] In general, there are many themes related to social transformation that can be taught from an interdisciplinary perspective drawing from this experience, including but not limited to socioeconomics, social class, race, culture, poverty, oppression, (in)equity, (in)equality, affirmative action, crime, and privilege.

Further, if teachers are in organizational cultures where they are able to plan together, the mathematics teachers could coordinate and work with the English language arts teachers to construct a letter to the police chief or perhaps even the local newspaper outlining their concerns about crime in their local communities. Posing questions about why violence is even occurring in their community provides space to make recommendations about what could be done to solve the challenges. Germane to the letter development, drawn from the data they collect about the number of liquor stores, gun shops, and street lights in their community, are elements of standards students should be learning and developing related to literacy (thesis statement development, collecting and supporting evidence, genres/ types of writing, and so forth).

On micro and macro levels, educators should consider the following in attempting to make sense of the robbery: curriculum (the *what* related to the robbery), instruction (the *how* in conveying instructional messages related to the robbery), sociology (the *where* of the robbery and its effects on the broader community as well as the school), and people (the *whom* influenced by the robbery—not just those immediately involved in the incident).

- *Curriculum.* On a micro level, teachers and other educators are challenged to construct and interpret the *what* of student learning in ways that deepen students' knowledge of poverty and related matters, perhaps to eradicate it. The teachers described in the case could not see, envision, construct, reconstruct, or interpret the robbery as a site of curriculum—what students should learn about. Accordingly, because teachers hold some power over the curriculum, they decide what students learn based on their own belief systems, worldviews, priorities, and conceptions about what matters in the curriculum. On a macro level, teachers must be able to negotiate what they are expected to teach, draw links, and make professional decisions to be responsive to the nature and needs of students.

- *Instruction.* On a micro level, *how* the curriculum is taught can have the potential to help students understand the content in ways that speak directly to the robbery. Instructional practices can also pique student interests in social conditions that allow them to develop skills that honor the expected curriculum. On a macro level, this means that teachers must have the subject-matter knowledge and instructional savvy to transform the expected curriculum to address the interests and lived experiences of students. The teachers described above did not understand how to draw connections between what they were expected to teach and what they likely needed to teach based on what had occurred in the community.

- *Sociology.* On a macro level, understanding the social context or location of the community and school plays a pivotal role in understanding poverty and education—both inside and outside of school variables. Poverty, resources, and what Tate advanced as "geography of opportunity" shape students' experiences and could potentially help teachers and other educators make curricula and instructional decisions responsive to the sociopolitical environment.[22] Moreover, teachers could support students in writing essays, perhaps to the local newspaper, detailing why the number of liquor stores and gun shops should decrease in order to decrease potential violence. Students would thus be acting on behalf of their community.

- *People.* Knowing who occupies particular social contexts (communities and schools) is essential, and thus it is critical to consider those in the community affected by the robbery. For instance, the teachers described in the cases seemed to have a particular view of their students and the students' ability to "deal with" the robbery. On a macro level, knowing who lives in material poverty and why sheds light on deep structural inequities that perpetuate conceptions of the "haves" and "have nots." The availability (or lack) of human and other resources either enables or stifles students' opportunities to deal with the reality of the robbery.

It is important to note that I am in no way encouraging teachers to ignore the standards or what they are professionally obligated to teach. I am not even suggesting that teachers should "teach" a robbery or the conditions that caused it. My major point is that situations like those the students experienced in the Perry community are potential spaces of curriculum and instructional scaffolding. Teachers can use the experiences that students have as opportunities to anchor standards they must teach in the classroom. However, I am stressing that when situations like a robbery present themselves, schools must respond to them in order to ensure that students' mental health and socioemotional needs are met so they can concentrate on learning.

CASE STUDY #6: "HOW CAN YOU AFFORD THOSE SHOES?"

Mrs. Garcia, an upper-middle-class Latina teacher of eight years, has worked in the same elementary school since the beginning of her career. This year, she moved up from second grade to fifth grade at her elementary school—having taught second grade for seven years. She had a pretty diverse group of students, although the majority of them were white and lived below the poverty line. She had expected her older students in fifth grade to be "more responsible" than what she observed and experienced with the younger students. For instance, she realized early as a teacher that her second graders would sometimes forget to bring their pencils, paper, or notebook to school. However, she was shocked and frankly disappointed that her fifth-grade students seldom brought their books to class and rarely had writing utensils, folders, or paper either.

Because she taught in a self-contained classroom, Mrs. Garcia had many conversations with the parents of her students. The parents would encourage their children to bring their materials to school, but the school culture was such that students seemed to have learned to function without them. In fact many teachers provided writing utensils for their students each day, so the students took advantage of this. Although all the students at the school wore uniforms (khaki pants and a standard blue or white shirt), they wore shoes of their choice. Again, although many of her students lived below the poverty line, Mrs. Garcia was shocked at the very expensive tennis shoes her students wore each day. Moreover, she often questioned how they were able to have the latest high-priced technology such as iPhones, iPads, and iPods. Mrs. Garcia often asked: "Why would you spend that much money on shoes?"

For their science projects, Mrs. Garcia asked each student to spend about $15 on materials that the school was not able to supply. The students complained and stressed they did not have the funds to purchase the items and that they would not do it. Mrs. Garcia was confused: why would not her students find the funds to purchase a few science project materials when they readily found money for shoes, phones, and tablets? She felt a bit "ganged up" on by her class when she engaged them in a discussion about why they felt they should not be responsible for purchasing the needed items. Besides, she believed that her students should be willing to "invest" in their "education" and earn the extra money needed to purchase the materials if their parents could not afford them.

Mrs. Garcia stated her position: "If you can spend a hundred and forty bucks for tennis shoes, you can certainly find fifteen bucks for your science project." She went on to explain the consequences if students did not complete the project: "If your project is not done well with the materials you need, you will fail the science project." Each day, she waited for students to bring in their science project materials, but they never did. What was this teacher to do? Should she have expected her students and their families to spend their own money for schoolwork when she realized most of them lived below the poverty line? Why or why not? Was the fact that her students (and their families) found funds to purchase other material items relevant to her request? In other words, did it matter that her students purchased expensive tennis shoes but refused to buy science project items? At what level should this issue be addressed? For instance, should Mrs. Garcia think about broader-level reforms to address the challenges she faced?

CASE STUDY #7: "WHY SHOULD I GIVE YOU ANOTHER NOTEBOOK?"

Ms. Redman, a black, middle-class teacher of eighteen years, prided herself on developing structure and rules in her sixth-grade middle school social studies classroom.[23] She held all her students to high expectations and her students tended to perform well. Although the school had historically been a lower-middle-class school environment with mostly Asian and white students, over the last few years many members of the community and parents of her students had begun struggling financially, and this year several of her students, including Li (an Asian student), were living below the poverty line. Nevertheless, Ms. Redman was resolute and steadfast in her decision making—she was determined to maintain high expectations and to treat all her students the same.

At the beginning of the academic year, Ms. Redman gave each student a blue notebook to keep their notes on various aspects of geography and world history. Li, typically a well-organized and hard-working student, had come to school several days without the notebook, and Ms. Redman explained to him that he needed to bring his notebook to class each day—which was the expectation of all the students. Eventually Li brought the notebook to school, but it was in poor condition. The seams were coming apart, the color had faded, and the pages were wrinkled. Li asked Ms. Redman for a new notebook. Ms. Redman, who saw herself as a fair teacher who believed in equality, wondered about the appropriateness of assigning Li a new notebook when the other students would not receive one. What message would this send? Would other students feel compelled to "ruin" their notebooks if she gave Li a new one? In what ways was Ms. Redman embracing an equality framework over an equity one?

Ms. Redman also worried about the implicit lesson Li would learn if she provided him a new notebook. He might believe that it was acceptable for him to damage property that was given to him and expect a replacement in the future. Given the circumstances, was it equitable to provide a new notebook for Li? Why or why not? What else should this teacher consider in making her decision?

CASE STUDY #8: "BUT I THOUGHT I WAS THE PRINCIPAL AT THIS SCHOOL . . ."

Mrs. Silverman, a white, upper-middle-class first-year principal but educator of nineteen years, witnessed now as a principal some of the challenges she had faced as a teacher in inner-city Chicago for fifteen years. Throughout her career, she had many students who lived in poverty, and a disproportionate number of them were black and brown. After teaching for many years, she had decided to pursue her graduate degree in administration in order to garner the power to actually make a difference for her students. When she was a teacher, she felt that her administrators (principals and assistant principals) did not always make decisions in the *best interests* of her students. She suspected that they had become jaded by bureaucratic structures that prevented them from being the types of educators they had entered the teaching field to become.

When she became an assistant principal, she was determined to work overtime to optimize student learning opportunities. She finally believed she would be able to support her teacher colleagues in developing innovative, creative, relevant, and responsive instructional practices. As an effective teacher herself and now an administrator, Mrs. Silverman was eager to help teachers recognize the "genius" of their students and draw from the students' many assets to support them. Unfortunately, however, Mrs. Silverman spent the majority of her time handling discipline problems—even though her title was "assistant principal for curriculum and instruction." She discovered that this title was meaningless, because all three assistant principals in the school were inundated with disciplinary slips. The focus was not on helping teachers to support student learning and development. They spent their time "dealing with discipline."

Finally, when Mrs. Silverman was promoted to full principal in the same community at a high school, she was again excited about her goal to become an instructional leader and support her assistant principals and teachers in ways that allowed them to also be instructional leaders who could reshape the culture away from so many disciplinary challenges. Early in the school year, she realized teachers needed to examine their own belief systems about race and poverty because these so powerfully influenced their practices. She found that too many of the teachers had low expectations for students, did not challenge them, complained about student "deficiencies," and were undermotivated to teach. She wondered, *How can students be excited about learning and coming to school each day when it is clear that the teachers themselves dread their jobs?* She immediately began to talk with the superintendents in her district in hopes of securing professional development monies for her faculty. Because the Title 1 funds were already tied up with previously established programs, she needed support from the district office, whose leaders had high hopes and expectations for her and her students. The district superintendent sent two messages to this new principal: focus on instruction, not the things tangential to teaching such as race, and do not expect anything "extra" for the work that needed to occur in the school. The district superintendent also questioned her decision to focus on race and poverty and encouraged her instead to "get the teachers" stronger in their content areas and to hold the students and parents "accountable" for their "poor" judgment and "bad behavior." What was this principal to do? How might she become a transformative leader in her school even when her district supervisor refused to support her in this work?

CONCLUSION

In this chapter, I have shared vignettes with themes of race, poverty, and socioeconomic status. These stories are representative of the kinds of challenges teachers, administrators, and students face in their experiences in different sociopolitical contexts across the United States, and perhaps beyond. In previous chapters, I have suggested both micro- and macrolevel reforms and strategies that address some of the issues explored in the cases. I encourage readers to think about the degree to which the reforms mentioned earlier might be relevant and also to consider the added dimensions of the cases not explored in the recommended reforms. For instance, what nuances are underexplored in the scenarios discussed? What else do we need to know in order to make informed decisions about the core of the cases? The idea is for teachers to think through situations they may encounter in the future (or have encountered in the past) in order to determine what can be done to better meet the needs of students—*all* students!

What the above cases and related discussion drawn from the literature suggest is that both teachers and administrators need training in how to connect with students, de-escalate conflicts, and ultimately keep students in class. There is a prisonlike ethos in many schools where teachers believe some students are not the right kinds of citizens to remain in the classroom—what might be considered "regular" society. So, these teachers refer students out of the classroom and expect someone else to deal with them. One teacher, Mrs. Foreman, in fact, wanted two of her African American female students to just "go away."

Further, teachers need to understand how to communicate effectively with students because many students will do what is necessary to "save face" with their peers. Students in middle and high school especially (like Tonya and Kimberly) care more about impressing their peers than their teachers. Thus, students who feel they are being "called out" or "disrespected" may retaliate by in fact being "disrespectful" or "rude" to the teacher. A vicious cycle ensues: teachers fight with students, and students fight against teachers—rather than working together. In the fight to end poverty and, quite frankly, discrimination, there needs to be a concerted, systematic effort at the school, district, and even the state level to study the referral patterns of teachers. Who refers whom, when, how often, and for what reasons? These data can help leaders, teachers, and institutions recognize referral patterns and systems that support—or handicap—certain students. We can no longer do nothing. Inevitably, students' lives are influenced by our lack of attention and action to many of the challenges discussed in this chapter.

CHAPTER 4

A Call to Action in Teacher Education

I BELIEVE IN THE POWER AND POTENTIAL of teacher education to help teachers confront race, racism, and poverty in the lives of preK–12 students. But what role can teacher education programs, both traditional and nontraditional, play in helping teachers build the knowledge, skill, insight, and perspective to teach effectively? How can we build knowledge from research to inform practices that ensure optimal opportunities for all students? This chapter is dedicated to both structural and pedagogical features of teacher education that have potential to support teachers in their fight to end poverty and racism. It focuses on actions and demonstrates the urgency of helping teachers support and develop students. From my perspective—based on my own research as well as my review of literature—no area has more power to improve the life chances of preK–12 children living in poverty than strong teacher preparation that prepares teachers to teach effectively. To be clear, most teachers have good intentions. They do the very best they can to provide optimal learning and social enhancement for their students. They purchase materials for their students from their personal budgets. They arrive at school early and stay late to plan lessons, grade papers, and work with students. They attend afterschool activities (such as football and soccer games, theatrical events, and band concerts) that showcase their students, even when they are not on duty as coaches, theater sponsors, or band directors. Some teachers even take on surrogate parental roles. Although teachers tend to have good intentions, good intentions are simply not enough for the work necessary to support all students. The taxing task of understanding, confronting, building knowledge about, and developing practices to assist children living in poverty and students of color can be daunting at best. Teachers need support to build practices that move them beyond good intentions, not blame for issues and barriers outside of their control.

While I argue that teacher education and teaching matter, I am not suggesting that these two factors alone can make measurable strides in reversing the deleterious effects of poverty and racism, which are deeply sewn within the fabric of society, and consequently education.[1] But I am stressing that teacher education programs can be better equipped to support teachers in the kinds of practices essential to their success in schools. I focus on three areas to consider as we prepare teachers with a heightened focus of the nexus between poverty and race:

1. *Macrolevel policies and practices.* What policies and expectations are established in preservice teacher education to cultivate microlevel practices that can propel teacher educators and teachers toward success in constructing educational opportunities for students living in poverty and those of color? How do teacher education programs support teachers after they have graduated?
2. *Microlevel practices.* How can teacher education cultivate the knowledge, abilities, mind-sets, and skills among teachers that ultimately contribute to effective practices with students?
3. *Enhanced knowledge base.* What structural impediments prevent teacher educators from doing more to prepare teachers to assertively fight poverty and racism? What needs to happen to improve what we know about preparing teachers to teach students living in poverty and students of color?

MACROLEVEL POLICY AND PRACTICE REFORMS

In this section, I focus on what teacher education programs in general can do to design experiences for teachers that are advantageous for them as well as preK–12 students. This discussion is intentionally shorter than subsequent sections because I realize there are many impediments to what I propose here, or what would be ideal given that the social context of teacher education programs varies. Thus, rather than focus too much attention on matters that may be outside the scope of these programs, I zone in on areas that can logically support microlevel practices to assist teacher educators and teachers.

For one, teacher education programs need to develop a commitment—*an explicit vision and mission*—to address the intersected nature of poverty and race. Although many teacher education programs claim to have a social justice orientation to their work, I argue that an explicit vision, and consequently mission, related to *poverty and race*—rather than a general, uncoordinated set of ideas about social justice or equity—are important to orient teacher educators to better meet the needs of teachers and students.

It is equally important for teacher educators themselves to study the manifestation, effects, influences, and consequences of race, poverty, and their intersecting nature. Put simply, we cannot assume that teacher educators have a sufficiently sophisticated or well-informed understanding of these issues to deepen teachers' knowledge and skills. Thus, teacher educators truly committed to these goals need to study the best research available on the intersecting nature of race and poverty as well as those factors both outside and inside of school that shape preK–12 student learning. This study then needs to be incorporated in the design of courses and related experiences for teachers. How often do teacher educators deliberately study the research and then make structural shifts in their courses and the broader teacher education program to improve teacher training? How often are teacher educators themselves provided with learning opportunities to extend their knowledge and skill repertoire? Moreover, how many programs provide the time for teacher educators to retool in order to better support the teachers they educate?

Structurally, teacher education programs need to be better equipped to provide teachers with a set of experiences that extend far beyond the traditional boundaries of subject matter and student development. Understanding the sociological, anthropological, and cultural aspects of student development as well as community aspects of student learning are also essential. Taking one course on multicultural education, culture, poverty, or race does not equip teachers to meet the needs of children living in poverty. Often such a course is constructed to meet some accreditation requirement. Ideally, teachers will undertake an integrated set of courses and experiences that speak directly to race and poverty as well as subject-matter and student development. Building teacher knowledge to address poverty and racism requires an interdisciplinary approach that integrates anthropology, cultural studies, area/ethnic studies, sociology, human development, and psychology.

In addition, teacher education programs cannot simply end when students graduate. An induction period—at least three years—is essential to supporting teachers after they have completed their programs.[2] This is especially critical for those working with underserved students living in poverty. To be effective, teachers must understand the sociopolitical ecology in which they teach. Teacher education programs need to be restructured to develop learning trajectories for their teachers for the first three to five years of their teaching. This support should be expansive, including one-to-one coaching as well as lesson modeling, where expert teachers demonstrate instructional moves that allow new teachers to learn. The literature outlines several competencies that are essential in the induction years (it is important to note that the following thematic areas should be explored through a combination of courses, or related experiences, not necessarily in one course:[3]

> *Understanding race, poverty, and teaching.* Seminars and experiences can provide insights about race, poverty, and teaching—especially learning opportunities that do not reinforce stereotypes about students and their families.

> *Action research.* Induction experiences are a time for teachers to identify and systematically study their own practices (drawing from data they collect themselves) in order to change and improve them. This ongoing self-study can help teachers understand problems that emerge and work to resolve them—either individually or in collaboration with other, perhaps more experienced, colleagues.

> *Classroom management.* Induction gives teachers experience with classroom management and disciplinary challenges, making it clear that classroom management is about developing effective relationships with students and using innovative teaching strategies—not trying to control students. Classroom management techniques are less about identifying specific routines and procedures and more about helping teachers develop knowledge about their students and curricula and instructional strategies that respond to their needs.

> *Parents and community.* Induction needs to help teachers understand, recognize, draw from, and be responsive to out-of-school realities and assets (working with parents, community organizations, and other local partners) that they can build on in curriculum development and instruction.

> *Understanding black and brown males.* Without generalizing or stereotyping, induction experiences need to help teachers understand

some of the challenges that black and brown males face inside and outside of school. Black and brown males continue to be underserved in communities and schools. These induction experiences should explore issues related to masculinity, identity, sexuality, social status, economic development, and achievement. By drawing from both the literature and the voices of the students themselves, teachers can build a robust knowledge about the range of needs of these students and develop instructional practices that address those needs. Moreover, this expanded knowledge about black and brown males could potentially help teachers keep students in the classroom rather than sending them to the office when conflicts emerge.

Mental health/counseling. Through induction, teachers should come to understand the psychological, social, emotional, and mental health challenges and trauma students experience on a daily basis and, perhaps more important, build the expertise to identify and address traumatic experiences. Induction needs to provide teachers with the tools to support their students as they work through psychological and emotional turmoil—especially until other personnel are available to assist.

Teacher wellness. In induction, teachers themselves need to be supported physically, emotionally, socioemotionally, cognitively, and affectively in order to effectively respond to and teach their students. Teacher wellness opportunities should be ongoing so that teachers can take care of themselves throughout their teaching journey— beyond the three to five years of induction. In addition to counseling and psychological support, teachers need to develop tools to deal with their own stress (such as exercise regimens) and learn how to de-escalate conflicts with their students (or possibly other colleagues, supervisors, parents, or community members).

Culturally relevant and responsive teaching. Teachers should draw from the work of Gay and Ladson-Billings to transform their curriculum into instructional practices that are relevant and responsive to their students and their particular social context.[4]

Relationship building. Through induction, teachers learn that their instruction is not tied solely to their ability to teach their subject matter. They must also be able to build the types of relationships with students, parents, students' family members, and community members that allow them to develop instructional practices that meet students' academic and social needs.

Leadership development. During the induction period teachers also need to learn leadership skills to work with their colleagues in building a school culture of success. This means developing their self-efficacy and conceptions of the type of school climate that allows them to be professionals—without having to follow a scripted curriculum, line by line. This leadership is essential to build morale and confidence among colleagues as well as students.

Study and organizational skills. Teachers have to be able to identify gaps in students' organizational and study skills and help students understand how to build those skills in the midst of teaching.

Social skills. In induction, teachers must develop skills to honor students' ability to navigate and negotiate social interactions, complement areas of strength, and disrupt social patterns that could be disadvantageous for students. Essential to this identification of social skills is teachers' ability to identify the social assets that students already possess. For instance, students' ability to negotiate challenging situations outside of school can be foundational for managing social interactions inside of school.

Deep, robust content knowledge. Through induction, teachers need to continue learning and deepening their knowledge in their respective content areas.

Innovative assessments of student learning. Teachers have to be guided to construct and deconstruct rubrics and other assessment tools that capture student learning, growth, and development. Although assessment tools tend to serve a diagnostic function in identifying what students do not know, innovative assessments allow students to showcase what they do know and how they think so that teachers can build on these areas.

Dialogic learning from students. In induction, teachers need to develop instructional and related habits that promote ongoing dialogue with students (and their parents). By talking about students' needs and teachers' expectations, teachers and students build relationships, and teachers develop knowledge and insights about how the curriculum and instruction could be reformed to better meet student needs. Adults often talk about students to their parents and teacher colleagues. However, this induction feature stresses the need for teachers to develop opportunities to talk *to* students, not only *about* them.

Ideally, *cohorts of teachers* would be developed within a particular school, thus providing opportunities for teachers to learn together in cohort models that could potentially transform troubling cultural practices embedded in schools. Further, what if teachers and principals learned and developed together in teacher education programs and then moved into the same preK–12 schools together? The idea is for teachers, leaders, and other educators to experience a common teacher education program tied to development and learning on poverty and race and then move into one school building together as they are supported through induction over the next three to five years. Such a model of teacher preparation where teachers, leaders, and other educators are prepared together and then coupled into a single school together would particularly work in schools that are being "turned around" or new schools that are developing. Designing teacher placement such that a critical mass enters the same school could help ensure that what teachers learn in their preservice education is not diminished by an established toxic, unstable, and dysfunctional environment. Regardless of how outstanding a preservice teacher education program is, teachers' knowledge, skills, understandings, commitments, and practices will be shaped in some powerful ways by the established broader context of the school in which they teach.

MICROLEVEL POLICY AND PRACTICE REFORMS

Teacher education programs can do much more to support teachers who work with children of color living in poverty. I focus in particular on what can happen in classroom settings to potentially influence teachers' thinking, beliefs, and mind-sets. Because so many teachers do not recognize how race manifests in their own lives and those of others, heightening this awareness and intensifying how they think about race have the potential to transform their practices with preK–12 students. These are my recommendations:

- Teacher education programs should develop and offer courses with a focus on race and poverty, and every teacher needs to be required to take the courses. Ideally, every teacher should take part in a well-designed program—not just disjointed courses that do not address the intersections of content, race, poverty, learning, development, and teaching.
- Teacher educators should build knowledge and experiences concerned with race and poverty throughout the entire teacher education programs.
- From the beginning of their teacher education experience, those learning to teach or to improve their teaching skills need to be exposed to real students, in real schools, in real time to help them build knowledge from effective skilled teachers, coaches, and leaders in working with students living in poverty. This knowledge should be developed through observing good teaching, practicing innovative instructional methods, and talking to students in schools about their social and academic needs.
- Teacher education progrms should equip teachers to systematically study their own practice to improve it.
- Teacher education programs should support teachers in understanding that they must work with the community in order to develop their knowledge of the needs and assets in the community and also to build alliances, advocacy, and resources that can make a difference for student learning and development.

As a concrete example, consider the following different ways in which a single situation could be interpreted and framed:

A high school student, Carla, works six to eight hours a day after school at a fast-food restaurant to help support her family financially. She passes all her classes and shows up at school every day, but her schoolwork is not exceptional.

A teacher's deficit perspective: Poor Carla. She works too many hours. Although she passes my class, she could do so much better if she spent more time studying and less time working. Her work could be better.

A teacher's asset perspective: Carla demonstrates the capacity to balance her schoolwork and her part-time job. I should talk with her about how I can assist her to make sure she is maximizing the class while she is working so hard in her part-time job. She is demonstrating the ability to balance school and work. This balancing act is commendable.

Curriculum Reform in Teacher Education

Certain kinds of classroom experiences in teacher education help teachers build knowledge of, empathize with, and see the relevance of issues of race and poverty. I encourage teacher educators to teach about race and poverty from an *interdisciplinary* and *multidisciplinary* perspective. They should anticipate some resistance but persist for the sake of preK–12 students as well as the teachers who will teach them.

In fields such as anthropology and sociology, people are expected to study race deeply because it is understood that race is a very real factor in people's lives; so, too, do I recommend this emphasis in teacher education, as professionals are being prepared to work with students whose experiences are shaped by their racial (and ethnic) identity. In their teacher education and training, teachers are too rarely expected to do any historical and deep contextual reading about race. Unfairly, teachers are often blamed for the underachievement and lack of success of their black and brown students when teacher education programs (both traditional and nontraditional) rarely provide opportunities for teachers to examine what race is and its salience for their work with students. How often, for instance, do teachers read historical texts such as Dubois's *Souls of Black Folk* or Woodson's *The Mis-education of the Negro* to understand the historical landscape of race in society and education and make connections to social and educational inequities?[5]

Unfortunately, the field of teaching is shaped by movements to deprofessionalize and de-skill teachers such that they are not expected to act as professionals in making decisions about student learning. Rather, due to increased "accountability" pressure, some teachers expect their professional training to be inundated with quick tricks for ways to teach particular content to students. However, teachers are and should be seen as professionals capable of making rational and appropriate decisions based on what they read and understand in their teacher education programs but also in the classroom in responding to their students.

The point is that rather than criticize teachers for their inability to empathize with and make astute pedagogical decisions for their racially diverse students, we need to examine the extent to which teacher education programs address race. In examining test scores, office referral patterns, absenteeism, graduation rates, and rates of suspension, a consistent focus should be placed on racial disparities, which continue to disenfranchise black and brown students. Rather than continuing to allow teachers to blame parents or the students themselves for these patterns, it is important to help them understand that these students are operating in educational systems that were *not* designed for them—historically or contemporarily. Students have complex racial identities that should be considered as teachers work to transform their practices. Yet, some teachers complete their educational training with few if any opportunities to really learn about race. Moreover, when teachers do study race, the learning tends to be superficial at best.[6] *Again, in practice, I have observed that it is the preK–12 schools that interrogate race and place it in the center of their professional development that make the most strides in their practices with students of color.* Thus, both preservice and inservice teacher education programs must make race a centerpiece of their curriculum for teachers in order to help address the racial imbalance in outcomes among various groups of students.

"Can We Get Over Race, Please?"

Though I am arguing for a reformed curriculum of teacher education with an interdisciplinary perspective, I want to stress how difficult it can be to engage teachers in issues of race—especially since many teachers believe we live in a postracial society. I was born and raised in the South. Although my parents did not have college degrees, I grew up with many material possessions and was expected to attend college. In short, my family valued education. My family was not rich, but I did not know what it meant not to have clothes to wear or food on the table. Race and conversations about race were common in my family as far back as I can remember.

I recall how one of my white classmates called me a nigger when I was in the fourth grade; my parents, mostly my father, had a very frank discussion with me about race and in particular, how racism worked on both the individual and systemic level. Interestingly, almost all my classmates in elementary school were black. Yet one of the very few white students had learned the word *nigger* and chose to articulate it with me. Although I recall not deeply understanding my dad's explanations of what the word meant and why it mattered, I remember the conversation resonating with me and connecting to experiences I had had. Moreover, in high school, I recall how one of my mathematics teachers literally taught to the "white side" of the classroom. All the black students in the class would discuss the teacher's actions but never complained about them to our parents or the school administration. I was disappointed and upset at times with this teacher and her actions. But I was never quite able to capture why this was happening, why I was so upset about it, and what, if anything, I should or could do about it.

In elementary school, I recall that most of my classmates received free or reduced-price lunch; I was one of very few students in my classes who did not. I remember a day when one of my fourth-grade friends who lived in the housing projects next to my elementary school rode the bus to my house after school so my dad could give him a ride to our football practice (he and I played on the same team). As we walked to my house from the bus stop, my friend asked me to point out my house to him. His response: "Wow—you live in a brick house, and it is not connected to another house. You must be rich." Of course, my family was far from wealthy, but I vividly recall that conversation and my friend's reaction to the fact that ours was a single-family home and was bricked on the front. This was not the norm at my school.

Having worked as a professor for more than a decade, I have taught in several different types of institutions and worked with a diverse range of teachers. I have taught in an elite, private, mostly white institution; an historically black university; three public, mostly white schools in the United States; and a public, mostly white institution abroad. In each case, I worked with preservice and inservice teachers—mostly to build skills in how to teach English language arts in public schools as well as how to teach with an equity focus. Many of my courses focused on diversity, and especially race. Again, my life experiences have shaped my courses, as has the reality of so many underserved students in preK–12 schools.

Subconsciously, I suspect I had gotten used to queries from my teacher education students (especially at the predominantly white institutions)

about my credentials, about whether I had taught before in public schools
and for how long, and even about my family background. However, I was a
bit caught off guard the third time I taught a particular required secondary
education course because it felt as if the students gathered before and after
class to protest the focus of the course. I did not apologize for emphasizing
issues of race as the class covered the different themes of the course. I often
thought about conversations I had with black and brown students in public
schools who were bored, undermotivated, and ignored in the educational
system as I planned and enacted the curriculum. I also thought often about
how my own family members were mistreated and underserved in schools
that saw them as numbers (perhaps statistics drawn from tests) rather than
developing human beings. To be sure, my curriculum and instructional
practices were deliberately shaped by and infiltrated with my racial identity.
For example, I had developed classroom experiences related to curriculum
development so that students were guided to consider the complexity and
centrality of race and racism. In what ways, for instance, were particular
genres of writing and canonical texts emphasized over others and why?
Who decided what got covered, for how long, and why? What role did the
race and socioeconomic status of those decision makers play?

Many of the students in this course (all but three of whom were white
women) were not happy about the emphasis on race. They were explicit:
"Why do you make everything about race?" "I thought this class was supposed to prepare me to become a teacher. I don't see how race and racism
relate to this course." Even more troubling for many of my students was my
direct emphasis on the educational experiences and needs of black males
in public school classrooms. Clearly, my own racial, ethnic, and gender
background played an enormous role in how I taught this class and what I
emphasized. The same point is true for teachers in public schools.[7] Teachers' own backgrounds strongly influence what they focus on as well. They
failed to understand this reality—one that almost guaranteed that black
and brown students would experience a curriculum that was grossly disconnected from their own racial, ethnic, and gender identities. Indeed,
when race was covered more generally, students were upset; some questioned the relevance of such a focus while others defaulted to silence. When
I guided the discussion to include black males, though, it appeared that an
even deeper sense of frustration, signaled through silence, permeated the
room. When one student said, "Kids are just kids. I don't think it's useful

for us to 'essentialize' any student or groups of students," I began to examine my own position. As an assistant professor on a tenure track early in my career, my concerns were deep rooted and multifaceted. I questioned whether I should allow the students to push me (or, as I felt, bully me) away from a focus that I knew to be gravely important for their own work as teachers and also for their students.

At the beginning of the course that semester, the students were loud and clear in their feedback. The themes of the student feedback were powerfully influential to me. On my end-of-semester evaluation, one student wrote:

> The professor is smart and knows a lot about teaching. I learned a lot. However, he focused too much on race, on African American students, and on African American male students particularly. This course was supposed to be about teaching *not* race!

The collective student feedback insisted that I must have an "agenda" because I found it important to focus on race in a course that they thought was "about teaching." They struggled to understand how central, connected, and salient race and teaching were. In fact, it seemed that they failed to understand that *race was about teaching, and teaching was about race*.

As a black male teacher educator, I had a pedagogical agenda that, in the students' view, conflicted with theirs: I wanted my students to learn the content and themes of the course and to gain insights about the interrelated nature of race to the other course content. The irony is that the students in the course never thought about how their agendas as white women could be very much in conflict with their black students; yet, their preK–12 students did not have the power to hurt these white teachers through teaching evaluations as did the students in my course. Besides, in my students' view, they had a right to contradict me and my curricula and pedagogical decisions because from their perspective, the class was about teaching, not race. They were "paying" me to teach them and to focus on what they wanted to cover—not what I knew was essential. How often do students in preK–12 classrooms have the opportunity to provide such feedback? Ironically, two of the students from that course emailed me years later sharing their "thanks" for shedding light on "eye-opening" experiences. They stressed how valuable the course had been in helping them "understand" their "minority" children in the classroom. At the time, my curriculum emphasis was irrelevant. After they began teaching, the emphasis was germane enough for them to write me a personal note. I received no note of apology, however, from any of the students who were sure to mark my teaching evaluations in a way that could have hurt my reviews for promotion and tenure.

I have found that although teachers may struggle to see the relevance of race, they are much more open to thinking about poverty and socioeconomics. I have also found that when I (and others in our courses) shared personal experiences that illuminate issues of race or poverty, or the nexus between race and socioeconomic status, teachers tended to be much more receptive. They were able to develop insights because the narratives made the issues salient. Thus, while some might reject opportunities for students to draw personal connections and provide stories that influence their lived experiences, narratives can be a door-opener for seeing the links between race and poverty. However, personal stories need to be well connected to broader matters, content, contexts, and constructs to help frame pedagogical relevance for teachers. Stories without theory could leave discussions at a surface level when narrative grounded in and connected to literature can be impactful.

Are You the Janitor?

As I walked into the building to my office, I passed the administrative assistant who works in another division. Before I was out of sight, this person, a middle-aged white woman whom I had greeted several times in the past, called me back to her work area. "Is that yours?" she asked, pointing to a janitorial cart with cleaning supplies near her workstation but in front of the doors to the main lobby. I replied, "Excuse me?" with more than a hint of confusion. "That cart right there—is that yours?" she asked. Still confused, I responded, "No, I am not the janitor." She replied: "Well, whoever it belongs to needs to move it. It is in the way sitting right there. It is blocking the doorway entrance." I had greeted this administrative assistant on several occasions in the past, carrying my briefcase and dressed in semiprofessional attire. In fact, she had always seemed cordial to me as we exchanged our "hellos" and "goodbyes" in the midst of busy days. Although she never engaged in conversation (she always seemed too busy to glance up from her computer), she always appeared friendly enough.

Had she not remembered our brief encounters in the past? Was she joking with me? As I reflected on the interaction, I concluded that this person assumed that I was the janitor, despite my professional dress. Could I not be a professor? That is, was I encountering what Ellison referred to as the "invisible man" phenomenon?[8] Had she decided who I must be based on her prejudgments of who performed custodial work in the building? What factors contributed to her thinking about me (my occupation, my role, my status at that university)?

It was no secret that many of the janitorial staff members in the building were (and had been) African American. It was also no secret that there were very few African American faculty members. To be clear, I am not degrading support staff. I respect the janitorial staff in all the institutions in which I have worked and appreciate their contribution. What I am suggesting is that because I am a black man, the administrative assistant relied on stereotypical assumptions about who I must be. Hurt, anger, and frustration were the emotions I felt after this experience.

Her perception of me was based on race, although my white colleagues with whom I shared the story rationalized it and convinced themselves— trying to convince me—that it was not. They concluded that surely the interaction meant something very different. Based on my experiences, this is unfortunately common. White people often try to rationalize raced experiences and turn them into something else. They do not want to believe that people are still racist and that people still experience racism on a daily basis. Many of those I shared the experience with did not believe the situation was about race at all. Moreover, although this experience was troubling and stands out as one of the moments that elucidates how race still matters, it is representative of the kinds of experiences I have had in different contexts all my life.[9] Not only was this experience about race, it was also about socioeconomic status. Most of the professors at the university were white and held a prestigious status in comparison to what this person perceived of the custodial worker.

Another personal experience illuminates this point. After retiring from General Motors after thirty-eight years of service, my father started a janitorial business where he worked to clean office buildings, including restrooms. When I visited my parents during holidays, I helped my father clean the buildings. The very way in which staff talked to me (with some people refusing to look up from their computers as I greeted them to pick up their trash) spoke directly to a social order that was established, perhaps unconsciously. I wanted to remind the folks who ignored me or treated me like I didn't matter what a janitor friend shared with me: "I may be picking up trash, but I am not trash."

This experience is important to consider as features of it can be thought about in a broader context. Imagine the numbers of black and brown students who experience situations where their racial identity and perhaps socioeconomic status are thwarted by ignorance. Teacher educators must be mindful of how such situations can influence students, and prepare teachers to develop heightened awareness of how these "microaggressions" can affect people of color. *Racial microaggressions* can be defined as "brief and commonplace daily verbal, behavioral, or environmental indignities, whether intentional or unintentional, that communicate hostile, derogatory, or negative racial slights and insults toward people of color."[10] Researchers have found that such microaggressions can take a toll on people of color, who can start to disconnect because the persistent aggressions are taxing and wear them down. In Smith, Yosso, and Solorzano's words: "The accumulative stress from racial microaggressions produces racial battle fatigue. The stress of unavoidable front-line racial battles in historically white spaces leads to people of color feeling mentally, emotionally, and physically drained."[11]

One high school student explained to me how he felt when he was constantly being followed around department stores while shopping at the local mall:

> That shit gets on my nerves. These damn white people follow me around the stores like I'm going to steal the clothes off their backs. The white boys are in the store and nobody's checking them. It's the brothers they following around, you know? The shit gets old. I'm sick of it! I've been working since I was twelve and saving. I can buy whatever I want in those damn stores . . . but you know it's because I'm a brother that they checking every move I make.

Another student I talked to in a predominantly white school shared how she felt her voice and perspectives were always ignored in her literacy classroom:

> It's like whenever I say something in class she [the teacher] is like 'that's interesting.' But when a white student says the same thing or makes the

same point, she's like 'that's a great point.' I'm thinking that's exactly what I just said. She always does that so I just stop talking [participating] in class because I'm tired of it.

In 1964, Fannie Lou Hamer delivered a provocative speech at the Williams Institutional CME Church in Harlem, New York. The title of her lecture was "I'm Sick and Tired of Being Sick and Tired."[12] Hamer, a black woman born in 1916 in Montgomery County, Mississippi, was a civil rights leader who worked tirelessly for voting rights for black people and other marginalized groups. In her speech, she talked about racist and sexist experiences she had encountered in Mississippi and also stressed that some in other cities across the United States still dealt with relentless discrimination against black people, and women in particular. A central point of her lecture was that some people were not "free" at all and that current conditions caused them to experience life in society in slave-like ways, even though federal mandates had begun to support rights for all U.S. citizens. She provided poignant stories of resilience of her family as they worked and fought through phobias and -isms both in their personal interactions in the South and in the workforce. The title of Hamer's speech metaphorically connects with the themes of the student comments above as well as my own experiences. Like Hamer, we are *sick and tired of being sick and tired* of racist, sexist, homophobic, xenophobic, hegemonic, classist, and inequitable structures and systems both inside and outside of education. And it is the obligation and responsibility of teacher education programs to help teachers understand and respond to these conditions. The environmental factors described above may well influence the socioemotional and physical health of those undergoing these taxing experiences.

WHAT CAN TEACHER EDUCATION COURSES DO?

What can teacher education courses actually do to fight poverty and racism? What assignments, in particular, can support preservice and inservice teachers? Most of the following examples are related to helping teachers build knowledge and awareness, although I realize this is perhaps a first step to a much more complex process of building practices. In addition to developing understandings of how microaggressions and racial battle fatigue influence their students of color, teachers (and teacher educators) need support to: (1) *understand the self in learning to teach*; (2) *acquire* knowledge about others; (3) identify and confront societal discourse; (4) develop caring relationships; and (5) build links to curriculum and instruction. Deliberately, many of the recommendations made in this chapter build on points made in previous chapters, related to what should happen in districts and schools.

Understanding the Self in Learning to Teach

The literature makes clear the importance of teachers' self-examination and awareness in meeting the needs of students.[13] Medina, Morrone, and Anderson explain the importance of helping teachers "examine their personal notions of urban schools and communities."[14] Woolfolk writes that "reflective teachers think back over situations to analyze what they did and why and to consider how they might improve learning for [all] their students."[15] Valli explains that "reflective teaching emphasizes the importance of teacher inquiry and counteracts a more limited interest in teachers' behavior without considering what is going on in their minds and hearts."[16] Researchers and theorists have attempted to bridge reflective thinking and race and stress the importance of teachers' thinking and beliefs in the cultural contexts of learning.[17] Moreover, the importance of self-reflection has been stressed for all teachers, not just white people.[18] Cultural and racial self-reflection is necessary for all teachers—even teachers of color, because many have internalized, validated, and reified pervasive, counterproductive stereotypes about themselves and others. They may have, in a sense, been brainwashed into believing dominant cultural negative misconceptions about themselves and others in their group.

Teachers should reflect on their own beliefs about students living in poverty and students of color as a way to improve their practices with those groups. Do they believe these students are capable of excellence in the classroom and beyond? Are teachers willing to accept that these students are not always or necessarily the problem in the classroom and that, as teachers, they may need to make some adjustments to meet their students' needs? A critical look at the self—a deep, introspective examination of one's personal worldview—is necessary. Teachers who engage in self-reflection realize that effective practice begins with the self, and they come to understand how they have some control over what they emphasize and teach in the curriculum.

Clearly, when teachers do not believe that their students living in poverty and/or their students of color are capable of meeting high expectations, these students are placed at an enormous disadvantage. Successful teachers know themselves, are willing to confront their biases, privileges, and misconceptions, and work to provide students with meaningful learning opportunities that address their needs.[19]

Although various assignments and experiences can build self-knowledge, I have found that having teachers engage in critical autobiographies, where they focus on their own race and socioeconomic backgrounds, helps them reflect on their own histories and current realities.[20] However, simply reporting episodes or experiences related to their race and past/present socioeconomic status only gets at a descriptive level and does not necessarily lead to *critical* examination. Posing questions about how they come to see themselves as individuals with a race and socioeconomic background is essential. I have learned that questions like the following build the kind of critical reflection in learning and developing as a teacher:

What is your racial background? How do you know?

In what ways does your racial background privilege you (or not) in society?

How and when did you first see yourself as a racial being? How do you know?

What is your socioeconomic background? How do you know?

What was your socioeconomic background growing up?

How has your socioeconomic background influenced your educational opportunities?

In what ways do your race and socioeconomic background shape your worldview, what you do, how you experience the world, and what you teach?

While understanding the self with regard to race, poverty, and socioeconomic status is crucial, working to understand another person's (perhaps a student) race and socioeconomic background and overall ways of experiencing the world is also necessary. Therefore, those in both professional development and teacher education programs need to continuously learn about their students and their families. However, I stress that teacher education needs to continuously shepherd teachers into examining themselves as a foundation to working with others. This reflective process must be ongoing as their situations and their ability to interpret their social positioning regarding race and socioeconomics shift over time.

Acquiring Knowledge About Others

I have found that many teachers enter teacher education courses with no conception of, interest in, or concern about acquiring knowledge about others, especially those who fall outside of their race and socioeconomic background.[21] Many teachers—especially preservice teachers—may have interacted mostly with people from their own grade schools or their neighborhoods, which might not be very diverse in terms of race and socioeconomic status. Thus, teacher education programs that endeavor to provide students with the understanding necessary to teach students of color living in poverty should consider that many of them will have little if any prior knowledge of other people's worldviews and ways of being in the world.[22]

This lack of insight and awareness of others can result in curricula and learning experiences that are overwhelmingly Eurocentric in their content and that omit the multiple contributions of people from other racial or ethnic backgrounds. Indeed, it is critical for teachers to acquire positive knowledge- and asset-based perspectives about their students. Many black students, for instance, are trendsetters (in terms of inventions, science, the arts, and the humanities); they are also giving, kind, smart, athletic, and compassionate. I have found that many black grade-school students often have very strong links to their families. Also, older students may care for their younger siblings or work full-time jobs, giving their earned money to their parents to help with bills.

In her qualitative study of eight recently retired African American teachers, Mitchell reminds us of the insight that teachers can share about students' experiences. The teachers in her study "were critically aware of the experiences of the students, both in and out of school, and of the contexts shaping these experiences."[23] These teachers were able to connect with students because they understood that what was occurring in school was often a direct result of the students' out-of-school experiences. They knew the reasons behind students' choices, which again supports the recommendation that teacher education programs prepare teachers to acquire knowledge about others—especially their students. Teachers should be equipped to research and, as Ladson-Billings puts it, *study their students.*[24] In Mitchell's words, the teachers "recalled situations in which factors outside of the school adversely affected students' behavior. They described students as listless because of hunger and sleepy because they worked at night and on weekends to help support younger siblings. They described students as easily distracted and sometimes belligerent because of unstable living environments."[25]

Obviously, all black students or students living below the poverty line do not experience the same things. Their experiences are as diverse as they are themselves. The point is that teachers need to acquire knowledge that might counter or complement or confirm what they believe about particular groups of people and cultural practices, and work to develop the skills to consistently acquire knowledge throughout their careers. These retired teachers understood the connection between home and school, and how students' feelings and consequently actions were impacted by their home circumstances. Again, teachers had to teach to the middle of the home and school. The teachers understood that many of their students were living in poverty, that some were doing drugs, and some were playing adult roles in their homes by bringing in money to support their families. The teachers used this knowledge to relate to and empathize with their students as well as decide what to focus on through instruction. For instance, as teachers acquire knowledge about their students, they may be less apt to send their students to the office when they misbehave or put their heads on their desks (because of fatigue), or to dismiss them as apathetic for mouthing off (which might really be due to stress at home).

But simultaneously, teachers must have high expectations of their students because curriculum rigor has been identified as one of the strongest in-school predictors of student achievement.[26] Thus, my point in presenting these ideas on the importance of acquiring knowledge about others is not to suggest that teachers should water down the curriculum, but rather, adapt the curriculum to fit the particular circumstances of their students. Responsive and adaptive curriculum practices are not synonymous with low expectations. To the contrary, the type of curriculum practices I am advancing aligns high standards with responsive, agile, and adaptive learning opportunities.

To help teachers acquire knowledge about others, I believe guided sentence stems are helpful. When my colleague, Margaret Smithey, and I developed a course that attempted to cover some of the issues discussed in this book, we thought carefully about the kinds of assignments and the types of experiences needed to support teachers in building knowledge about diversity broadly, and equity in particular.[27] Margaret Smithey had taught for many years and conducted research at both the preK–12 and teacher education level; I had teaching experience and had been conducting research in schools as well. As we constructed the course, we relied on Sleeter's insightful suggestions to design backwards the kinds of experiences teachers needed to be successful in high-poverty environments.[28] So, we drew from what we had learned (effective teaching and learning) in preK–12 classrooms to shape our decisions and course design in teacher education. We found that when we left assignments open ended, allowing our teachers to draw meaning related to diversity without explicit guidance (especially early in the course), they focused on tangential matters—often not focusing much, if at all, on issues of race in particular. But providing explicit guidance through sentence stems directed teachers to focus on matters we found especially germane to their learning and development: acquiring knowledge about others. Because this was not a one-time exploration, we wanted to support teachers in ways that encouraged them to continually study others.

The following examples of sentence stems particularly address the intersecting nature of race and poverty:

1. Insights I have had about my role as a [white, middle-class teacher— or whatever racial/socioeconomic background applies] working with students of color and/or students of color living in poverty are . . .
2. Issues of race/poverty/socioeconomic status that have emerged from the curriculum in my classroom are . . .
3. Issues of race/poverty/socioeconomic status that have emerged from my students' learning needs are . . .
4. I am/am not committed to addressing issues of race and poverty in my classroom because . . .
5. Ways for me to deepen my knowledge about students of color living in poverty are . . .

Of course, for preservice teachers who are not yet in the classroom, the sentence stems can be framed for what they will do or what they think about their practices once they are actually teaching.

Identifying and Confronting Societal Discourse

Issues of race and socioeconomic status are also topics of public discourse, outside of schools. However, again, the historical, structural, and systemic dimensions of race and the deep meanings of race and racism are rarely examined in teacher education programs. Some believe that these societal realities have little to do with teachers and their teaching. However, I am suggesting that it is teachers' beliefs and worldviews about societal occurrences that can help them shape and reassess how they work with students living in poverty and those of color. Consider table 4.1, which describes what certain people expressed—their language—and how the public responded, as well as the financial consequences of their word choice. In this sense, words are political positions and actions that have important meaning and consequence.[29]

The six incidents in the table provide a snapshot of the kinds of racial matters that emerge in society—many, though by no means all, in sport. Race and racism can be ingrained in the words that people use, although that language may seem tangential to hate or racism. People may claim that they have no malice or negative intent in what they say. But words carry deep meaning and intent and they are forms of practice.

Just as race and racism can manifest in society through language and other behaviors, so can they emerge in the classroom. These manifestations may be covert or implicit, but are still prevalent. What I have found is when teachers are provided space to think about these societal occurrences and to position themselves within the story lines, they begin to analyze such occurrences in society (and hopefully in their work with students), and they also develop tools to recognize when and how discourse shapes beliefs. Thus, I recommend that teacher education programs use incidents such as those in table 4.1 to identify and confront societal realities of racism through discourse and thus help teachers recognize language that can have devastating effects on students and also build empathy with those in less powerful positions (such as students and families). Regardless of how teachers position themselves in reaction to the statements above (or similar ones), providing space for teachers to think through these discourses is essential, and can be used as a pedagogical tool in teacher education. Teachers' beliefs and positions regarding the racialized statements and actions taken are important sites of examination for their work.

TABLE 4.1   Public Incidents of Racial Language and Consequences

Incident	Result
April 1987: Al Campanis, LA Dodgers' general manager, told ABC's *Nightline* that African Americans may not have the abilities necessary to be field managers or general managers or the resilience to swim well.	Campanis apologized and resigned soon thereafter.
January 1988: "Jimmy the Greek" Snyder, sports analyst and oddsmaker, said that black people are "bred to be better athletes," dating back to slavery when "the owner would breed his big black man with his big woman so that he would have a big black kid."	Snyder apologized but was fired after 12 years with CBS.
April 1997: After Tiger Woods became the first black person to win the Masters, Fuzzy Zoeller, PGA golf pro, said that Woods is a "little boy" and suggested that he not serve "fried chicken . . . or collard greens" at the Masters dinner.	Zoeller lost Kmart's sponsorship; Woods accepted his apology.
September 2003: Rush Limbaugh, conservative talk show host, said Donovan McNabb gets good press because "the media has been very desirous that a black quarterback do well."	Limbaugh resigned under pressure, saying he regretted causing "discomfort to his ESPN colleagues."
November 2006: Michael Richards, actor and comedian, yelled out racial epithets during his standup comedy act, including calling four black patrons in the audience niggers after they supposedly were disrespectful to Richards during his act.	Richards apologized on David Letterman's *Late Show* on CBS as well as to Jesse Jackson and Al Sharpton.
November 2006: Michael Irvin, ESPN football analyst, talked about the Dallas Cowboys' 21–14 win and suggested that Cowboys' quarterback Tony Romo must have some "brother down in the line somewhere" to play as well as he does.	Irvin apologized but was still fired by ESPN.

Source: Adapted from L. Petrecca and G. Strauss, "Imus Flap a Matter of Black, White, and Green," *USA Today*, April 11, 2007.

Developing Caring Relationships

As discussed in depth in previous chapters, it is also essential for teacher education programs to develop teachers who are caring and empathic in their work with students living in poverty and students of color. Caring relationships are established, according to Weinstein, by teaching strategies that "draw from a wide range of methods; they are challenging and intensive, flexibly applied, [and] responsive to student obstacles encountered in learning."[30] In describing some common characteristics of care among the thirteen teachers in his study, Brown reported,

> These . . . teachers create caring classroom communities by showing a genuine interest in each student. They gain student cooperation by being assertive through the use of explicitly stated expectations for appropriate student behavior and academic growth. And these teachers demonstrate mutual respect for students through the use of congruent communication processes.[31]

Quite often, teachers enter classrooms secretly afraid of their students because they have never known anyone who "looked, talked, or acted like [their students]."[32] It is difficult for teachers to care about individuals they fear. Ennis examined issues of confrontation among ten urban high schools that enrolled approximately 110,000 students from lower- to middle-class families.[33] Her findings revealed possible outcomes when teachers feel unsupported by their administrators; some 50 percent of the teachers in the study reported that they did not teach certain content topics "because of the confrontations that such topics generate with specific students."

I have found that the best way for teachers to build caring, empathetic relationships with students is through their conversations with them. Assignments in teacher education that allow teachers to talk with students about their experiences, likes and dislikes, goals, interests, dreams, and so forth enable teachers to perceive their students as real people and build connections with them. Providing broad frameworks or categories for posing questions to students—for instance, students' family structure, home responsibilities, and successes and challenges in their schoolwork—can all help teachers develop caring dispositions and practices. However, it is also important that teachers maintain a professional distance and not intrude while supporting their underserved students. Indeed, a central task of teacher education is to help teachers understand the important role of care in their practices and to continue building caring dispositions while demonstrating their concern and empathy for students through what they teach, what they expect of their students, and how they teach.

Building Links to Curriculum and Instruction

If these topics are addressed independently without cultivating an understanding of how the above recommendations matter in what and how they teach, teachers may view them as unimportant to their real work. It is important for teacher education programs to help teachers recognize how race, socioeconomic status, and poverty are germane to curriculum and instruction. Of course, the curriculum should reflect the broader society as well as the racial and ethnic background of those in a classroom.[34] What teachers cover, how much time they spend on aspects of the curriculum, whether the curriculum materials are appropriate and accurate representations of the people being portrayed and their experiences from various racial and ethnic backgrounds—all are necessary considerations in developing the curriculum and teaching it.

At the heart of what a teacher chooses to emphasize in the curriculum is teacher identity—who teachers are and how they represent their worldview to others influences what they teach and what students learn. In this way, teachers do have some control over what gets covered in the curriculum, even with the push for Common Core Standards and pacing guides.[35] Race, socioeconomic status, and teachers' experiences in these areas can have an impact on what teachers decide to emphasize in lessons.

Making connections between effective teaching of students living in poverty, issues of race, and Common Core Standards is also an essential task of teacher education. For instance, the following principles and themes are among those in the Common Core Standards movement: (1) Writing, (2) Drawing from Data/Information to Substantiate Points, (3) Scientific Method, (4) Gathering Data/Research/Substantiate Points, (5) Presentations, (6) Listening, (7) Speaking, (8) Constructing/Representing Data (Tables, Charts, Graphs), (9) Information Texts, (10) Critical Thinking, (11) Problem Solving, and (12) Analytical Thinking. Indeed, the curriculum and instructional practices of teachers committed to addressing poverty and racism can be linked to Common Core Standards. Making these connections is essential as teachers will be more apt to develop transformative practices to address the needs of students living in poverty and students of color if they are provided strategies and ideas for linking their practices to these standards.

Studying Racial Demography Trends

Teachers in teacher education, educators in schools, and students in preK–12 schools need to examine how the profile of the U.S. population is shifting and how their perspectives, knowledge, and understanding need to grow to function effectively both inside and outside of the classroom. Consider table 4.2.

An examination of the table data reveals that Hispanic and Latino representation in U.S. society from 2000 to 2010 increased from 12.5 to 16.3 percent. Conversely, the white population decreased from 75.1 to 72.4 percent. Such an increase would suggest that the trend will continue and these data should be investigated at different times to help educators and students better understand the world as they know it as well as the coming demographic changes that will certainly inform the world as they *will* know and experience it. I stress here that not only teachers but also students should use these demographic trends as instructional sites of learning.

ENHANCING THE KNOWLEDGE BASE

The previous three sections of this chapter have focused on macrolevel and microlevel recommendations that I believe are essential in contributing to district-, school-, and classroom-level fights against poverty and racism. In this section, I examine challenges we in teacher education face in building a more robust and sustainable knowledge base in the field of teacher education regarding poverty and racism. Cochran-Smith and Zeichner draw similar critiques about the field of teacher education in general.[36] In teacher education, we face

- *An epistemological issue:* It is difficult to study teacher education with an emphasis on race and poverty because it is not clear what topics the different teacher education programs cover, whether traditional or nontraditional. How do we know what we know regarding teaching students of color and those living in poverty, and what worldviews are privileged over others in our studies in teacher preparation?

TABLE 4.2 U.S. Population by Hispanic or Latino origin and by race, 2000 and 2010

	2000 Number	2000 Percentage of total population	2010 Number	2010 Percentage of total population	Change, 2000 to 2010 Number	Change, 2000 to 2010 Percent
Hispanic or Latino origin						
Total U.S. population	281,421,906	100.0	308,745,538	100.0	27,323,632	9.7
Hispanic or Latino	35,305,818	12.5	50,477,594	16.3	15,171,776	43.0
Not Hispanic or Latino	246,116,088	87.5	258,267,944	83.7	12,151,856	4.9
White alone	194,552,774	69.1	196,817,552	63.7	2,264,778	1.2
Race						
Total U.S. population	281,421,906	100.0	308,745,538	100.0	27,323,632	9.7
One race	274,595,678	97.6	299,736,465	97.1	25,140,787	9.2
White	211,460,626	75.1	223,553,265	72.4	12,092,639	5.7
Black or African American	34,658,190	12.3	38,929,319	12.6	4,271,129	12.3
American Indian and Alaska Native	2,475,956	0.9	2,932,248	0.9	456,292	18.4

Asian	10,242,998	3.6	14,674,252	4.8	4,431,254	43.3
Native American and other Pacific Islander	398,835	0.1	540,013	0.2	141,178	35.4
Some other race	15,359,073	5.5	19,107,368	6.2	3,748,295	24.4
Two or more races[a]	6,826,228	2.4	9,009,073	2.9	2,182,845	32.0

Source: U.S. Census Bureau, *Overview of Race and Hispanic Origin: 2010,* 2010 Census Briefs, Census Publication C2010BR-02, Table 1: Population by Hispanic or Latino Origin and by Race for the United States: 2000 and 2010 (Washington, DC: U.S. Government Printing Office, 2011), http://www.census.gov/prod/cen2010/briefs/c2010br-02.pdf.

[a] In the 2000 U.S. Census, a data processing error resulted in an overstatement of the Two or More Races population by about 1 million people (about 15 percent) nationally, which almost entirely affected race combinations involving Some Other Race. Therefore, data users should assess with caution observed changes in the Two or More Races population and race combinations involving Some Other Race between the 2000 and 2010 census data. Changes in specific race combinations not involving Some Other Race, such as white *and* black or African American or white *and* Asian, generally should be more comparable.

- *A theoretical issue:* It is difficult to build theory about the effects and influences of teacher education regarding students of color and those living in poverty because the literature and knowledge base are somewhat scattered. The theoretical issue is at least threefold: What relevant and useful analytic tools are, could be, and should be employed to explain teacher education practices for/with students living in poverty and students of color? How do we build theoretical knowledge *from the ground up* to conceptualize practices in teacher education for students living in poverty, their families, and students/families of color? And how do we theorize about students living in poverty and those of color in preK–12 sociopolitical contexts for teacher education?

- *A practice issue:* It is unclear how practices such as student teaching and practicum experiences are carried out across different teacher education programs. Moreover, at present, there is no way to gauge the links between what teachers are learning in teacher education and their actual practices (in preK–12 schools) with students—and specifically with students living in poverty or from lower socioeconomic backgrounds and students of color.

- *A racial demographic issue among teacher educators:* The racial demographic of teacher educators is also a concern in thinking about what gets covered in teacher education programs, especially because students of color are too often on the margins of teaching and learning. Some teacher educators are underprepared themselves to prepare teachers to teach for equity.[37] Thus we need to be concerned about the racial demography of teacher educators themselves. We cannot assume that teacher educators are committed, capable, or automatically prepared to educate teachers to meet the complex needs of preK–12 students; nor can we assume that they are committed philosophically, theoretically, practically, or empirically to develop, enact, and study a curriculum that is consistent with the needs of students living in poverty and students of color. The idea here is that having a more racially diverse cadre of teacher educators could potentially better prepare teachers for racially diverse students and those living in poverty.

- *A racial demographic issue among teachers in preK–12 classrooms:* In addition to the demographic challenges in teacher education, teacher education programs are also faced with the arduous task of helping to diversify the preK–12 teaching force. Teacher education programs should think seriously about building pipeline programs that recruit racially diverse teachers into teacher education as professors.

- *A research issue:* Collectively, the epistemological, theoretical, and practice issues discussed above can make it difficult to meaningfully study teacher education with an emphasis on race and poverty. How do we study teacher education in a way that deepens and broadens our knowledge about theory, research, policy, and practice for students of color and those living in poverty? How can we build research agendas that allow us to know more about, theorize with more sophistication, and develop practices that contribute to palatable, sustainable, and productive teacher education programs that truly meet the needs of all students?

- *A discourse/language dissonance issue:* Related to epistemology, it is difficult to build a strong knowledge base because there is no consistent, common vocabulary in teacher education.[38] The varied constructs that different teacher education researchers and programs employ in their studies and program structures make it difficult to draw logical connections between and among them. This could have real implications for what we know (and consequently do) regarding students of color and those living in poverty. Cochran-Smith and Zeichner reported the difficulty in expanding the knowledge base in teacher education because of the inconsistency of language used by researchers.[39] It is difficult to build knowledge about the preparation of teachers for students living in poverty, for instance, because of the variation of discourse used in the field. When I reviewed the literature, I found that researchers used free- and reduced-priced lunch, socioeconomic status, class, and poverty quite interchangeably to represent similar ideas. Many of the studies I reviewed were unclear just what they meant by poverty, and researchers draw from varying data points to denote poverty. For instance, while free and reduced-price lunch were used as proxies for poverty in many studies, this was not the case in others.

CONCLUSION

Although teacher education has its challenges, I still believe that its effectiveness is one of our best chances to ensure that every child receives an education that makes a difference in his or her life. Addressing the challenges in teacher education for students of color and those living in poverty, as outlined above, requires engagement from a range of stakeholders and professionals. Confronting these challenges requires that those from different communities, preK–12 teachers, policy makers, and researchers all have input into what gets addressed and how in the preparation of teachers. With so much criticism of teacher education, teacher educators should be leaders in discussing what teacher education is and its potential influence across the United States and beyond. As Freire explains, it matters who has a seat at the table for discussions regarding those who are consistently underserved in and beyond education, especially when conversations have the potential to address oppression, power, privilege, and the marginalization of so many students who are poorly educated in public schools across the country. The interests of those who participate in the discourse are important to consider.[40] As discussed earlier, people's worldviews have a direct influence on their personal, political, and professional agendas and identities. In addressing the challenges we face in teacher education, we need to hear from multiple voices both through the empirical, theoretical, and practice literature and beyond it. Those involved in the conversation decide what gets discussed in meaningful ways, how much time is spent on particular issues, and what courses of action will be taken to address perspectives and especially problems that are shared. Indeed, as teacher educators, we must develop the collective wisdom to ensure that every teacher is well prepared to meet the needs of every student—for the benefit of us all. Teacher education programs have the potential to:

- Help teachers shift their belief systems from viewing students living in poverty as problems to those capable of academic and social success.
- Help teachers understand how to interpret their subject matter in ways that allow them to teach the material in rigorous and developmentally appropriate ways to particular groups of students.
- Help teachers develop the tools necessary to work collaboratively with their colleagues to build the kinds of learning environments that can ensure students reach their full capacity to learn because there is collective effort to do so.
- Help teachers after their preservice education in ways that allow them to continue to develop professionally for the benefit of their students but also to systematically study the influence of teacher education programs in order to improve.

The time is now. The issues are pervasive. The need for teacher education to centralize issues of race and poverty in the preparation of teachers is urgent!

CHAPTER 5

Conclusion

Anyone who has ever struggled with poverty knows how extremely expensive it is to be poor.

—James A. Baldwin

Education in this country is about how to maintain the status quo and to perpetuate racism.

—Jane Elliott

Once you know better, you should do better!

—Maya Angelou

T HROUGHOUT THIS BOOK, I have argued for a renewed sense of urgency in the fight against poverty and racism in education and our schools. Focusing on poverty and race and their intersected nature has promise rather than concentrating exclusively on outcomes—especially test scores—that are separated from the material realities of those living in poverty and the ways racism prevents us from addressing the causes of underachievement. I use the noun *fight* to express a level of aggression that I believe is necessary to overcome the challenges we face. In this sense, I stress that fight be conceptualized as a verb to actually, consciously do something we have not been able to do. I have suggested throughout that our fight should not be with students or their parents. So often, educators are quick to pass the blame for students' lack of success to their parents (or virtually anything outside the school walls). Parents and family structure are often essential aspects of student success. However, addressing the influence and effects of poverty and racism will likely prove much more useful than playing a blame game with parents or students. This revitalized fight—on poverty and racism—is about how structural inequality and inequity prevent too many of our students from reaching their full capacity to succeed, socially as well as academically.

To address the intersected nature of poverty and race, I have outlined several specific ways that schools, districts, and even states committed to addressing real problems of poverty can be successful. In chapters 1 and 2, I provide macro- and microlevel recommendations for specific reforms to help educators build synergy in the fight against poverty and various forms of racism. Conceptualized from some of the best research on practice in the field as well as my own research, these reforms include understanding and practicing equitable decision making, understanding and responding to neighborhood conditions, reducing class size, and rethinking and reforming inflexible and narrowed curricula. On a classroom level, I consider the following as essential in the fight against poverty and racism: infusing language arts across the curriculum, building and sustaining meaningful relationships, developing teachers' knowledge and skills beyond academic content, and teaching and cultivating student social and study skills.

The focus of the book then shifts to specific cases that I have constructed from the research literature, conversations I have had with colleagues and preK–12 teachers, and my own research. The purpose of these case studies is to provide contextually rich, nuanced accounts of classroom and school-related situations that teachers and other educators could encounter in their own classrooms. My goal is not to offer a static, scripted panacea to the problems presented. Rather, the purpose is to provide vignettes that allow teachers and other educators to draw from insights shared in previous chapters as well as their own professional repertoire. The stories range from preschool through high school and address issues of race, poverty, and their interrelated nature. For instance, how might a middle school teacher address a group of students who will not (whether or not they are capable financially) purchase additional science materials for a project, but have bought expensive tennis shoes and technology (iPads, and iPhones)? Moreover, what challenges and potential solutions are embedded in a committed building principal who wants to address poverty and racism in her school but is not supported by her superintendent and other district officials?

I then shift the emphasis to teacher education because I believe in the power of teacher education programs to help teachers meet the needs of students living in poverty. In chapter 4, I focus on achievable steps teacher educators can take to develop and reform their programs with heightened attention to issues of race and poverty and their connections. In my original drafts, the macrolevel reforms I outlined for teacher education programs were much more complex and would have required additional funding mechanisms and even perhaps reorganization of university fiscal planning. I decided to revise that section because I realize teacher education programs are somewhat limited given broader institutional financial bureaucracies that are far beyond the control and scope of most in teacher education. Thus, I focused instead on macrolevel shifts that teacher educators could address, such as developing an overt and comprehensive vision statement and a related mission (action) focused on fighting poverty and racism.

In chapter 4 I also provide some insights about what is necessary to prepare teachers to teach all students effectively. For example, much is available in the research literature regarding practice on what teacher education courses can do to support teachers in this effort. In addition to reforming the teacher education curriculum with increased emphases on poverty and race, I also stress the importance of the following: understanding the self in learning to teach; acquiring knowledge about others; identifying and addressing societal discourse; developing caring relationships; and helping teachers see links to curriculum and instruction especially linked to standards. The chapter ends with analyses and critiques of the field of teacher education in terms of building and enhancing our knowledge base (what we know) and epistemology (how we know what we know). I provide some recommendations regarding the knowledge base in preparing teachers to effectively teach students living in poverty and those of color.

"THE POWER OF ONE—EVERY STUDENT MATTERS"

In the introduction, I wrote about the joy that many prekindergarten and kindergarten children exhibit on their first day(s) of school. They tend to want to attend school and are ready for the new adventures of their educational journey. As preschool-aged children, they have watched older students walk to school and stand on sidewalks waiting for buses. They have interacted with their older siblings and developed an intuitive sense of what school is and will be. However, over time, many students begin to disengage, feel disconnected, and essentially hate being in school. A short conversation with many students would reveal that they attend school because they do not have a choice.

Parents and students alike surely must take some responsibility in students' disengagement and school disconnect. However, educators and others who make decisions about education should examine critically why some children—too often those living below the poverty line and those of color—come to hate school.

When I taught high school English, one day I experienced a situation that I can only now understand more deeply and draw insights from that can shed light on how the educational system too often fails to meet the needs of students. Jeffrey, one of my ninth-grade students, was always difficult to teach. He was highly intelligent, but it seemed that his daily goal was to disrupt the learning in the classroom. He was African American and lived below the poverty line. He and I did not have a great relationship, a reality that was mostly my fault because I was the adult without the necessary tools to help and connect with him. He constantly teased his classmates, would arrive to class late, consistently wanted to be excused to go to the restroom, and was aggravating overall because he wanted to focus on what I perceived as nonsense while I was charged with teaching English I. Jeffrey had failed ninth grade twice, and my class was the third time he would have to read *Romeo and Juliet* and develop the five-paragraph essay. It's important to note that students had to pass English to be promoted to the next grade in high school.

One day, Jeffrey entered the classroom in his usual manner. He decided on this day that he would not complete his "quiz" that had been scheduled for several weeks. I insisted: work on your quiz, or I will have to send you out. He shared with me clearly and precisely: "I'm going to sit here and not bother anybody, but I am *not* going to do the quiz." I took it personally as his classmates looked on to see what I would do. I persisted: "Jeff, if you don't get started, I'm going to . . . " And then it happened—he jumped up, pushed over his desk, and exclaimed: *"Fuck this and fuck you!"* I was shocked! We had experienced some challenges over the months, but we had never had such an exchange. I was appalled, offended, and admittedly a little embarrassed. In many ways, I knew there was something peculiar about this exchange and Jeffrey's reaction. But I also realize now, after reflecting over the years, that I was thinking not only about Jeffrey but also my own ego. Who did he think he was? How could he use such language with his teacher? Had I not been supportive enough of him? Did I not consistently give him chance after chance to succeed? Had I not been working hard to build a relationship with Jeffrey, even though he refused to meet me halfway? Moreover, how could he use such language with me and in such a tone in front of his classmates? How was I going to bounce back from this situation and regain my respect from the other students in the class if something drastic did not happen? Would Jeffrey's reaction begin to manifest with other students in the class?

Clearly, as I reflect now on this episode, I realize that my challenges and concerns were mostly about me—my ego—than Jeff's real-life struggles. I realize now that Jeff was probably much like many of the students I observed when he was in preschool and kindergarten. He was probably a student who was curious about what school would offer him. He probably wanted an experience that would propel him to develop knowledge and skills that would be fulfilling and that would complement his gifts, interests, and intellect. However, over time, despite his being highly capable and intelligent, school and educational systems failed him, and consequently he failed himself as he grew older.

Unlike many students in his situation (having failed English I more than once), Jeffrey continued to come to school each day. If Jeff really meant "fuck this" he probably would not have continued to show up. Besides, although he was in ninth grade, he was old enough to quit school if he wanted to, as the educational structure and responses would surely have been fuel enough for him to drop out. He kept showing up, though, for a reason. As a novice, first-year teacher, I thought he was coming to school to bother people (and make my life miserable). I had implicitly decided that he wanted to ruin the educational experience of everybody in the class. But as I reflect on the situation now, I think he kept coming because he wanted to be there and desired support. He was showing up so that I (and his other teachers) would have to respond to the fact that Jeffrey was experiencing situations that far exceeded his ability or willingness to complete a quiz. And so I failed him on that day, and I pushed him out of the classroom. He left the mobile classroom, slamming the door. I wrote out an extensive referral for him but never turned it in. Two days later, Jeffrey showed up again and declared: "I'm ready to take the quiz now." I found an unmarked exam, gave it to him, taught my lesson, and Jeffrey passed it. But most important, he passed the class, English I. Unfortunately, though, he did not stay in school. I wonder what role I played, albeit unintentional, in his decision to leave. Although I have many success stories from my days in the classroom, I sometimes find myself wondering what life is like for Jeffrey, sixteen years later. Although his story is one embedded in a sea of successful experiences I had with students as a teacher, his story matters. Every child matters!

TOWARD COLLECTIVE INTERESTS, INSIGHTS, AND CAPACITY

Put simply, I believe the next steps to revitalizing a war against poverty and racism in schools are for different constituencies to adopt some of the reforms and suggestions outlined throughout this book. It is also important for those involved to document and study aspects of the recommendations. This should be done in a descriptive manner, where researchers and practitioners describe the nature of the implementation and its success and/or failure. In addition, investigations need to incorporate varying aspects of the recommendation to the exclusion of others. In what ways do some of the recommendations and reforms succeed in comparison to or absence of others?

Moreover, I believe it is also essential for educators at different levels (state, district, and school) to converse about transforming an entire district. There are outstanding teachers in nearly every school and district throughout the country. The problem is, these teachers go inside their classrooms, close their doors, and teach—with no chance for other teachers/educators to learn from and with them. District-level reforms with common commitments to combat poverty and racism can allow teachers to build *collective capacity* and develop practices that have lasting benefits as students experience teachers with similar mind-sets, visions, missions, and expectations from the early grades throughout high school. That is, what if an entire district—funneled through individual schools—were committed to improving the educational experiences of children living in poverty?

In 2008, the Children's Defense Fund published a report entitled *Cradle to Prison Pipeline*. The report identified race and poverty as the most salient underlying factors contributing to the prison pipeline. Other contributing factors include:

- Inadequate access to health coverage
- Gaps in early childhood development
- Disparate educational opportunities

- Intolerable abuse and neglect
- Unmet mental and emotional problems
- Rampant substance abuse
- An overburdened, ineffective juvenile justice system

These problems were identified as overwhelmingly prevalent in black and brown communities. To address these challenges and particularly to disrupt the cradle-to-prison pipeline, the Children's Defense Fund wrote the following recommendations:

- End poverty through investments in high quality education for every child, livable wages for families, income supplements like the Earned Income and Child Tax Credits, job training and job creation, and work supports like child care and health coverage.
- Ensure every child and pregnant woman has access to affordable, seamless, comprehensive health and mental health coverage and services.
- Make early childhood development programs accessible to every child by ensuring such programs are affordable, available and of high quality.
- Help each child reach his/her full potential and succeed in work and life, by ensuring our schools have adequate resources to provide high quality education to every child.
- Expand prevention and specialized treatment services for children and their parents, connect children to caring permanent families, improve the quality of the child welfare workforce and increase accountability for results for children.
- Reduce detention and incarceration by increasing investment in prevention and early intervention strategies, such as access to quality early childhood development and education services and to the health and mental health care children need for healthy development.[1]

Although these recommendations were written several years ago, they are still relevant today. Indeed, interdisciplinary perspectives that focus on a range of issues from early childhood development to health care to workforce development are essential in building collective capacity to meet the needs of students living in poverty. In addition to these recommendations, I would add the following, which are discussed in the preceding chapters:

- Develop comprehensive training and support for substitute teachers because in many schools with high numbers of students living below the poverty level and students of color, substitute teachers frequently are called to fill in for teachers who are absent.
- Build aggressive, robust professional development avenues for entire schools that help teachers and other staff build knowledge and skills regarding poverty and race. These professional development sessions should be offered to all personnel, including janitors, cafeteria workers, parental organizers, and so forth.
- Support teachers in building their own mental and physical health by providing wellness programs and health incentives that promote psychological, emotional, and physical wholeness and well-being.
- Increase the number of qualified adults in every classroom. (Although people tend to question the fiscal logistics of this recommendation, my response is that we could afford to have more adults in schools if we decreased the amount of money we commit to building and operating prisons.)
- Significantly increase financial compensation for all early childhood educational providers.
- Increase early childhood and elementary teachers' capacity to help young children develop knowledge and insight about issues of race and poverty.

DEVELOPING STUDENT KNOWLEDGE AND SOCIAL ACTION

Although as adults we often believe children are not aware of how poverty affects them or how racism is manifest in their lives or those of others, children are much more astute about these issues than we might give them credit. One day, I promised my daughters to take them to the pool in our racially diverse neighborhood. As we changed into our swimsuits, they asked me to take their hair down from their braided ponytails so that they could, in their words, wear their hair "like [their] friends at school." In essence, they were asking to wear their hair like their white friends did. To be clear, my wife and I read bedtime stories to our daughters about the beauty of their hair and skin, encouraging them to love it and themselves, and we regularly comment to them on how beautiful and especially smart they are. But on this day, they wanted hair like their white friends'.

Moreover, one evening as I read a bedtime story to my daughters, one of them whispered that one of their white classmates had told them they are "black" and that it was "a secret." At the time, the children were three years old. Again, although many believe race is irrelevant and inconsequential among young children, the evidence simply negates these assertions. For instance, the pivotal work of Kenneth and Mamie Clark in the 1940s, which showcased a "white bias" among the children in their study of young children's doll selection, demonstrates that young children do think about race even when adults do not have explicit conversations with them about it.[2] In the famous study, black children frequently selected white rather than black dolls to play with and attributed more-positive traits to the white dolls.

More recently, CNN asked Margaret Beale Spencer of the University of Chicago to conduct an updated version of the Clark doll-test studies with black and white children. She and her research team found white bias among the 133 children (of both races) in the study.[3] Put simply, what this data reveal is that some black children internalize whiteness as being more intelligent, smart, and/or friendly. Moreover, this research also shows that race matters, even for young children across ethnicities, because white bias can develop at an early age. However, racial-identity development is rarely on the curricular agendas in preschools, for either adults or children.

In an effort to build collective expertise and capacity to seriously do something to redress poverty and racism, students themselves must also be included. Collective work and engagement that makes a difference involves and invokes the lives, experiences, and contributions of students, too. Thus I conclude this book by emphasizing that we develop district and school communities that provide learning opportunities for students about the nature of poverty and racism in age-appropriate ways, beginning at an early age.

In previous chapters, I stressed the importance of adults learning about poverty and race in order to transform their work. I purposely conclude this book with the recommendation that students themselves have opportunities to learn about poverty and racism to build their capacity to consciously do something to fight them. The idea is that as students in preK–12 environments build knowledge about poverty, race, and racism, they may be more apt to take action against them, not only in their own lives but also beyond as they work to transform their communities. Hopefully, this recommendation will ensure that we are raising conscientious individuals willing to fight against hegemony and other forms of discrimination wherever they might encounter them. It is essential to remember that neutrality among each of us is actually a form of action—that is, when one takes a neutral stance, he or she is actually supporting racism and other forms of discrimination. Thus, neutrality is not an option in the fight to end racism and the effects of poverty.

Similar to questions about when it is most developmentally appropriate for students to discuss and learn about race in the curriculum are questions about the appropriateness of discussions related to poverty and socioeconomic status.[4] Although districts and teachers may opt not to have discussions or develop curriculum materials and instructional practices about poverty, students do think about these issues, even at an early age.[5] While their communication may not be as forthcoming, sophisticated, or nuanced as that of older students, young children know that differences exist between people. Students recognize disparities in resources and materials available to them in comparison to others.[6] So, should we ignore this knowledge just because adults feel uncomfortable and underprepared to address it? According to Haberman (who spent his career investigating underserved students in urban schools), students should indeed be engaged in questions like, Why are some people poor while others are rich? What is poverty and how do people get out of it?[7] Indeed, starting the journey of collective work with young children is our best chance that these students will grow up to make society a more just place to live.

Learning about poverty and racism is only part of what is essential for collective interests and capacity to improve the world. A related step necessary to support student development is for districts and schools to cultivate experiences that compel students to action—to do something about the "isms" and challenges they face, with race and poverty at the core. Students should learn how to understand, interpret, and read the world and the word (the various texts they encounter), and work to mobilize themselves and others out of poverty and against racism.[8] To be clear, the word, in Freire's discussion, is more than reading textbooks in school. The world is also a text that should be read just as individual students are texts to be read and interpreted. In addition, students should be empowered to recognize and speak out against structures that perpetuate poverty and racism when they and others in their community experience them. Districts and schools need to construct the learning environment in a way that showcases and honors what students know about poverty and race.

Building a context where the entire district is committed to helping teachers and students develop skills to recognize how situations they witness and experience have impacts far beyond themselves as individuals is an essential aspect of building community-focused citizens committed to transforming the world. Again, students move from a self-motivated perspective, where they are concerned only about themselves, to a more collective one where they realize that when other people live in poverty or experience racism, we all are at a disadvantage.

A FINAL WORD FORWARD

How does one end a book on poverty and race that makes an explicit call to educators to rally together to fight poverty and racism in our schools? This is a difficult book to conclude because I realize how essential these issues and reforms are for the benefit of preK–12 students. However, I want to stress that while I encourage teachers to center on race and poverty as they think about their curriculum development and instructional practices, I also caution them to do so with integrity, attention, and concern for the populations with whom they work. Stereotyping and positioning populations of color in deficit, "at risk," and inferior ways can misrepresent the nuances and complexities that manifest in diverse populations of students. There is no one monolithic story that captures the essence of people of color or those living in poverty. However, we must carefully confront the intersection of race and poverty, not ignore it, if we want to have a better chance of ensuring that all students succeed and that society consequently improves for all.[9] Until we pose the tough questions and engage in the analytic and critical work to solve the "race and poverty problem" in U.S. schools, we will likely continue to see disparities.

Finally, human suffering because of poverty should be unacceptable and, frankly, embarrassing in a country that is as resource wealthy as the United States. No child should have to suffer from the lack of resources necessary to function successfully in and out of school. Shame on us for allowing poverty to continue! My final question to readers of this book is: What are we committed and prepared to do to end poverty and racism for our students, all of whom deserve an equitable education?

Notes

FOREWORD

1. "Executive Paywatch: High-Paid CEOs and the Low-Wage Economy," AFL-CIO, http://www.aflcio.org/Corporate-Watch/Paywatch-2014.
2. Kimberlé W. Crenshaw, *Demarginalizing the Intersection of Race and Sex: A Black Feminist Critique of Antidiscrimination Doctrine, Feminist Theory and Antiracist Politics* (Chicago: University of Chicago Legal Forum, 1989), 139–167.
3. H. L. Shaefer and K. Edin, *Extreme Poverty in the United States, 1996 to 2011*, National Poverty Center, Policy Brief 28, February 2012, http://npc.umich.edu/publications/policy_briefs/brief28/.
4. Children's Defense Fund, *The State of America's Children 2014 Report*, 2014, http://www.childrensdefense.org/child-research-data-publications/state-of-americas-children/.

INTRODUCTION

1. M. J. Shujaa, ed. *Too Much Schooling, Too Little Education: A Paradox of Black Life in White Societies* (Trenton, NJ: African World Press, 1994).
2. J. S. Coleman, *Equality and Achievement in Education* (Boulder, CO: Westview Press, 1969); J. S. Coleman, "Social Capital in the Creation of Human Capital," *American Journal of Sociology* 94 (1988): 95–120.
3. S. J. Caldas and C. Bankston III, "Effect of School Population Socioeconomic Status on Individual Academic Achievement," *Journal of Educational Research* 90, no. 5 (1997): 269.
4. L. Darling-Hammond, foreword to *Handbook of Urban Education*, eds. H. R. Milner and K. Lomotey (New York: Routledge, 2014).
5. W. E. B. DuBois, *The Souls of Black Folk* (New York: Fawcett, 1903); C. G. Woodson, *The Mis-Education of the Negro* (Washington, DC: Associated Publishers, 1933).
6. N. J. Nakkula and E. Toshalis, *Understanding Youth: Adolescent Development for Educators* (Cambridge, MA: Harvard Education Press, 2006), 123.

7. G. Ladson-Billings, "From the Achievement Gap to the Education Debt: Understanding Achievement in U.S. Schools," *Educational Researcher* 35, no. 7 (2006): 3–12.

8. A. M. Pritchard, "A Common Format for Poverty: A Content Analysis of Social Problems Textbooks," *Teaching Sociology* 21, no. 1 (1993): 42–49.

9. T. Coldarci, "Do Smaller Schools Really Reduce the 'Power Rating' of Poverty?" *Rural Educator* 28, no. 1 (2006): 1–8.

10. R. D. Goddard, S. J. Salloum, and D. Berebitsky, "Trust as a Mediator of the Relationships Between Poverty, Racial Composition, and Academic Achievement: Evidence from Michigan's Public Elementary Schools," *Educational Administration Quarterly* 45, no. 2 (2009): 292–311.

11. V. Battistich, D. Solomon, K. Dong-il, M. Watson, and E. Schaps, "Schools as Communities, Poverty Levels of Student Populations, and Students' Attitudes, Motives, and Performance: A Multi-level Analysis," *American Educational Research Journal* 32, no. 3 (1995): 627–658.

12. M. S. Page, "Technology-Enriched Classrooms: Effects on Students of Low Socioeconomic Status," *Journal of Research on Technology in Education* 34, no. 4 (2002): 389–409.

13. M. J. Kieffer, "Catching Up or Falling Behind? Initial English Proficiency, Concentrated Poverty, and the Reading Growth of Minority Learners in the United States," *Journal of Education Psychology* 100, no. 4 (2008): 851.

14. R. K. Toutkoushian and T. Curtis, "Effects of Socioeconomic Factors on Public High School Outcomes and Rankings," *Journal of Educational Research* 98, no. 5 (2005): 259–271, 320.

15. R. B. Howse, G. Lange, D. C. Farran, and C. D. Boyles, "Motivation and Self-regulation as Predictors of Achievement in Economically Disadvantaged Young Children," *Journal of Experimental Education* 71, no. 2 (2003): 151.

16. K. Klopfenstein, "Beyond Test Scores: The Impact of Black Teacher Role Models on Rigorous Math Taking," *Contemporary Economic Policy* 23, no. 3 (2005): 416–428.

17. I am grateful to Dean Larry Davis and the Center for Race and Social Problems at the University of Pittsburgh for helping to elucidate this important point.

18. J. M. Henslin, *Essentials of Sociology: A Down-to-Earth Approach*, 5th. ed. (Boston: Pearson, 2004); J. Kozol, *Savage Inequalities: Children in America's Schools* (New York: Crown Publishers, 1991).

19. U.S. Census Bureau, 2005; V. Burney and J. Beilke, "The Constraints of Poverty on High Achievement," *Journal for the Education of the Gifted* 31, no. 3 (2008): 295–321, 385.

20. Philanthropy News Digest, "U.S. Poverty Rate Fell to 14.5 Percent in 2013, Report Finds," September 17, 2014, http://philanthropynewsdigest.org /news/u.s.-poverty-rate-fell-to14.5-percent-in-2013-report-finds.

21. U.S. Census Bureau, "How the Census Bureau Measures Poverty," http://www.census.gov/hhes/www/poverty/about/overview/measure.html.
22. E. O. McGee and M. B. Spencer, "Theoretical Analysis of Resilience and Identity: An African American Engineer's Life Story," in *Thinking Comprehensively About Education: Spaces of Educative Possibility and Their Implications for Public Policy*, eds. E. Dixon-Román` and E. W. Gordon (New York: Routledge, 2012), 161–178; R. Payne, *A Framework for Understanding Poverty* (Highlands, TX: Aha! Process, 1996).
23. M. Haberman, "Urban Schools: Day Camps or Custodial Centers?" *Phi Delta Kappan* 82, no. 3 (2000): 203–208.
24. K. Burch, "A Tale of Two Citizens: Asking the Rodriguez Question in the Twenty First Century," *Education Studies* 32, no. 3 (2001): 264.
25. J. Anyon, "Social Class and the Hidden Curriculum of Work," *Journal of Education* 162, no. 1 (1980): 366–391; J. Anyon, *Ghetto Schooling: A Political Economy of Urban Educational Reform* (New York: Teachers College Press, 1997); Kozol, *Savage Inequalities*; Haberman, "Urban Schools."
26. J. Anyon, "Social Class and the Hidden Curriculum of Work"; R. Rothstein, *Class and Schools: Using Social, Economic, and Educational Reform to Close the Black-White Achievement Gap* (Washington, DC: Economic Policy Institute, 2004).
27. L. Weis and N. Dolby, *Social Class and Education: Global Perspectives* (New York: Routledge, 2012).
28. Henslin, *Essentials of Sociology.*
29. D. Y. Ford, *Recruiting and Retaining Culturally Different Students in Gifted Education* (Waco, TX: Prufrock Press, 2013).
30. Henslin, *Essentials of Sociology.*
31. Anyon, "Social Class and the Hidden Curriculum of Work."
32. A. Munin, *Color by Number: Understanding Racism Through Facts and Stats on Children* (Sterling, VA: Stylus, 2012); C. DeNavas-Walt, B. D. Proctor, and J. C. Smith, U. S. Census Bureau, Population Reports, P60-236, *Income, Poverty, and Health Insurance Coverage in the United States: 2008* (Washington DC: U.S. Government Printing Office, 2009), http://www.census.gov/prod/2009pubs/p60-236.pdf.
33. Munin, *Color by Number.*
34. Ibid.
35. D. T. Slaughter-Defoe and K. G. Carlson, "Young African American and Latino Children in High-Poverty Urban Schools: How They Perceive School Climate," *Journal of Negro Education* 65, no. 1 (1996): 60–70.
36. G. Ladson-Billings and B. Tate, "Toward a Critical Race Theory of Education," *Teachers College Record* 97, no. 1 (1995): 47–67.
37. C. E. Cooper, R. Crosnoe, M. A. Suizzo, and K. Pituch, "Poverty, Race, and Parental Involvement During the Transition to Elementary School," *Journal of Family Issues* 31, no. 7 (2009): 859–883.

38. A. J. Artiles, J. K. Klingner, and W. F. Tate, "Representation of Minority Students in Special Education: Complicating Traditional Explanations," *Educational Researcher* 35, no. 6 (2006): 3–5; W. J. Blanchett, "African American and Other Students of Color in Special Education," in *Handbook of Urban Education*, eds. H. R. Milner and K. Lomotey (New York: Routledge, 2014), 271–283; P. A. Noguera, "Schools, Prisons, and Social Implications of Punishment: Rethinking Disciplinary Practices," *Theory into Practice* 42, no. 4 (2003): 341–350; C. O'Connor and S. D. Fernandez, "Race, Class, and Disproportionality: Reevaluating the Relationship, Poverty and Special Education Placement," *Educational Researcher* 35, no. 6 (2006): 6–11.

39. J. E. Davis, W. J. Jordan, "The Effects of School Context, Structure, and Experiences on African American Males in Middle and High School," *Journal of Negro Education* 63, no. 4 (1994): 570–587; R. J. Skiba, R. S. Michael, A. C. Nardo, and R. L. Peterson, "The Color of Discipline: Sources of Racial and Gender Disproportionality in School Punishment," *Urban Review* 34, no. 4 (2002): 317–342.

40. Milner, *Start Where You Are, but Don't Stay There.*

41. A. C. Lin and D. Harris, "The Colors of Poverty: Why Racial and Ethnic Disparities Persist," National Poverty Center Policy Brief 16, January 2009.

42. A. Lareau, *Unequal Childhoods: Race, Class, and Family Life* (Berkeley, CA: University of California Press, 2003).

43. G. Ladson-Billings, "Fighting for Our Lives: Preparing Teachers to Teach African American Students," *Journal of Teacher Education* 51, no. 3 (2000): 206–214.

44. Haberman, "Urban Schools."

CHAPTER 1

1. H. R. Milner, *Start Where You Are, but Don't Stay There* (Cambridge, MA: Harvard Education Press, 2010).

2. D. A. Bell, "*Brown v. Board of Education* and the Interest-Convergence Dilemma," *Harvard Law Review* 93, no. 3 (1980): 518–533; D. A. Bell, "Serving Two Masters: Integration Ideals and Client Interests in School Desegregation Litigation," *Yale Law Journal* 85, no. 4 (1976): 470–516; W. F. Tate, G. Ladson-Billings, and C. A. Grant, "The *Brown* Decision Revisited: Mathematizing Social Problems," *Educational Policy* 7 (1993): 255–275.

3. W. G. Secada, "Agenda Setting, Enlightened Self-interest, and Equity in Mathematics Education," *Peabody Journal of Education* 66, no. 2 (1989): 23.

4. M. Roza, *How Districts Shortchange Low-Income and Minority Students* (Washington, DC: The Education Trust, 2006), 11.

5. R. Wiener and E. Pristoop, *How States Shortchange the Districts That Need the Most Help* (Washington, DC: The Education Trust, 2006), 9.

6. Roza, *How Districts Shortchange Low-Income and Minority Students*, 12.

7. G. Liu, *How the Federal Government Makes Rich States Richer* (Washington, DC: The Education Trust, 2006), 2.

8. J. Kozol, *Savage Inequalities: Children in America's Schools* (New York: Crown Publishers, 1991).

9. Roza, *How Districts Shortchange Low-Income and Minority Students*, 9.

10. Liu, *How the Federal Government Makes Rich States Richer*.

11. Roza, *How Districts Shortchange Low-Income and Minority Students*, 11.

12. J. E. Ryan, "Schools, Race, and Money," *Yale Law Journal*, 109, no. 2 (1999): 315.

13. G. W. Bracey, "Money Matters: No It Doesn't, Yes It Does," *Phi Delta Kappan* 79, no. 2 (1997): 162–164; P. A. Noguera and L. Wells, "The Politics of School Reform: A Broader and Bolder Approach for Newark," *Berkeley Review of Education* 2, no. 1 (2011): 5–25; R. C. Nyhan and M. G. Alkadry, "The Impact of School Resources on Student Achievement Test Scores," *Journal of Education Finance* 25 (Fall 1999): 211–227.

14. Noguera and Wells, "The Politics of School Reform."

15. T. Walker, "The Opportunity Gap in Education Is Growing," *NEA Today*, April 19, 2012, http://neatoday.org/2012/04/19/report-the-opportunity-gap-in-education-is-growing/.

16. J. Anyon, *Radical Possibilities: Public Policy, Urban Education, and a New Social Movement* (New York: Routledge, 2005); M. Haberman, "The Pedagogy of Poverty Versus Good Teaching," *Phi Delta Kappan* 73, no. 4 (1991): 290–294; Kozol, *Savage Inequalities*; J. Kozol, *The Shame of a Nation: The Return of Apartheid Schooling in America* (New York: Crown Publishing, 2005); J. MacLeod, *Social Reproduction in Theoretical Perspective. Ain't No Makin It: Aspirations and Attainment in a Low-Income Neighborhood* (San Francisco: Westview Press, 1995); Milner, *Start Where You Are, but Don't Stay There.*

17. W. F. Tate, "'Geography of Opportunity': Poverty, Place, and Educational Outcomes," *Educational Researcher* 37, no. 7 (2008): 397–411.

18. A. Munin, *Color by Number: Understanding Racism Through Facts and Stats on Children* (Sterling, VA: Stylus, 2012), 29.

19. Kozol, *Savage Inequalities*; H. R. Milner, "Policy Reforms and De-professionalization of Teaching," February 28, 2013, National Education Policy Center, http://nepc.colorado.edu/publication/policy-reforms-deprofessionalization; R. Suskind, *A Hope in the Unseen: An American Odyssey from the Inner City to the Ivy League* (New York: Broadway, 1998); Cass, "Held Captive."

20. R. M. Nooe and D. A. Patterson, "The Ecology of Homelessness," *Journal of Human Behavior in the Social Environment* 20, no. 2 (2010): 105–152.

21. S. Finley and M. Diversi, "Critical Homelessness: Expanding Narratives of Inclusive Democracy," *Cultural Studies, Critical Methodologies* 10, no. 1 (2010): 4–13.

22. B. A. Lee, K. A. Tyler, and J. D. Wright, "The New Homelessness Revisited," *Annual Review of Sociology* 36 (2010): 505.

23. B. Duffield, "The Educational Rights of Homeless Children," *Educational Studies* 32, no. 3 (2001): 324.

24. Ibid., 325.

25. Nooe and Patterson, "The Ecology of Homelessness," 105.

26. Finley and Diversi, "Critical Homelessness," 7.

27. L. Mawhinney-Rhoads and G. Stahler, "Educational Policy and Reform for Homeless Students: An Overview," *Education and Urban Society* 38 (2006): 289.

28. Ibid., 292.

29. Ibid., 290.

30. *2011 Annual Homeless Assessment Report to Congress*, November 2012, U.S. Department of Housing and Urban Development, Office of Community Planning and Development, https://www.onecpd.info/resources /documents/2011AHAR_FinalReport.pdf.

31. Anyon, *Radical Possibilities*; C. M. Payne, *So Much Reform, So Little Change: The Persistence of Failure in Urban Schools* (Cambridge: Harvard Education Press, 2008).

32. L. Delpit, *Other People's Children: Cultural Conflict in the Classroom* (New York: New Press, 1995); L. Delpit, *Multiplication Is for White People: Raising Expectations for Other People's Children* (New York: New Press, 2012); G. Gay, *Culturally Responsive Teaching: Theory, Research, and Practice*, 2nd ed. (New York: Teachers College Press, 2010); T. C. Howard, *Why Race and Culture Matter: Closing the Achievement Gap in American Classrooms* (New York: Teachers College Press, 2010); G. Ladson-Billings, *The Dreamkeepers: Successful Teachers of African American Children*, 2nd ed. (San Francisco: Jossey-Bass, 2009); Milner, *Start Where You Are, but Don't Stay There.*

33. Delpit, *Multiplication Is for White People.*

34. Ladson-Billings, *The Dreamkeepers.*

35. S. Konstantopoulous, "Effects of Teachers on Minority and Disadvantaged Students' Achievement in the Early Grades," *Elementary School Journal* 110, no. 1 (2009): 108.

36. R. Reichardt, "Reducing Class Size: Choices and Consequences," policy brief, Mid-continent Research for Education and Learning, Aurora, CO, 2001; Nyhan and Alkadry, "The Impact of School Resources on Student Achievement Test Scores."

37. Haberman, "The Pedagogy of Poverty Versus Good Teaching."

38. Gay, *Culturally Responsive Teaching*; T. C. Howard, *Why Race and Culture Matter: Closing the Achievement Gap in American Classrooms* (New York: Teachers College Press, 2010); Ladson-Billings, *The Dreamkeepers.*

39. C. Jepsen and S. Rivkin, "Class Size Reduction and Student Achievement," *Journal of Human Resources* 44, no. 1 (2009): 223–250.

40. Milner, *Start Where You Are, but Don't Stay There*; H. R. Milner, "Critical Race Theory and Interest Convergence as Analytic Tools in Teacher

Education Policies and Practices," *Journal of Teacher Education* 59, no. 4 (2008): 332–346.

41. E. Graue, K. Hatch, K. Rao, and D. Oen, "The Wisdom of Class-Size Reduction," *American Education Research Journal* 44, no. 3 (2007): 670–700.

42. E. W. Eisner, *The Educational Imagination: On the Design and Evaluation of School Programs* (New York: MacMillan College Publishing, 1994); G. McCutcheon, *Developing the Curriculum: Solo and Group Deliberation* (Troy, NY: Educators' Press International, 2002).

43. A. Ede, "Scripted Curriculum: Is it a Prescription for Success?" *Childhood Education* 83, no. 1 (2006): 31.

44. K. King and S. Zucker, "Curriculum Narrowing," Pearson Education, 2005, http://www.pearsonassessments.com/NR/rdonlyres/D3362EDE-7F34-447E-ADE4-D4CB2518C2B2/0/CurriculumNarrowing.pdf.

45. D. Srikantaiah, *How State and Federal Accountability Policies Have Influenced Curriculum and Instruction in Three States: Common Findings from Rhode Island, Illinois, and Washington* (Washington, DC: Center on Education Policy, 2009), 2, http://www.cep-dc.org/displayDocument.cfm?DocumentID=217.

46. C. D. Jerald, *The Hidden Costs of Curriculum Narrowing* (Washington, DC: Center for Comprehensive School Reform and Improvement, 2006), 5, http://www.centerforcsri.org/files/CenterIssueBriefAug06.pdf.

47. G. Cawelti, "The Side Effects of NCLB," *Educational Leadership* 64, no. 3 (2006): 64–68.

48. P. Smagorinsky, A. Lakly, and T. S. Johnson, "Acquiescence, Accommodation, and Resistance in Learning to Teach Within a Prescribed Curriculum," *English Education* 34, no. 3 (2002): 187–211. Also see J. Westheimer, "No Child Left Thinking: Democracy at-Risk in American Schools," *Colleagues* 3, no. 2 (2011): 8; A. Luke, A. Woods, and K. Dooley, "Comprehension as Social and Intellectual Practice: Rebuilding Curriculum in Low Socioeconomic and Cultural Minority Schools," *Theory into Practice* 50, no. 2 (2011): 157–164.

49. Smagorinsky et al., "Acquiescence, Accommodation, and Resistance in Learning to Teach Within a Prescribed Curriculum," 198–199.

50. M. S. Crocco and A. T. Costigan, "The Narrowing of Curriculum and Pedagogy in the Age of Accountability: Urban Educators Speak Out," *Urban Education* 42, no. 6 (2007): 512.

51. E. Dutro, "What 'Hard Times' Means: Mandated Curricula, Class-Privileged Assumptions, and the Lives of Poor Children," *Research in the Teaching of English* 44, no. 3 (2010): 255.

52. P. Freire, *Pedagogy of the Oppressed* (New York: Continuum, 1998).

53. Dutro, "What 'Hard Times' Means," 257.

54. A. E. Lewis, "There Is No 'Race' in the Schoolyard: Colorblind Ideology in an (Almost) All White School," *American Educational Research Journal* 38, no. 4 (2001): 781–811; Milner, *Start Where You Are, but Don't Stay There.*

55. Gay, *Culturally Responsive Teaching*; Ladson-Billings, *The Dreamkeepers.*

56. G. Gay, "Culturally Responsive Teaching: Principles, Practices, and Effects," in *Handbook of Urban Education*, eds. H. R. Milner and K. Lomotey (New York: Routledge, 2014).

57. K. Hinton and T. Berry, "Literacy, Literature and Diversity," *Journal of Adolescent & Adult Literacy* 48, no. 4 (2004): 286.

58. A. T. Tatum, "Engaging African American Males in Reading," *Educational Leadership* 63, no. 5 (2006): 45.

59. L. S. Cook and K. B. Amatucci (2006). "A High School English Teacher's Developing Multicultural Pedagogy," *English Education* 38, no. 3 (2006): 220–244.

60. E. Buendia, A. Gitlin, and F. Doumbia, "Working the Pedagogical Borderlands: An African Critical Pedagogue Teaching Within an ESL Context," *Curriculum Inquiry* 33, no. 3 (2003): 291–293.

CHAPTER 2

1. K. Gutierrez, P. Baquedano-Lopez, and C. Tejeda, "Rethinking Diversity: Hybridity and Hybrid Language Practices in the Third Space," *Mind, Culture, and Activity* 6, no. 4 (1999): 286–303.

2. Ibid.

3. R. Payne, *A Framework for Understanding Poverty* (Highlands, TX: Aha! Process, 1996).

4. R. Bomer, J. Dworin, L. May, and P. Semingson, "Miseducating Teachers About the Poor: A Critical Analysis of Ruby Payne's Claims About Poverty," *Teachers College Record* 110, no. 12 (2008): 2497–2531; P. Gorski, "The Classist Underpinnings of Ruby Payne's Framework," *Teachers College Record Online*, February 9, 2006 (retrieved from www.tcrecord.org, ID number:12610); R. J. Murnane, "Improving the Education of Children Living in Poverty," *The Future of Children* 17, no. 2 (2007): 161–182; N. Osei-Kofi, "Pathologizing the Poor: A Framework for Understanding Ruby Payne's Work," *Equity & Excellence in Education* 38 (2005): 367–375.

5. Gorski, "The Classist Underpinnings of Ruby Payne's Framework."

6. O. Lewis, "The Culture of Poverty," *Scientific American* 215 (1966): 19–25; O. Lewis, The *Children of Sanchez: Autobiography of a Mexican Family* (New York: Random House, 1961); O. Lewis, *Five Families: Mexican Case Studies in the Culture of Poverty* (New York: Basic Books, 1959).

7. G. Ladson-Billings, *The Dreamkeepers: Successful Teachers of African American Children*, 2nd ed. (San Francisco: Jossey-Bass, 2009).

8. Osei-Kofi, "Pathologizing the Poor."

9. H. R. Milner, *Start Where You Are, but Don't Stay There: Understanding Diversity, Opportunity Gaps, and Teaching in Today's Classrooms* (Cambridge, MA: Harvard Education Press, 2010).

10. Payne, *A Framework for Understanding Poverty*, 4.
11. J. Kozol, *The Shame of a Nation: The Return of Apartheid Schooling in America* (New York: Crown Publishing, 2005); Milner, *Start Where You Are, but Don't Stay There.*
12. G. Ladson-Billings, "From the Achievement Gap to the Education Debt: Understanding Achievement in U.S. Schools," *Educational Researcher* 35, no. 7 (2006): 3–12.
13. J. Anyon, "Social Class and the Hidden Curriculum of Work," *Journal of Education* 162, no. 1 (1980): 366–391; L. Darling-Hammond, *The Flat World and Education: How America's Commitment to Equity Will Determine Our Future* (New York: Teachers College Press, 2010); J. M. Henslin, *Essentials of Sociology: A Down-to-Earth Approach*, 5th ed. (Boston: Pearson, 2004).
14. Lewis, "The Culture of Poverty"; Payne, *A Framework for Understanding Poverty.*
15. K. Gutierrez and B. Rogoff, "Cultural Ways of Learning: Individual Traits and Repertoires of Practice," *Educational Researcher* 32, no. 5 (2003): 19–25.
16. A. H. Dyson and C. Genishi, *The Need for Story: Cultural Diversity in Classroom and Community* (Cambridge, MA: Harvard University Press, 1994).
17. P. Noguera, "Building the Capacity of Schools to Meet Students' Needs," inaugural fall lecture, November 2013, Center for Urban Education, University of Pittsburgh, Pittsburgh, PA.
18. Although most of the discussion is situated within a U.S. context, it is important to note that studies about poverty and language arts are not exclusive to a U.S. context. For instance, in a Canadian study of first-grade students in ten high-poverty schools, Haughey, Snart, and da Costa (2001) designed three interventions to determine their effectiveness in raising the achievement of students. Using test scores as the measure, students in the study made "noteworthy" (p. 301) improvements in the areas of writing and reading. The interventions were designed to focus on reducing class size through literacy instruction, continuous professional development, and intensified focus, specifically on literacy instruction.
19. J. Edmondson and P. Shannon, "Reading Education and Poverty: Questioning the Reading Success Equation," *Peabody Journal of Education* 73, no. 3/4 (1998): 104–126.
20. M. A. Adler and C. W. Fisher, "Early Reading Programs in High-Poverty Schools: A Case Study of Beating the Odds," *The Reading Teacher* 54, no. 6 (2001): 616–619.
21. Ibid.
22. G. Ladson-Billings, "'Why Can't We Read Something Good?' How 'Standards,' 'Testing,' and Scripted Curricula Impoverish Urban Students," Invited Address, National Reading Conference, December 2009, Albuquerque, NM.
23. Ibid.

24. L. Delpit, *Other People's Children: Cultural Conflict in the Classroom* (New York: New Press, 1995).
25. Ibid.
26. A. Valenzuela, *Subtractive Schooling: U.S.-Mexican Youth and the Politics of Caring* (Albany, NY: State University of New York Press, 1999.
27. K. Lepi, "This Is How Teens Are Using Social Media," *Edudemic*, July 23, 2013, http://www.edudemic.com/2013/07/this-is-how-teens-are-using-social-media/.
28. L. Delpit and J. K. Dowdy, eds., *The Skin That We Speak* (New York: New Press, 2008).
29. P. Freire, *Pedagogy of the Oppressed* (New York: Continuum, 1998).
30. Delpit, *Other People's Children.*
31. Ibid.
32. National Council of Teachers of English, *Reading and Writing Across the Curriculum* (Urbana, IL: National Council of Teachers of English, 2011).
33. A. N. Applebee and J. A. Langer, "What Is Happening in the Teaching of Writing?" *English Journal* 98, no. 5 (2002): 18–28.
34. NCTE, *Reading and Writing Across the Curriculum.*
35. C. Keys, "Revitalizing Instruction in Scientific Genres: Connecting Knowledge Production with Writing-to-Learn in Science," *Science Education* 83, no. 2 (1999): 115–130.
36. NCTE, *Reading and Writing Across the Curriculum.*
37. G. Gay, *Culturally Responsive Teaching: Theory, Research, and Practice*, 2nd ed. (New York: Teachers College Press, 2010); Ladson-Billings, *The Dreamkeepers*; Milner, *Start Where You Are, but Don't Stay There.*
38. D. T. Slaughter-Defoe and K. G. Carlson, "Young African American and Latino Children in High-Poverty Urban Schools: How They Perceive School Climate," *Journal of Negro Education* 65, no. 1 (1996): 60–70.
39. K. V. Hoover-Dempsey and H. M. Sandler, "Why Do Parents Become Involved in Their Children's Education?" *Review of Educational Research* 67 (1997): 3–42.
40. Some studies conflate ethnic and racial categories. C. E. Cooper, R. Crosnoe, M.-A. Suizzo, and K. Pituch, "Poverty, Race, and Parental Involvement During the Transition to Elementary School," *Journal of Family Issues* 31, no. 7 (2009): 859–883.
41. M. Foster, "Race, Class, and Gender in Education Research: Surveying the Political Terrain," *Educational Policy* 13, no. 1/2 (1999): 77–85.
42. L. Gutman and V. Mcloyd, "Parents' Management of Their Children's Education Within the Home, at School, and in the Community: An Examination of African American Families Living in Poverty," *Urban Review* 32, no. 1 (2000): 1–24.
43. B. A. Jacob and L. Lefgren, "In Low-Income Schools, Parents Want Teachers Who Teach," *Education Next* 7, no. 3 (2007): 59–64.

44. A. Milne and L. A. Plourde, "Factors of a Low-SES Household: What Aids Academic Achievement?" *Journal of Instructional Psychology* 33, no. 3 (2006): 183–193.

45. P. A. Halsey, "Parent Involvement in Junior High Schools: A Failure to Communicate," *American Secondary Education* 34, no. 1 (2005): 57–69.

46. Ladson-Billings, *The Dreamkeepers.*

47. L. S. Shulman, "Knowledge and Teaching: Foundations of the New Reform," *Harvard Educational Review*, February 1987, 1–22.

48. J. A. Banks, "Teaching Literacy for Social Justice and Global Citizenship," *Language Arts* 81, no. 1 (2003):18–19.

49. P. A. Noguera and L. Wells, "The Politics of School Reform: A Broader and Bolder Approach for Newark," *Berkeley Review of Education* 2, no. 1 (2011): 5–25.

50. H. R. Milner, "Analyzing Poverty, Learning, and Teaching Through a Critical Race Theory Lens," *Review of Research in Education* 37, no. 1 (2013): 1–53; J. Anyon, *Radical Possibilities: Public Policy, Urban Education, and a New Social Movement* (New York: Routledge, 2005); Noguera and Wells, "The Politics of School Reform."

CHAPTER 3

1. U.S. Department of Education, 2011–2012 Civil Rights Data Collection, http://ocrdata.ed.gov.

2. C. A. Samuels, "PreK Suspension Data Prompt Focus on Intervention," *Education Week*, October 2014, http://www.edweek.org/ew/articles/2014/04/02/27ocrprek.h33.html.

3. J. E. Davis and W. J. Jordan, "The Effects of School Context, Structure, and Experiences on African American Males in Middle and High School," *Journal of Negro Education* 63, no. 4 (1994): 570–587; P. A. Noguera, "Preventing and Producing Violence: A Critical Analysis of Responses to School Violence," *Harvard Educational Review* 65, no. 2 (1995): 189–212; R. H. Sheets, "Urban Classroom Conflict: Student-Teacher Perception: Ethnic Integrity, Solidarity, and Resistance," *Urban Review* 28, no. 2 (1996): 165–183; R. J. Skiba, R. S. Michael, A. C. Nardo, and R. L. Peterson, "The Color of Discipline: Sources of Racial and Gender Disproportionality in School Punishment," *Urban Review* 34, no. 4 (2002): 317–342.

4. Skiba et al., "The Color of Discipline."

5. A. Gregory, R. J. Skiba, and P. A. Noguera, "The Achievement Gap and the Discipline Gap: Two Sides of the Same Coin?" *Educational Researcher* 39, no. 1 (2010): 59–68; C. W. Lewis, B. R. Butler, I. I. Bonner, A. Fred, and M. Joubert, "African American Male Discipline Patterns and School District Responses Resulting Impact on Academic Achievement: Implications for

Urban Educators and Policy Makers," *Journal of African American Males in Education* 1, no. 1 (2010): 7–25; R. J. Skiba et al., "Race Is Not Neutral: A National Investigation of African American and Latino Disproportionality in School Discipline," *School Psychology Review* 40, no. 1 (2011): 85.

6. Skiba et al., "The Color of Discipline."
7. R. J. Skiba, R. L. Peterson, and T. Williams, "Office Referrals and Suspension: Disciplinary Intervention in Middle Schools," *Education and Treatment of Children* 20 (1997): 295.
8. C. S. Weinstein, M. Curran, and S. Tomlinson-Clarke, "Culturally Responsive Classroom Management: Awareness into Action," *Theory into Practice* 42, no. 4 (2003): 269–276.
9. H. R. Milner, "Classroom Management in Urban Classrooms," in *The Handbook of Classroom Management: Research, Practice and Contemporary Issues*, eds. C. M. Evertson and C. S. Weinstein (Mahwah, NJ: Lawrence Erlbaum, 2006), 491–522.
10. L. Delpit, *Other People's Children: Cultural Conflict in the Classroom* (New York: New Press, 1995); L. Delpit, *Multiplication Is for White People: Raising Expectations for Other People's Children* (New York: New Press, 2012).
11. Weinstein, Curran, and Tomlinson-Clarke, 270.
12. E. O. McGee, "Dying to Succeed: The Extreme Price of STEM College Success for Black Students," in press; L. D. Caldwell, A. Sewell, N. Parks, and I. A. Toldson, "Before the Bell Rings: Implementing Coordinated School Health Models to Influence the Academic Achievement of African American Males," *Journal of Negro Education* 78 (2009): 204–215.
13. P. A. Noguera, "Preventing and Producing Violence: A Critical Analysis of Responses to School Violence," *Harvard Educational Review* 65, no. 2 (1995): 189.
14. P. A. Noguera, "Schools, Prisons, and Social Implications of Punishment: Rethinking Disciplinary Practices," *Theory into Practice* 42, no. 4 (2003): 342–343.
15. Ibid., 343.
16. H. Grossman, *Classroom Behavior Management in a Diverse Society* (Mountain View, CA: Mayfield Publishing, 1995), 142.
17. J. Duncan-Andrade, "Note to Educators: Hope Required When Growing Roses in Concrete," 2012, Harvard Education Alumni Association, http://www.youtube.com/watch?v=8z1gwmkgFss.
18. McGee, "Dying to Succeed."
19. Duncan-Andrade, "Note to Educators."
20. http://ocrdata.ed.gov.
21. W. F. Tate, "'Geography of Opportunity': Poverty, Place, and Educational Outcomes," *Educational Researcher* 37, no. 7 (2008): 397–411.
22. Ibid.

23. I am thankful to Adrienne Dixon for sharing important insights related to this story with me.

CHAPTER 4

1. H. R. Milner, "Teacher Reflection and Race in Cultural Contexts: History, Meaning, and Methods in Teaching," *Theory into Practice* 42, no. 3 (2003): 173–180; H. R. Milner, "Reflection, Racial Competence, and Critical Pedagogy: How Do We Prepare Preservice Teachers to Pose Tough Questions?" *Race, Ethnicity, and Education* 6, no. 2 (2003): 193–208; H. R. Milner, "Stability and Change in Prospective Teachers' Beliefs and Decisions About Diversity and Learning to Teach," *Teaching and Teacher Education* 21, no. 7 (2005): 767–786; H. R. Milner, "Preservice Teachers' Learning About Cultural and Racial Diversity: Implications for Urban Education," *Urban Education* 41, no. 4 (2006): 343C–375; H. R. Milner, "Disrupting Deficit Notions of Difference: Counter-Narratives of Teachers and Community in Urban Education," *Teaching and Teacher Education* 24, no. 6 (2008): 1573–1598; H. R. Milner, "What Does Teacher Education Have to Do with Teaching? Implications for Diversity Studies," *Journal of Teacher Education* 60 no. 1/2 (2010): 118–131.
2. M. Cochran-Smith and K. Zeichner, eds. *Studying Teacher Education: The Report of the AERA Panel on Research and Teacher Education* (Mahwah, NJ: Lawrence Erlbaum Associates, 2005).
3. G. Gay, *Culturally Responsive Teaching: Theory, Research, and Practice*, 2nd ed. (New York: Teachers College Press, 2010); M. Haberman, "The Pedagogy of Poverty Versus Good Teaching," *Phi Delta Kappan* 73, no. 4 (1991): 290–294; T. C. Howard, *Why Race and Culture Matter: Closing the Achievement Gap in American Classrooms* (New York: Teachers College Press, 2010); G. Ladson-Billings, *The Dreamkeepers: Successful Teachers of African American Children*, 2nd ed. (San Francisco: Jossey-Bass, 2009); H. R. Milner, *Start Where You Are, but Don't Stay There* (Cambridge, MA: Harvard Education Press, 2010).
4. Gay, *Culturally Responsive Teaching*; Ladson-Billings, *The Dreamkeepers*.
5. W. E. B. DuBois, *The Souls of Black Folk* (New York: Fawcett, 1903); C. G. Woodson, *The Mis-Education of the Negro* (Washington, DC: Associated Publishers, 1933).
6. Milner, *Start Where You Are, but Don't Stay There*.
7. H. R. Milner, "Developing a Multicultural Curriculum in a Predominantly White Teaching Context: Lessons from an African American Teacher in a Suburban English Classroom," *Curriculum Inquiry* 35, no. 4 (2005): 391–427.
8. R. Ellison, *Invisible Man* (New York: Vintage, 1947).
9. G. Ladson-Billings and B. Tate, "Toward a Critical Race Theory of Education," *Teachers College Record* 97, no. 1 (1995): 47–67.

10. D. W. Sue et al., "Racial Microaggressions in Everyday Life: Implications for Clinical Practice," *The American Psychologist* 62, no. 4 (2007): 271, doi:10.1037/0003-066X.62.4.271.
11. W.A. Smith, T.J. Yosso, and D.G. Solórzano, "Challenging Racial Battle Fatigue on Historically White Campuses: A Critical Race Examination of Race-Related Stress," in *Faculty of Color: Teaching in Predominantly White Colleges and Universities*, ed. Christine A. Stanley (Bolton, MA: Anker Publishing, 2006), 299–327.
12. F. L. Hamer, "I'm Sick and Tired of Being Sick and Tired," speech delivered with Malcolm X at the Williams Institutional CME Church, Harlem, New York, December 20, 1964, http://www.crmvet.org/docs/flh64.htm.
13. K. Zeichner and D. Liston, *Reflective Teaching* (Mahwah, NJ: Lawrence Erlbaum Associates, 1996).
14. M. A. Medina, A. S. Morrone, and J. A. Anderson, "Promoting Social Justice in an Urban Secondary Teacher Education Program," *The Clearing House* 78, no. 5 (2005): 208.
15. A. Woolfolk, *Educational Psychology*, 7th ed. (Boston: Allyn & Bacon, 1998), 8.
16. L. Valli, "Listening to Other Voices: A Description of Teacher Reflection in the United States," *Peabody Journal of Education* 72, no. 1 (1997): 67.
17. T. C. Howard, "Telling Their Side of the Story: African American Students' Perceptions of Culturally Relevant Teaching," *Urban Review* 33, no. 2 (2001): 131–149; H. R. Milner, "Teacher Reflection and Race in Cultural Contexts: History, Meaning, and Methods in Teaching," *Theory into Practice* 42, no. 3 (2003): 173–180; F. A. Rios, *Teacher Thinking in Cultural Contexts* (Albany, NY: State University of New York Press, 1996).
18. B. D. Tatum, "Professional Development: An Important Partner in Antiracist Teacher Education," in *Racism and Racial Inequality: Implications for Teacher Education*, eds. S. H. King and L. A. Castenell (Washington, DC: AACTE, 2001), 51–58.
19. Gay, *Culturally Responsive Teaching*.
20. L. Johnson, "'My Eyes Have Been Opened': White Teachers and Racial Awareness," *Journal of Teacher Education* 53, no. 2 (2002): 153–167.
21. Milner, *Start Where You Are, but Don't Stay There*.
22. C. I. Bennett, *Comprehensive Multicultural Education: Theory and Practice*, 3rd ed. (Boston: Allyn & Bacon, 1995); M. Cochran-Smith, "Color Blindness and Basket Making Are Not the Answers: Confronting the Dilemmas of Race, Culture, and Language Diversity in Teacher Education," *American Educational Research Journal* 32 (1995): 493–522; G. Ladson-Billings, *Crossing Over to Canaan: The Journey of New Teachers in Diverse Classrooms* (San Francisco: Jossey-Bass, 2001).
23. A. Mitchell, "African-American Teachers: Unique Roles and Universal Lessons," *Education and Urban Society* 31, no. 1 (1998): 105.

24. Ladson-Billings, *The Dreamkeepers.*
25. Mitchell, "African-American Teachers."
26. P. E. Barton, *Parsing the Achievement Gap: Baseline for Tracking Progress* (Princeton, NJ: Educational Testing Services, 2003).
27. See H. R. Milner and M. Smithey, "How Teacher Educators Created a Course Curriculum to Challenge and Enhance Preservice Teachers' Thinking and Experience with Diversity," *Teaching Education* 14, no. 3 (2003): 293–305.
28. C. E. Sleeter, "Preparing Teachers for Culturally Diverse Schools: Research and the Overwhelming Presence of Whiteness," *Journal of Teacher Education* 52, no. 2 (2001): 94–106.
29. P. Freire, *Pedagogy of the Oppressed* (New York: Continuum, 1998).
30. R. S. Weinstein, "High Standards in a Tracked System of Schooling: For Which Students and with What Educational Support? *Educational Researcher* 25, no. 8 (1996): 18.
31. D. F. Brown, "Urban Teachers' Use of Culturally Responsive Management Strategies," *Theory into Practice* 42, no. 4 (2003): 282.
32. L. Weiner, *Preparing Teachers for Urban Schools: Lessons from Thirty Years of School Reform* (New York: Teachers College Press, 1993).
33. C. D. Ennis, "When Avoiding Confrontation Leads to Avoiding Content: Disruptive Students' Impact on Curriculum," *Journal of Curriculum and Supervision* 11 (1996): 145.
34. J. A. Banks, "Citizenship Education and Diversity: Implications for Teacher Education," *Journal of Teacher Education* 5, no. 1 (2001): 5–16.
35. G. McCutcheon, *Developing the Curriculum: Solo and Group Deliberation* (Troy, NY: Educators' Press International, 2002).
36. Cochran-Smith and Zeichner, *Studying Teacher Education.*
37. M. M. Merryfield, "Using Electronic Technologies to Promote Equity and Cultural Diversity in Social Studies and Global Education," *Theory and Research in Social Education* 28, no. 4 (2000): 502.
38. Cochran-Smith and Zeichner, *Studying Teacher Education.*
39. Ibid.
40. Freire, *Pedagogy of the Oppressed.*

CHAPTER 5

1. Children's Defense Fund, *America's Cradle to Prison Pipeline Report*, October 10, 2007, http://www.childrensdefense.org/child-research-data-publications /data/cradle-prison-pipeline-report-2007-full-highres.html, 1.
2. https://abagond.wordpress.com/2009/05/29/the-clark-doll-experiment/.
3. http://www.cnn.com/2010/US/05/13/doll.study/.
4. A. E. Lewis, "There Is No 'Race' in the Schoolyard: Colorblind Ideology in an (Almost) All White School," *American Educational Research Journal* 38, no.

4 (2001): 781–811; H. R. Milner, *Start Where You Are, but Don't Stay There* (Cambridge, MA: Harvard Education Press, 2010); b. hooks, *Where We Stand: Class Matters* (New York: Routledge, 2000).

5. J. A. Chafel, "Children's Views of Poverty: A Review of Research and Implications for Teaching," *Educational Forum* 61, no. 4 (1997): 360.

6. J. Anyon, "Social Class and the Hidden Curriculum of Work," *Journal of Education* 162, no. 1 (1980): 366–391.

7. M. Haberman, "The Pedagogy of Poverty Versus Good Teaching," *Phi Delta Kappan* 7, no. 4 (1991): 290–294.

8. P. Freire, *Pedagogy of the Oppressed* (New York: Continuum, 1998).

9. See H. R. Milner, "Race, Culture, and Researcher Positionality: Working Through Dangers Seen, Unseen, and Unforeseen," *Educational Researcher* 36, no. 7 (2007): 388–400.

About the Author

H. Richard Milner IV is the Helen Faison Endowed Professor of Urban Education, Professor of Education, Professor of Sociology, Professor of Social Work, Professor of Africana Studies, and Director of the Center for Urban Education at the University of Pittsburgh. His research, teaching, and policy interests are urban education, teacher education, African American literature, and the sociology of education. In particular, Professor Milner's research examines policies and practices that support teacher success in urban schools.

Professor Milner's work has appeared in numerous journals, and he has published five books. His award-winning book, *Start Where You Are but Don't Stay There: Understanding Diversity, Opportunity Gaps, and Teaching in Today's Classrooms* (Harvard Education Press, 2010), represents years of research and development. In 2006, Professor Milner received an Early Career Award in recognition of his distinguished program of education research from the American Educational Research Association. Professor Milner has appeared on the top two hundred Edu-Scholar Public Presence Ranking, published by *Education Week* (#95 in 2013, #88 in 2014, and #89 in 2015). In 2012, Professor Milner was honored with The Ohio State University College of Education and Human Ecology Distinguished Alumnus Award. Currently, he is editor-in-chief of *Urban Education* and coeditor of the *Handbook of Urban Education*, published by Routledge Press in 2014.

Index

accents, 86

accountability, 60, 62, 110, 112, 133–134, 151, 181

achievement gap, 9, 23, 25–26, 175

action research, 146

adaptability, 106

Advanced Placement students, 19

affirmative action, debates over, 9–10

affluent families, 17–18, 97, 98–99

affluent schools, instructional practices in, 17–18, 20–21

African American families
  low-income, 21–22
  middle-class, 23
  parental involvement in, 97–98

African American students. *See also* students of color
  disciplinary actions and, 119–129
  experiences of, 162–163
  extracurricular activities and, 97, 98
  preschool, 114–115
  relationship building and, 94–95
  underperforming, 115–116

afterschool programs, 39

analytical thinking skills, 108

Angelou, Maya, 29, 175

Asian families
  low-income, 21
  parental involvement in, 97

assessments, 56, 148. *See also* standardized tests

asset-based perspectives, 151, 162

assistant principals, 139–140

asthma, 40

Baldwin, James A., 175

black males. *See also* African American students
  challenges facing, 146–147
  racial microaggressions and, 156–159

brown males. *See also* Latino students
  challenges facing, 146–147

Brown v. Board of Education, 8, 33

career skills, 108–109

case studies, 113–142
  of classroom conflicts, 113–129
  elementary school, 115–117
  high school, 119–121
  middle school, 117–119
  preschool, 114–115
  robbery impact, 129–137
  school leadership, 139–140
  school supplies, 136–139

character, 84

charter schools, 101

child development, 1–2

children. *See also* students
  attitudes of, toward school, 1–3
  homeless, 43–48
  race and, 182–185
  valuing, 3

Civil Rights Data Collection, 115

teacher education programs *(cont.)*
race and, 149–173
self-examination and, 160–162
societal discourse and, 165–166
teachers, 26. *See also* educators
attitudes of, toward race, 4, 23,
149–151
blame of, 7
class size and, 51–56
cohorts of, 149
communication by, 73–74
connections between parents and,
99–102, 111, 146
critical self-examination and
reflection by, 110
cross-disciplinary collaboration by,
79–81, 135
de-skilling, 151–152
disciplinary practices of, 113–129,
141
dispositions of, toward students,
110
elementary, 79–80
expectations of, 18–19, 20, 71, 110,
111, 118–119, 140, 163
home lives of students and, 67–69
impact of, 29–30, 33
induction period for, 145–149
knowledge about students of,
162–164
knowledge and skills of, 102–103
language used by, 110
moods of, 73
parental expectations of, 98
professional development for,
30–32, 39, 55, 130–132, 134,
140
quality of, 54
racially diverse, 171
role of, 2, 25, 30–31, 67–68
school-dependent students and,
50–51
scripted curriculum and, 58–63

self-examination and awareness by,
160–162
students' views about, 71–72
writing instruction and, 88–94
teacher-student relationships, 6, 30,
94–95, 141, 147–148, 167–168
teacher wellness programs, 147
teaching
class size and, 51–56
culturally relevant and responsive,
147
individualization of, 55
race, poverty, and, 146
reflective, 160–162
technology integration, 82–83
terminology, 26–27
test performance, 5–6, 24, 53–54, 68,
98, 133–134, 175
test-taking strategies, 108
text messaging, 82–83
theme, 84
thesis statement, 84
time management, 108
Title I funds, 36–37
transportation issues, 46
traumatic events, 129–137

upward mobility, 2
urban poverty, 41–43
urban schools, 5–6, 38
urban students, 41, 42

violence, in the community, 129–137
vocabulary, 86–88

white bias, 183
white families, low-income, 21–22
whiteness, 9, 97, 183
white students, 4, 41, 97
whole-class discussions, 89–90
workforce stratification, 19–20
work responsibilities, 49
writing instruction, 89–94